PLASTICITY IN THE CENTRAL NERVOUS SYSTEM
Learning and Memory

PLASTICITY IN THE CENTRAL NERVOUS SYSTEM
Learning and Memory

Edited by

James L. McGaugh
University of California, Irvine

Federico Bermúdez-Rattoni
Roberto A. Prado-Alcalá
Universidad Nacional Autonoma de Mexico

LAWRENCE ERLBAUM ASSOCIATES, PUBLISHERS
1995   Mahwah, New Jersey

Lawrence Erlbaum Associates, Inc., Publishers
10 Industrial Avenue
Mahwah, New Jersey 07430

Library of Congress Cataloging-in-Publication Data

Plasticity in the central nervous system : learning and memory /
    edited by James L. McGaugh, Federico Bermúdez-Rattoni, Roberto A.
    Prado-Alcalá.
        p.   cm.
    Includes bibliographical references and index.
    ISBN 0-8058-1573-2 (alk. paper)
        1. Learning.   2. Memory.   3. Neuroplasticity.   I. McGaugh, James L.
    II. Bermúdez-Rattoni, Federico.   III. Prado-Alcalá, Roberto A.
    OP408.P53   1995
    612.8′2—dc20   95-32064
                                                                 CIP

Books published by Lawrence Erlbaum Associates are printed on acid-free paper,
and their bindings are chosen for strength and durability.

Printed in the United States of America
10 9 8 7 6 5 4 3 2 1

Contents

Preface

Research exploring the brain functions that enable learning and memory has greatly accelerated in recent years. The rapid pace of research was catalyzed by the development of new neurobiological and behavioral techniques, as well as by new conceptual and theoretical approaches to the study of the relationship between brain and behavior. The chapters in this book reflect current theoretical approaches to the study of brain and memory and provide new insights concerning the cellular bases of memory and the differential involvement of brain systems in different forms of memory.

In the opening chapter, John Garcia discusses current strategies used in experiments investigating learning and memory and emphasizes the critical importance of pursuing behavioral research in a biological context. Behavioral neuroscience research requires special efforts to link the findings of behavioral and brain research. The success of recent behavioral neuroscience research in bridging this critical gap is amply demonstrated in the subsequent chapters of the book.

The chapters by McGaugh and colleagues, Izquierdo, and Prado-Alcalá then discuss pharmacological approaches to the study of brain and memory. McGaugh's chapter summarizes recent research examining the interaction of peripheral adrenergic and central noradrenergic system with cholinergic, opioid peptidergic, and GABAergic systems in regulating memory storage. Findings of studies investigating the effects of intra-amygdala injections of drugs, as well as lesions of amygdala nuclei, indicate that the amygdala is involved in integrating the neuromodulatory systems activated by learning experiences and regulating memory storage in other brain regions. Studies investigating the effects of drugs administered into the amygdala, entorhinal cortex, or hippocampus after training provide a temporal analysis of the participation of these brain regions in the storage of information. Izquierdo's research using this strategy suggests that these brain regions are differentially involved in the storage of different kinds of information. In research using a similar strategy, Prado-Alcalá has found that memory can be influenced by posttraining pharmacological activation or inactivation of several brain regions and suggests that information storage requires the activation of each of several functionally connected structures. Further, his findings that extensive training reduces the influence of posttraining pharmacological treatments suggest that extensive training accelerates the formation of the functional connections.

Chapters in the second section review experiments using a variety of techniques, including brain lesions, brain grafting, and electrophysiological recording, to investigate the role of different brain regions in learning and memory.

Intracerebral grafting has emerged as a useful experimental tool in investigating brain function. In addition, the ability to restore functioning through neuronal grafting has provided a promising approach for treating brain disease or injury. Studies of the recovery of the capacity for aversively motivated learning, summarized by Bermúdez-Rattoni and his colleagues, indicate that recovery is accelerated by homotopic fetal brain grafts, as well as by a combination of homotopic brain grafts and nerve growth factor. The chapter by Gage and his co-workers summarizes findings indicating that intracerebral grafting of cells genetically modified to secrete neurotropic factors results in restored learning and memory functioning in aged rats and improves learning in young rats with brain damage.

Bures' chapter reveals the usefulness of temporary functional inactivation of brain regions in studies of brain systems involved in memory. Functional ablation can block critical brain regions during specific phases of learning and/or retrieval. Research using such techniques has revealed that reversible lesions are particularly suitable for identifying and analyzing the neural processes mediating the formation or modification of memory. In his chapter, Thompson summarizes research using permanent, as well as reversible, lesions in combination with electrophysiological recording, to determine the neural circuitry essential for classical conditioning of the eyelid and nictitating membrane response. The findings provide compelling evidence that the memory trace for this response is formed within a localized region of the cerebellum (the anterior interpositus and overlying cortex).

A review of the neuropsychological findings on amnesia in humans and laboratory animals, considered together with relevant anatomical and physiological evidence, is presented in the chapter by Eichenbaum, Young, and Bunsey. The findings suggest that neocortical association areas of the brain maintain short-term memory for specific items and events, prior to processing by the hippocampus, and are also the final locus of long-term memory. In his chapter, Fuster emphasizes the role of the cortex in memory. His research suggests that the dorsolateral frontal cortex is involved in two complementary functions: short-term memory, which is the temporary active memory of events required for forthcoming acts, and short-term set, which is the preparation of motor systems.

The third section of the book concerns molecular analyses of events associated with memory formation. Dudai and his colleagues summarize research examining the molecular events underlying the development of conditioned taste aversion (CTA). The finding that microinjections of a protein synthesis inhibitor into the insular cortex attenuate memory of a new taste is consistent with previous evidence suggesting that this cortical region is involved in mediating this form of memory. CTA training also modulates a set of substrates of tyrosine kinase in synaptic complexes and induces the expression of the immediate early gene c-fos in this brain region. In the final chapter, Rose summarizes a series of time-dependent molecular changes seen in chicks' brains after training in an aversive task. An initial biochemical cascade occurring in the hyperstriatum ventrale within the first 30 minutes after training involves several changes, including up-regulation of glutamate-NMDA receptors, opening of calcium channels, release of putative retrograde messengers, phosphorylation of pre- and postsynaptic protein kinase c substrates and the switching on of transcription factors. A second wave of protein and glycoprotein synthesis, occurring in a different brain region, appears several hours following training. Thus, it appears that training induces task-dependent, as well as time-dependent, biochemical alterations in different brain regions.

In providing up-to-date summaries of research investigating brain mechanisms underlying learning and memory, these chapters help to place current findings in their appropriate theoretical contexts. In doing so, they should further stimulate research into understanding how the brain makes memory.

We wish to acknowledge and thank Ms. Nancy Collett for her extensive and invaluable assistance in planning and coordinating the organization of the symposium that resulted in these chapters. Thanks to Jodie Hittner and Barry Setlow for preparing the indexes. We also thank the National Institute of Mental Health, the Mexican Society of Physiological Sciences, the Mexican Academy of Scientific Research, and the National Council of Science and Technology (CONACYT-Mexico) for financial support.

James L. McGaugh
Federico Bermúdez-Rattoni
Roberto A. Prado-Alcalá

1 Brain and Behavior: Bridging the Barranca

John Garcia
University of California, Los Angeles

> *In point of fact only one thing in life is of actual interest for us—our psychical experience. But its mechanism has been and still remains wrapped in mystery. All human resources—art, religion, literature, philosophy, and historical science—have combined to throw light on this darkness. Man has at his disposal yet another powerful resource— natural science with its strictly objective methods.*
>
> —Pavlov (1904)

So spoke I. P. Pavlov in 1904 at Stockholm in the final paragraph of his Nobel Prize address introducing classical conditioning as a new method for studying *mind* by precisely controlling learned behavior and noting the concomitant neural activity (Kaplan, pp. 56–57). Following Pavlov, scientists have concentrated on either the peripheral or central aspects of the behaving animal, and generally shunned the mind and its vagaries. As a result, there are two great mountain ranges of literature, one on behavioral research and the other on brain research, with a huge chasm, or barranca, separating them. Buried at the bottom of the barranca lies the unifying concept of mind.

The mind baffles us because none of us has direct access to the mind of another human. Quite simply, we have direct access to our own minds and we know that we conceal and disguise our own thoughts and motives, presenting a false front to others, so we are certain that others lie to us as well. Great effort is expended in detecting lies and extracting the truth from others, but no one has come up with a foolproof method.

We behavioral neuroscientists, whose occupation title reflects the barranca, need to keep a constructive attitude toward *mind*. Building sure bridges across the behavior-brain barranca and illuminating it with strictly objective methods

1

what Pavlov called *our psychical experience* is the essential task of behavioral neuroscience. Whether it is fair or not, our research will ultimately be judged according to how much light we shed on that singular enigma called *mind*. For our task, the adjective *behavioral* is overly restrictive; we should be known for what we are, *mental neuroscientists*.

I suggest to start that we accept mind as a causal agent. Curiously, abnormal brains and deranged minds are generally accepted as causes of aberrant behavior, whereas sound brains and normal minds are suspect. Second, we should give up the absolutist position that we must have direct access to other minds. It is an illusory shibboleth; most scientific principles based on indirect inferences. Third, I suggest we get on with our job of locating the mind and the organized brain mechanisms it uses for controlling behavior.

The foundations of mental neuroscience were laid down over three centuries ago. Nevertheless, how we project minds onto other organisms still raises epistemological issues and endless arguments. I cannot define exactly the kind of brain organization we're looking for, because *mind* must be defined only by future empirical research. For now I can only provide you this basic axiom:

> Mind is a manifestation whose validity is a function of its locus, such that no amount of evidence can disprove its existence in me and you, or prove its existence in them out there.

THE LANGUAGE BARRANCA

Historically, scientists turned their backs on the barranca, choosing either behavior or the brain, and over the centuries developed two objective languages with little or no functional relevance to each other.

On one side, the language developed by behavioral psychologists is in a constant state of flux, so that each new generation scarcely understands what the older generation was talking about. Behavioral theorists speak of *stimulus* and *response*, by which they mean *cause* and *effect*. When looking at any two events in a reliable behavioral sequence, the first event is the stimulus and the second event is the response, but the second event is also a stimulus for subsequent events. Furthermore, each response generates internal feedback stimuli, and thus a cascade of responses. The only way to clear up this muddle is to specify the afferent and efferent paths involved, but such specificity is viewed as a reductionistic and physicalistic surrender of liberated psychology to imperial biology. Still that's better than a flight into the lofty abstractions of logical models and mathematics preferred by some theorists of pure behavior and pure cognition.

On the other side of the barranca, the neuroanatomists developed a language to describe the brain that is stable, concrete, and archaic. Their language emphasizes the form and structure of landmarks in the brain without much regard for their functions, resulting in a colorful melange that is very difficult for students to memorize. The cerebrum is described as some strange fruit marked by a deep fissure running fore and aft and wrapped in two mothers, one tough and the other tender. It sits atop a stem with a little cerebrum attached directly below and to the rear. The interior of the brain is filled with a wondrous mix of rooms, hollows, tracts, bodies, nets, sea horses, almonds, worms, teats and tails, organized so that there is one of everything down the middle and two of everything down the sides.

Given the infinite human capacity to generate neologisms, metaphors, and translations, these semantic problems will clear up naturally as research progresses. As I will point out further, the attempt to establish permanent definitions and logical schemes has interfered with empirical research in mental neuroscience.

MICHELLE AND *HERMISSENDA*

Let us first contemplate the awesome size of the barranca as portrayed by Alkon (1992) in his book, *Memory's Voice: Deciphering the Mind Brain Code*. Alkon interlaces a sensitive psychiatric case history of a childhood friend, Michelle, with his search for fundamental brain mechanisms of learning and memory in the sea slug, *Hermissenda*. He does so with insight and literary skill, but covering over the barranca with a seamless tapestry of plausibility concealing the enormous task of closure before those who stand on either one precipice or the other.

Michelle grew up under an oppressive violent father, who used his overwhelming power to beat his little girl savagely and belittle her psychologically. As a child, unable to escape the pain and humiliation, she tried to be good, but was only rewarded with more punishment. As an adolescent, she strove for perfection, but was met with contempt and abuse. As a beautiful, talented young woman, she finally broke free of her tormentor in an emotional explosion, but she was never free of the coping mechanisms engraved on her mind during development, and thus, memory became her tormentor. Her fate led her through feelings of guilt and futility, to alcoholism and suicide. In a time when it is fashionable to attribute such problems to heredity, Alkon reminds us that a normal, healthy human can be incapacitated by residual memories of a hostile environment. Such enduring memories, incorporating species-specific emotions and motor patterns modified by personal experience, must reflect a complex mental system pervading the central nervous system.

Hermissenda, the Pacific sea snail also has its problems, but it lives in a world far different from Michelle's. About 3cm in length and gracefully slender, it explores the movements and chemicals in its watery environment with a crown of tentacles and wears a coat of featherlike appendages that increase its diffusion surface for respiration and elimination. It clings to the substrate with a muscular foot resisting currents threatening to overturn it as it creeps along the sea floor.

After studying a number of organisms, Alkon selected *Hermissenda* because of its relatively simple nervous system. He explored its receptors and traced its nervous pathways for years until he had comprehensive wiring diagrams for its visual system, optic ganglia, and vestibular system, including the interactions of these structures with the right and left side of the snail's brain. Employing Pavlov's general strategy, Alkon selected a visual conditioned signal (CS) and bodily rotation as the unconditioned stimulus (US); two events that are not likely to be coincidental in the natural world of the sea snail. He then traced the flow of signals through the nervous system and noted the changes occurring as a result of light-rotation pairing, establishing the acquisition and retention of a new association in the brain.

This is excellent research, and if he specifies how *Hermissenda* learns and remembers in a complete and convincing manner, Alkon deserves the highest accolades of science. But, he will have to go beyond the mechanisms by which cells live and communicate with each other, to reveal the entire mental structure by which *Hermissenda* learns and remembers how to cope with turbulence in its world, before we can see how *Hermissenda* relates to Michelle and her turbulent world. A maelstrom of change occurred as the two species diverged and adapted to vastly different environments. Some features were modified, some were lost and some were gained. However, there is the implicit assumption, perhaps unwarranted, that the basic circuitry remained relatively stable for eons so that the basics of human mind can be found in an invertebrate.

SEARCHING FOR NEUROBEHAVIORAL UNITS

Following four centuries of discourses on the associative *mind* by the empirical philosophers, Pavlov brought the association of ideas into the objective reality of a dog in the laboratory. He conditionally paired an auditory stimulus (S) eliciting the orienting response (R) with a gustatory S evoking a salivary R. After training a dog to salivate at the sound of the auditory S, Pavlov concluded that a new connection had been established between the auditory system and the salivary system in the dog's brain.

Pavlov emphasized that in observing the conditioned salivary reflex he was studying the *mind* of the dog. The saliva exquisitely matched the nature of the oral stimulation and the expectations of the animal, ranging from a thin fluid for flushing sand out of the mouth to a slick mucin for lubricating dry food. Pavlov wrote, "We see here facts which are exact and constant and which seem to imply intelligence. But the entire mechanism of this intelligence is plain? (Kaplan, pp. 61–62).

As soon as Pavlov presented his classic paradigm, Thorndike offered a variant known as *instrumental conditioning*. Rather than an auditory S, Thorndike followed by a movement (R) executed by a hungry cat with food to elicit eating (R). He thought of conditioning in terms of R-R connections between associated responses and he specified that the arbiters of responses, rewards and punishments were the neurons of the brain. S-S and R-R conditioning paradigms remain the most popular neurobehavioral manipulations to this day because of the repetitive numerical data they generate. But that may be their greatest weakness. Learning may come from a sudden insight, an all-or-none process without practice. If so, a one-trial procedure may be more appropriate.

Of all the American learning theorists, Hull (1943) followed Pavlov most faithfully. Hull chose not to work on the neural connections himself, but rather, he postulated intervening neural events from behavioral data to guide the work of others working on the brain. Hull's hypothetical postulates, couched in neurological terms, resided in the brain and were anchored to inputs (S) by afferent neural interaction and to outputs (R) by variations in excitatory and inhibitory reaction potentials. These input and output vagaries made Hull's theory difficult to falsify. His ultimate goal was to establish the S-R connection as the basic unit of behavior.

As Hull's system evolved, it became more behavioral and less neural, until Spence (1947), the dominant Hullian advocate of the time, abandoned the brain, saying, ". . . psychologists have come to realize that the explanation of behavioral events does not *necessarily* involve reduction to its physiological determinants." Meanwhile, Skinner (1938) excoriated the mind, along with S-S conditioning. Claiming he had the natural unit of behavior, Skinner took over R-R conditioning, renaming it *operant conditioning*. Manipulating the behavior of hungry pigeons with food rewards, he tried to persuade us that human behavior follows the same laws and is essentially mindless.

The problem with Skinner's denial is that the broad view of pigeons doing their own thing creates a suspicion that pigeons, like humans, have species-specific minds. That is true for almost any organism we come to know intimately. Jay B. Best once remarked to me, "The more I look at a flatworm, the more it seems to be a human in a flatworm suit." That may explain why after years of looking at insects, entomologists Kinsey (Kinsey, Pomeroy, & Martin, 1948) and Wilson (1975) suddenly turned their attention to human social behavior and made a great impact on psychology.

The issue facing the mental neuroscientist is similar to that faced by the S–R behaviorists in search of the unit of conditioning. Can learning and memory be adequately explained by unitary elements such as changes in a neuron, or in a synapse, or in the formation of a protein? I once heard Eric Kandel make a dismal prediction that learning may be accomplished by the "housekeeping activities" of neurons. If so, the goal of neuroscience is to describe the complex circuitry of neurons supporting holistic mind-systems.

Skinner's Radical Behaviorism

Skinner (1989, 1990) was the most prominent and most adamant proponent of mindless behaviorism. He was articulate but directed his argument towards an archaic view of mind that no scientist holds today. In 1989, he drew from his background as a college English major to argue that mentalistic terms spring from behavioristic roots. To say that thinking is a form of operant responding under the control of environmental contingencies is not an answer. It is simply a restatement of Freud's basic question, "What good comes to this patient from these thoughts?"

In 1990 Skinner accepted natural selection of species morphology and species behavior, but he cuts a piece of the evolutionary action out for himself. Natural selection, he said, ". . . prepares a species only for a future that resembles the past." That fault is corrected by a "second type" of evolution, namely, "operant conditioning, through which variations in the behavior of the individual are selected by features of the environment that are not stable enough to play any part in evolution."

Of course, unstable features play an evolutionary role by selecting individuals who learn and remember how to cope with such unstableness. That was fully discussed by Darwin and the evolutionists before and after him (Garcia y Robertson & Garcia, 1987). Some of the individuals who could learn and remember arrived in Skinner's laboratory in the form of pigeons prepared by natural selection to deal with the unstableness in his operant feeding schedules. Skinner (1990) did not discuss the contributions of evolutionary adaptation to conditioned responses, as Pavlov did, and that proved to be the source of his errors, tending to bury important variables in a singular concept. For example, reinforcement is vital to operant conditioning, but many reinforcers are species-specific or response-specific, and such specificity was not stressed even in the pigeon.

The pigeon, like other organisms, cannot deal with changes falling outside the range of unstableness found in its evolutionary niche. In nature the hungry pigeon searches for a seed that provides the target to peck, the signal to peck, and the reinforcement to peck in one convenient package. In the Skinner box, if these three features were presented together approximating the evolutionary condition, the pigeon performed well; but if they were spread far apart, the pigeon failed at arrangements that other species handle with ease. The pigeons's failure tells us something about the pigeon's mind and brain: Apparently when looking for seeds, the pigeon must catch all three features in a single glance, just as did its ancestors (Garcia & Garcia y Robertson, 1985).

Mental neuroscientists can profit by studying Skinner's mistakes. Subjects must be selected and studied with care, so must their adaptive behavioral functions. For certain functions, a wide variety of organisms may serve as subjects. For example, toxiphobic conditioning has been profitably studied in a wide range of vertebrate and invertebrate species, from primates to mollusks. However, even under the threat of poison, human behavior is a poor analogue for the wide range of snail behaviors, as under starvation, pigeon behaviors are poor analogues for human behaviors. Research on any given function in any one species can serve as a preliminary step to research in another species only when structural homologies underlying the given behavioral function are understood in terms of comparative anatomy and adaptive evolution. In toxiphobic conditioning, those homologies reside in the neural controls of ingestion and gut common to so many species. Beginnings toward that end have been made in the snail (Gelperin, Chang, & Reingold, 1978) and the rat (Garcia, Lasiter, Bermudez-Rattoni, & Deems, 1985).

Cognitive Maps and Animal Minds

Fortunately, the mind was kept alive and well by Tolman, who was also studying the behavior of rats in mazes. Tolman (1951) discussed concepts such as purpose, cognition, and the behavioristic theory of ideas. He described the vacillation of the rat at a choice point just before it switched to the correct path and wrote "whenever an organism at a given moment of stimulation shifts then and there from being ready to respond in some relatively less differentiated way to being ready to respond in some relatively differentiated way, there is consciousness" (pp. 64–65). The flash of insight, when the organism exults, "Aha, that's it!" is surely the birth of a new memory and whoever adequately specifies that singular moment mechanistically in the brain may also exult, "Aha!" and buy a ticket to Sweden.

Tolman believed that a rat did not acquire a chain of S-R units as it learned the correct path through the maze. Rather he believed that the hungry rat acquired a *cognitive map* showing the location of the food within the environmental field. The critical evidence came from place learning experiments, where animals abandon their habitual circuitous pathways to take a new short cut to the food. Tolman (1951) describes the brain's acquisition of a cognitive map as follows: "The stimuli, which are allowed in . . . are usually worked over and elaborated into a tentative, cognitivelike map of the environment . . . indicating routes and paths and environmental relationships, which finally determines what responses, if any, the animal will finally release" (pp. 244–245).

Unit connectionism in animal psychology ended without fanfare when the followers of the Clark Hull tradition reached a consensus with Tolman's cognitive camp followers. Two prominent S-R theorists serve as exemplars. Maltzman (1977) searched for the basic conditioning process in humans looking at a list of words. One item served as the CS, and it was followed by the US. The conditioning was monitored by the galvanic skin response (GSR). He found that shock reinforcement was not needed, a tone signaling the significance of the CS served just as well as pain. The conditioned response did not necessarily spread to the word immediately preceding the verbal CS, more often than not, it spread along semantic dimensions to words not on the list. For example, if the CS was *leaf*, conditioning spread to *twig* and *tree*. Maltzman concluded that he could not obtain true classical conditioning in humans with verbal materials, because his subjects perceived the entire conditioning schedule as a puzzle to be solved.

Rescorla (1988), after building an illustrious career conditioning animals, reached a conclusion that fits well with Maltzman's findings and Tolman's cognitive map. Rescorla favored "an analogy between animals showing Pavlovian conditioning and a scientist identifying the cause of a phenomenon." He described the organism as an information seeker using perceptual relations and preconditions to form a representation of its environment. Rescorla's description is reminiscent of Tolman's (1951) declaration, "I . . . intend to go ahead imagining how, *if I were a rat, I* would behave as a result of such . . . a demand. . . ." (pp. 163–164).

Today the cognitive map is widely accepted in animal psychology and behavioral biology. Even Skinner offered a weak concession. Emil Menzel (1978) reported B. F. Skinner's comment that map concepts are limited to learning that can be conceptualized in spatial terms (p. 418). Menzel replied that he was hard put to think of any problem that cannot be conceptualized in spatial terms.

The handling of spatial problems in a maplike way by various species is the most convincing objective data cited in the recent volume, *Cognitive Ethology: The Minds of Other Animals*, edited by Carolyn A. Ristau (1991). In the introduction, Donald Griffin writes: "Simple conscious thinking may be an efficient and economic mode of operation by which the central nervous systems enable animals to cope with the multiple problems of finding food, avoiding predators, finding mates and raising young. If so, it may be most advantageous for animals with small brains" (p. 3). Note that these multiple problems require the spatial strategies tested in Tolman's mazes, and conceptualized in his notion of the cognitive map. Yet only three of the fourteen chapters contributed to Ristau (1991) by various authors mentions Tolman. Only one chapter does so adequately. Yoerg & Kamil refer to him as "perhaps the first cognitive psychologist" (p. 277). The Romans were right, fame is fleeting!

BRAIN ANATOMY AND MIND INTEGRITY

For those of us interested in the mind-brain problem, split-brain studies have been most illuminating. The original study in cats with sectioned callosa. Myers and Sperry (1958) demonstrated that when inputs were limited to one hemisphere of the brain, that hemisphere could learn and remember a habit while the other hemisphere was kept ignorant or acquired another habit, as if two minds now dwelled in one cat skull.

Split-brain humans became available when commissure section proved to be effective in limiting the spread of epileptic seizures (Bogen, Fisher, & Vogel, 1965). The results of tests gave rise to notions of two minds in the same skull (Gazzaniga, 1970). The left hemisphere was described as linguistically fluent, analytically thoughtful, happy with an aptitude for fine motor skills, whereas the right hemisphere was inarticulate, holistically creative, given to anger and sadness, and good at gross motor movement. As more split-brain patients were studied by more investigators using more methodologies, the description of two minds in one skull became mired in questions of relativity, individual differences, preexisting conditions and semantic nuances, in other words, the same ambiguities plaguing the study of one mind in one skull in the area of *personality*.

Burghardt (1991) describes the behavior of a two-headed snake with two brains and two minds. The snake, named IM for instinct and mind, was closely observed for the first five years, involving over 400 feedings on small prey, while it grew a 20-fold increase in weight. The most pronounced difference between the heads was in their preference for size of prey; the left head struck more often at smaller prey, whereas the right head struck more often at larger prey, but the heads often struck simultaneously and attempted to swallow the same prey, lengthening the ingestion from minutes to an hour or more. Neither head learned to relinquish its hold on the prey and avoid the delay, despite the fact that, by either route, the food was going to the same gut and ultimately satisfying the hunger of both brains. Burghardt (1991) concludes, "Today, at 14 years of age, IM's two heads still fight over prey. I have become convinced that the two behavioral outcasts, instinct and mind, have much in common and that they are intimately connected" (p. 84).

Cognitive mapping must also be represented in the brain because thinking in spatial terms evolved naturally in a world where food, shelter, and mates were distributed in space. True, these goals were also distributed in linear time, but the sense of time is not as precise as the sense of space. Therefore, time is often converted into spatial cues such as the apparent movements of the sun, moon, and stars. Humans use sun dials, clock faces, and calendars to map time, because individual differences in estimates of lapsed time are unreliable compared to estimates of spatial displacements.

Accordingly, Olton (1979) resurrected and refurbished the 1945 model radial-arm maze for testing place learning, a source of data for Tolman, my sainted professor. It was like seeing a renovated 1945 automobile, gleaming with fresh paint and running like new. The radial arm maze has a central starting platform for the hungry rat, with arms radiating outward like spokes on a rimless wheel. Morsels of food are placed at the end of each arm, and not replaced during the test, so the optimal strategy for the rat is to visit each arm once and not visit any arm twice.

Tests indicate a functional similarity in working memory (i.e., the mind) between rat and human. Choices made at the beginning of the test session and at the end of the test session are remembered better than choices made in the middle of the session, resembling the effects seen in humans memorizing lists of words. The proactive effect interferes with remembering subsequent words and the retroactive effect interferes with previous words. Old rats, like old people, show deficits in recent memory, a fact to which I can testify.

The hippocampus plays an important role in spatial memory tested in the rat.

Specific lesions in the hippocampus or its connections to the rest of the brain severely disrupt performance on the radial arm maze. Cholinergic input from the medial septal area to the hippocampus is critical for memory. Of course, the trouble for investigators is that everything in the brain seems to be connected to everything else, but it is clear that if you wish to disrupt memory in man, monkey, rat, or bird, the hippocampus is a good place to start (Harvey & Krebs, 1990).

Conscious and Unconscious Mental Streams

In our laboratory, my students, associates and I pursued the problem of food selection for some 40 years before I fully appreciated the fact that we were dealing with a confluence of both conscious and unconscious streams of mentation in the brain of the rat (Garcia, 1990). We were studying the effects of whole-body exposure to hours of low levels of ionizing rays that were imperceptible according to popular radiological opinion, when we stumbled blindly onto food selection. Such exposures bathe the animal internally and externally to a diffuse flood of ionization without disturbing its routine behaviors of eating, drinking, copulating or sleeping, seemingly verifying the erroneous notion that rats and people are insensitive to x-rays (Garcia y Robertson & Garcia, 1985).

Experimentation demonstrated that, however diffuse the radiant energy might be, the rat responds in specific ways in keeping with its evolutionary history. First, the rat immediately senses the onset and offset of minute levels of ionizing radiation as an odd innocuous odor, and its olfactory system soon habituates to radiation exposure. Second, after hours of low-level exposure, radiation becomes noxious, but the animal does not attempt to avoid the rays; instead, it is apt to alter its diet. Radiation exposure mimics the effects of poison and the rat employs the ancestral toxiphobic wisdom evolved over eons in the natural world, where plants employ toxins to fend off herbivores. Thus, there must also be a toxiphobic mind system.

When the accumulation of circulating radiation by-products reaches a sufficient level, be it in exposures of hours or minutes, nausea will ensue in an hour or two. Histamine released by the gut is the major culprit. Nausea, a mental brain system, will cause a taste aversion without the rat's awareness and in the absence of any responses, operant or otherwise (Bermudez-Rattoni, Forthman, Sanchez, Perez, & Garcia, 1988). This inherited toxiphobic strategy protects the gut in all vertebrates.

The complete toxiphobic mentality involves Pavlovian CS-US conditioning plus feedback (FB) mechanisms which are part of the chain of events following ingestion of a toxic food US. The nauseous FB selectively attaches itself to any salient taste US. Anatomically, the afferent fibers carrying nausea signals, via the vagus and area postrema, and the taste fibers are intimately entwined, meeting in the solitary nucleus and reporting to the same cells in the parabrachial area. The toxiphobic system also includes elements in the hypothalmus and the limbic system. It is part of the food selection mind-brain system that pushes palatability in positive as well as negative directions. New food, followed by a nutritious FB, will taste better the next time it is encountered. The gustatory neocortex plays a modulatory role, which has been disrupted by lesions and restored functionally and structurally by transplants of fetal brain cells (Bermudez-Rattoni, Fernandez, & Escobar, 1989).

Skin defense is also a CS–US–FB mind-brain system stemming from the long evolutionary interaction of prey with predators. The charge of the predator, particularly the vibrations in the substrate alerts the prey with a danger CS. The impact of fang and claw on the skin of the prey acts as a pain US. An endogenous analgesic FB modulates the pain even in unconscious prey (Terman, Shavit, Lewis, Cannon, & Liebeskind, 1984). It is theorized that pain is diminished to facilitate escape reactions and subsequently pain sensitivity is increased to immobilize the wound for healing (Bolles and Fanselow, 1982).

THE BEGINNINGS OF MENTAL NEUROSCIENCE

Choosing "the beginning" of any movement in science has very little validity because *science*, the empirical investigation of one's niche, had a long continuous history before humanoid forms of life appeared on this earth. I choose two early steps in mental neuroscience which are as relevant today as when they were initiated, namely, the specific energies of nerves and psychophysics.

The doctrine of specific energies yielded both a classic principle and a classic error. Locke (1632–1704) noted that the qualities of sensations resided within ourselves, and not in the external world. Berkeley (1685–1753) took this idea to its ultimate conclusion with his subjective idealism, holding that the material earth had no existence beyond our sensations (as a clergyman, he assigned the external world to the mind of God). By creating a dogmatic solipsism beyond refute, Berkeley lost the heuristic viewpoint of internal-external interactions leading to concepts of adaptation and evolution. Others made better use of the doctrine, notably Helmholtz (1821–1894) who studied the minimal number of colored lights (three) required to produce the entire chromatic spectrum, and reasoned that there must then be three primary color receptors in the eye.

That our sensory systems select only a narrow band of the available energy and convert that band into a qualitative sensation is now a classic principle. The underlying assumption is that the receptors become focused on the most informative band of available energy by natural selection during the evolution of the organism in its niche. Premature specification is the classic error. The quality of sensation does not arise from differential energies within each sensory system. Selection and quality reside within the specific receptor and its terminus in the brain.

Psychophysics is really an extension of the research on specific energies initiated by Fechner (1801–1887) which developed into the field of sensation and perception. The various parameters of the physical stimulus were varied and the subject was required to report on sensations. Subjects were trained to attend to their internal solipsistic feelings and to avoid the *stimulus error*, the identification of the external physical manipulations by the experimenter. Psychophysics reached its culmination under Titchener (1867–1927) who, in his own fashion, repeated Berkeley's dogmatic error. The goal of psychophysics, he claimed, was to reveal the structure of the mind; to ravel out the elemental processes from the tangle of consciousness by vivisection, yielding structural, not functional results. Again, the injunction against investigating what the structural elements were for, was an gratuitous rejection of adaptive hypotheses.

Perhaps the best example of the power of psychophysics and trained introspection comes from Mach (1838–1916), a true polymath, if ever such existed. Mach is immortalized with Mach numbers for his work in physics, and famed in philosophy for ridding science of its metaphysical presumptions. He also left his indelible mark on psychophysics, writing a treatise on the analysis of sensation and the relation of the physical to the psychical. He argued that physical quantities were ultimately based on psychological sensations, and he generally challenged the distinction between objective and subjective perceptions.

Mach noticed that the visual boundary between a light and a dark area is enhanced by a band of brighter light on the illuminated side, and by a band of deeper shade on the darkened side. Measurements proved that these *Mach bands* did not exist physically, therefore he reasoned that they were of psychical origin. Before Ramon y Cajal described the synapse and Sherrington described neural integration, Mach postulated that the bands resulted from excitatory and inhibitory forces at work in the visual system (Ratliff, 1965).

Eventually, Mach bands led to a flurry of neurophysiological research on cellular network arrangements. The bands appeared everywhere. In impressionistic painting, artists painted in Mach bands to achieve brilliant figures against dark grounds. Similar enhancement of contours and boundaries were discovered in the sensory systems of touch and audition. Even in the olfactory system, the onset of a novel odor is strong, and soon fades away, even though its physical traces still hang in the air. That partially accounts for the rat's immediate detection of x-ray onset, and its failure to associate x-rays with the nausea occurring hours later.

One of the most interesting concepts from the beginning of mental neuroscience is the *unconscious inference* posited by Helmholtz to emphasize that the sensory system does not simply reflect the narrow range of stimulation to which it is tuned, but rather it infers from, or adds to, the stimulation without the subject's awareness. Mach bands are only one example of unconscious inference. The apparent movement induced by the alternate flashing of two lights, as in a railroad crossing signal, is another visual inference. Apparent movement can also be obtained on the skin by tapping one point first, followed by repeated tapping of a second nearby point, inducing a hopping sensation between the two points. Another compelling skin illusion is produced by a combination of warm and cold stimulation, producing the sensation of a searing burn.

These illusions are immediate and cannot be dispelled by reasoning or additional contextual information. For example, in movies, where the action is created by a series of flickering still pictures, the wheels of the wagon persist in appearing to turn backward, even as the wagon races forward with the enemy in hot pursuit. Such sensory phenomena demonstrate that physical stimuli are transformed by peripheral neural mechanisms into sensations that never existed in the world outside.

INTROSPECTIVE BEHAVIOR AND MENTAL PROJECTIONS

The advent of behaviorism was two steps forward towards objectivity and unified mental neuroscience, but one step backward in its dogmatic rejection of structuralism and trained introspection. Perhaps introspection is a narrow method, but it is vital to neuroscience. Nevertheless the behavioristic polemic still rages on. In his last paper, Skinner (1990), says, "Introspection has never been very satisfactory, however, philosophers have acknowledged its inadequacies while insisting that it is the only means to self-knowledge. Psychologists once tried to improve it by using trained observers and the brass instruments of which William James had such a low opinion. Introspection is no longer much used."

I wonder what William James would have said about the Skinner box. Today's brass instruments are electronic and are held in high opinion by Skinner's followers. Introspection is the same as ever and is used every day in neuroscience. The researcher refers to a feature of the environment, or to a state of the subject's body, and asks directly or by implication, "How do you feel about that?" Such inquiries are indispensable for the science of the mind.

The rebuttal of Skinner's argument came from Sperry (1993) who spent a lifetime studying the neuroanatomical control of behavior. He wrote, "subjective mental states as emergent interactive properties of brain activity became irreducible and indispensable for explaining conscious behavior and get primacy in determining what a person is and does."

We must give Skinner credit for developing operant technology, a marvelously efficient method for investigating many aspects of behavior, especially the sensory capacities of animals. In our laboratory, for example, we used Skinner's methods to demonstrate that rats can detect x-rays, and to identify the sensitive area in the olfactory system. We must also credit the many investigators who united operant methods with introspection, or with ethology, in creative ways to generate informative data. Operant conditioning, like introspection, has a certain limited validity as a method of inquiry, but it cannot be raised to the level of a theoretical formulation for correcting evolution, explaining all learning and memory, and obliterating psychical data.

A final word on the adaptive value of inferring causality and projecting minds onto other organisms: The classic associative principles of contiguity, similarity, and causality have some of the immediacy of unconscious inferences. Hume (1711–1779) argued cogently that successive events were not held together by the glue of causality. Neither are physical events held together by the glue of contiguity or the glue of similarity. The glue is psychical. Associations are all subjective inferences. Natural selection apparently favors individuals who behave as if contiguous events are connected and who respond in habitual ways to events that appear similar to familiar events in the past. Individuals who, in times of need or stress, seek out objects that in the past satisfied the need, or reduced the stress are also favored. Thus, contiguity, similarity, and causality are adaptive unconscious mnemonic devices for bringing psychical order out of external chaos. As such, associations are impressed by natural selection into the learning and memory mechanisms of the brain via the genes.

The projection of mind onto external objects is also widespread in humans. When observed in primitive people and children it is called *animism*. When an all-knowing mind is projected to the heavens or onto any complex imagery, animism becomes *religion*. Such religiosity is not limited to clergy and patriots. Scientists also project all-powerful minds into their abstract creations. To quote one recent example, Hawking (1990) called the most brilliant theoretical physicist since Einstein, wrote, "Yet if there is a complete unified theory, it would also presumably determine our actions. And so the theory itself would determine the outcome of our search for it! And why should it determine that we come to the right conclusions from the evidence? Might it not equally well determine that we draw from the wrong conclusion? Or no conclusion at all?" (p. 12).

Seeing minds is a mnemonic device that assembles all that is known about the universe, or about a single organism, into a coherent unitary memory. Such projections are both subjective and adaptive. Therefore they have a structural network in the brain. I believe that other organisms also have minds. I have always thought so. Perhaps I had no choice but to think so.

REFERENCES

Alkon, D. L. (1992). *Memory's voice*: Deciphering the mind-brain code. New York: Harper Collins.

Bermúdez-Rattoni, F., Fernandez, J., & Escobar, M. L. (1989). Fetal brain transplants induce recovery of morphological and learning deficits of cortical lesioned rats. In L. E. Canedo, L. E. Todd, & J. Jaz (Eds.), *Cell function and disease* (pp. 261–273). New York: Plenum.

Bermúdez-Rattoni, F., Forthman, D. L., Sanchez, M. A., Perez, J. L., & Garcia, J. (1988). Odor and taste aversions conditioned in anesthetized rats. *Behavioral Neuroscience, 102*, 726–732.

Bogen, J. E., Fisher, E. D., & Vogel, P. J. (1965). Cerebral commissurotomy: A second case report. *Journal of the American Medical Association, 194*, 1328–1329.
Bolles, R. C., & Fanselow, M. S. (1982). Endorphins and behavior. *Annual Review of Psychology, 33*, 87–101.
Burghardt, G. M. (1991). Cognitive ethology and critical anthropomophism: A snake with two heads and hog-nosed snakes that play dead. In C. A. Ristau (Ed.), *Cognitive ethology: The minds of other animals* (pp. 53–90). Hillsdale, NJ: Lawrence Erlbaum Associates.
Garcia, J. (1990). Learning without memory. *Journal of Cognitive Neuroscience, 2*, 287–305.
Garcia, J., & Garcia y Robertson, R. (1985). The evolution of learning mechanisms. *American Psychological Association: Master Lecture Series, 4*, 191–243.
Garcia, J., Lasiter, P. S., Bermúdez-Rattoni, F., & Deems, D. A. (1985). A general theory of aversion learning. In N. Braveman & P. Bronstein (Eds.), *Annals of the New York Academy of Sciences: Experimental assessment and clinical application of conditioned taste aversions* (pp. 3–41). New York: New York Academy of Sciences.
Garcia y Robertson, R., & Garcia, J. (1987). Darwin was a Learning theorist. In R. C. Bolles & M. D. Beecher (Eds.) *Evolution and learning* (pp. 17–38). Hillsdale, NJ: Lawrence Erlbaum Associates.
Garcia y Robertson, R., & Garcia, J. (1985). X-rays and learned taste aversions. In T. G. Burish, S. M. Levy, & B. E. Meyerowitz (Eds.), *Cancer, nutrition and eating behavior: A biobehavioral perspective* (pp. 11–41). Hillsdale, NJ: Lawrence Erlbaum Associates.
Gazzaniga, M. S. (1970). *The bisected brain.* New York: Appleton-Century-Crofts.
Gelperin, A., Chang, J. J., & Reingold, S. C. (1978). Feeding motor program in *Limax*: I. Neuromuscular correlates and control by chemosensory input. *Journal of Neurobiology, 9*, 285–300.
Griffin, D. (1991). Progress towards a cognitive ethology. In C. A. Ristau (Ed.), *Cognitive ethology: The minds of other animals* (pp. 3–6). Hillsdale, NJ: Lawrence Erlbaum Associates.
Harvey, P. H., & Krebs, J. R. (1990). Comparing brains. *Science, 249*, 140–146.
Hawking, S. W. (1988). *A brief history of time.* New York: Bantam.
Hull, C. L. (1943). *Principles of behavior.* New York: Appleton-Century-Crofts.
Kaplan, M. (1966). *Essential works of Pavlov.* New York: Bantam.
Kinsey, A. C., Pomeroy, W. B., & Martin, C. E. (1948). *Sexual behavior in the human male.* Philadelphia: Saunders.
Maltzman, I. (1977). Orienting in classical conditioning and generalization of the galvanic skin response to words: An overview. *Journal of Experimental Psychology: General, 106*, 111–119.
Menzel, E. W. (1978). Cognitive mapping in chimpanzees. In S. H. Hulse, W. K. Honig, & H. Fowler (Eds.), *Cognitive processes in animal behavior* (pp. 375–422). Hillsdale, NJ: Lawrence Erlbaum Associates.
Myers, R. E., & Sperry, R. W. (1958). Interhemispheric communication through the corpus callosum: Mnemonic carry-over between the hemispheres. *Archives of Neurology and Psychiatry, 80*, 298–303.
Olton, D. S. (1979). Mazes, maps, and memory. *American Psychologist, 34*, 583–596.
Ratliff, F. (1965). *Mach bands: Quantitative studies on neural networks in the retina.* San Francisco: Holden-Day.
Rescorla, R. A. (1988). Pavlovian conditioning: It's not what you think it is. *American Psychologist, 43*(3), 151–160.
Ristau, C. A. (1991). *Cognitive ethology: The minds of other animals.* Hillsdale, NJ: Lawrence Erlbaum Associates.
Skinner, B. F. (1938). *The behavior of organisms.* New York: Appleton-Century.
Skinner, B. F. (1989). The origins of cognitive thought. *American Psychologist, 44*, 13–18.
Skinner, B. F. (1990). Can psychology be a science of mind? *American Psychologist, 45*, 1206–1210.
Spence, K. W. (1947). The role of secondary reinforcement in delayed reward learning. *Psychological Review, 54*, 1–8.

Sperry, R. W. (1993). The impact and promise of the cognitive revolution. *American Psychologist*, *48*, 878–885.

Terman, G. W., Shavit, Y., Lewis, J. W., Cannon, T., & Liebeskind, J. C. (1984). Intrinsic mechanisms of pain inhibition: Activation by stress. *Science*, *226*, 1270–1277.

Tolman, E. C. (1951). *Collected papers in psychology.* Berkeley: University of California Press.

Wilson, E. O. (1975). *Sociobiology: The new synthesis.* Cambridge, MA: Harvard University Press.

Yoerg, S. I., & Kamil, A. C. (1991). Integrating cognitive ethology with cognitive psychology. In C. A. Ristau (Ed.), *Cognitive ethology: The minds of other animals* (pp. 271–289). Hillsdale, NJ: Lawrence Erlbaum Associates.

2 Involvement of the Amygdala in the Regulation of Memory Storage

James L. McGaugh
Larry Cahill
Marise B. Parent
University of California, Irvine

Michael H. Mesches
Karin Coleman-Mesches
Juan A. Salinas

There is general agreement that the amygdala is involved in learning and memory. The evidence supporting this conclusion has come primarily from studies of the effects of lesions of the amygdala on learning and memory in animals and human patients (Sarter & Markowitsch, 1985). There is also a growing consensus that the amygdala is of special and perhaps even unique importance in mediating affectively influenced memory (Davis, 1992b; Kesner, 1992; LeDoux, 1992; McGaugh, 1992). There are, however, several views concerning the specific role that the amygdala plays in mediating the influence of affect on learning and memory. Evidence that amygdala lesions impair learning and memory in animals trained in appetitively, as well as aversively, motivated learning tasks has suggested that the amygdala may serve to link stimuli with rewards (Aggleton & Passingham, 1982; Everitt & Robbins, 1992; Gaffan, 1992; Hiroi & White, 1991; Jones & Mishkin, 1972) and/or that the amygdala may be a locus of the neural changes underlying affective memory (Davis, 1992a; LeDoux, 1992).

The findings summarized in this chapter suggest an alternative role for the amygdala in memory: They suggest that the amygdala plays a role in regulating memory storage in other brain regions. The central hypothesis is that emotionally arousing stimulation activates the amygdala and that such activation results in modulation of the storage of recently acquired information. Although there is substantial evidence suggesting that memory storage, particularly storage of affective memory, may occur within the amygdala (Davis, 1992a; Izquierdo et al., 1993; Kim, Campeau, Falls, & Davis, 1993; LeDoux, 1992), other findings suggest that the amygdala influences memory storage occurring in other brain systems (Packard, Williams, Cahill, & McGaugh, 1995). Such evidence suggests that the amygdala may serve to ensure that the strength of memories will

17

be related to their emotional significance (McGaugh, 1990, 1992). A critical feature of this view of the role of the amygdala in learning and memory is that the amygdala regulates the storage of recently acquired information that may include, but is not restricted to, the specific affective response induced by the experience.

AMYGDALA STIMULATION AND INACTIVATION

Although studies of the effects of brain lesions have been important in efforts to understand the role of the amygdala in memory, interpretations of the findings of lesion studies are complicated by the fact that electrolytic, radio frequency, or neurotoxic lesions of the amygdala alter processes other than those directly involved in memory. Thus, it is difficult to determine which effects of such lesions on acquisition and retention performance are specifically attributable to memory. Experiments using treatments that induce temporary alterations in amygdala functioning have been useful in dissociating amygdala influences on memory from other effects on retention performance. The results of experiments using posttraining treatments that temporarily alter amygdala functioning are particularly instructive because in such experiments the functioning of the amygdala is normal during the training and during the retention test.

Amygdala Stimulation

Extensive evidence indicates that posttraining electrical stimulation of the amygdala can impair or enhance retention (Kesner & Wilburn, 1974; McGaugh & Gold, 1976). Findings indicating that the degree of the memory-modulating influence of the amygdala stimulation, whether enhancing or impairing, is greatest when the stimulation is administered shortly after training, support the view that the stimulation influences memory storage processes and is not due to other influences on retention performance (McGaugh & Herz, 1972). Furthermore, in experiments using the same stimulation parameters, posttraining electrical stimulation either enhances or impairs retention, depending on the footshock intensity used in the inhibitory avoidance training: With low footshock, retention is enhanced; with high footshock, retention is impaired (Gold, Hankins, Edwards, Chester, & McGaugh, 1975). Additionally, amygdala stimulation that impairs retention in normal rats enhances retention in adrenal demedullated rats (Bennett, Liang, & McGaugh, 1985; Liang, Bennett, & McGaugh, 1985).

These findings were the first to suggest the possibility that the amygdala may be involved in modulating memory storage processes. That is, if posttraining electrical stimulation produced only retrograde amnesia, it could be argued that the stimulation simply disrupted memory storage processes because of abnormal activity in the amygdala and consequent influences in brain regions activated by the amygdala. The evidence that the stimulation can enhance retention suggests that memory storage may normally be regulated by experience-induced variations in amygdala activity.

Amygdala Inactivation

Several recent experiments have investigated the role of the amygdala in memory by temporarily inactivating the amygdala with infusions of sodium channel blockers immediately after training. Bucherelli, Tassoni, and Bures (1992) reported that posttraining intra-amygdala infusions of tetrodotoxin produced retrograde amnesia in rats trained in an inhibitory avoidance task. Experiments in our laboratory (Parent & McGaugh, 1994) examined the effects of infusing lidocaine into specific amygdala nuclei after training. Rats with cannulae in either the central nucleus or the basolateral complex of the amygdala were given a single training trial in an inhibitory avoidance task, and lidocaine was infused, bilaterally, immediately, 6 hours after training or 24 hours after training; retention was tested 2 days later. As shown in Fig. 2.1, lidocaine infused into the basolateral complex produced retrograde amnesia: Retention was not affected by lidocaine infused into the central nucleus. The memory impairment produced by infusions administered into the basolateral complex depended on the delay of the injections after training, as well as the footshock intensity used in training. In groups given a low footshock, memory was impaired by lidocaine administered either immediately or 6 hours, but not 24 hours, after training. Additionally (results not shown) in animals trained with a higher footshock intensity, memory was impaired only when lidocaine was infused immediately after training. These results are consistent with those of Bucherelli et al. (1992) and suggest that the basolateral complex of the amygdala is of particular importance in regulating memory storage processes. The findings are also consistent with extensive evidence suggesting that

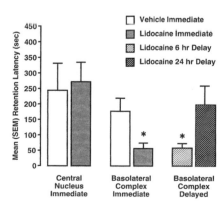

FIG. 2.1. The effects of immediate posttraining and delayed infusions of lidocaine hydrochloride into the central nucleus or basolateral complex on 48-hr retention of inhibitory avoidance. Lidocaine infused into the basolateral amygdala induced retrograde amnesia when administered immediately or 6 hr, but not 24 hr, after training (from Parent et al., 1994). *$p < .05$, compared with the vehicle injected group.

memory consolidation processes are influenced by variations in training conditions (McGaugh & Gold, 1976; McGaugh & Herz, 1972). The findings also suggest that the higher intensity footshock may produce greater activation of the amygdala and that the increased activity may accelerate memory storage.

In another recent experiment (Salinas, Packard, & McGaugh, 1993), we found that posttraining inactivation of the amygdala induced by lidocaine also impaired rats' memory for a change in reward magnitude. Rats trained to run a straight alley for a food reward decrease their running speeds (i.e., increase response latencies) and show emotional distress when the amount of reward is decreased (Amsel, 1962: Crespi, 1942). That is, the reward reduction is aversive even though the animals continue to receive a reward. In our experiment, rats with amygdala cannulae were trained with a reward of 10 pellets on each of six daily trials until running latencies stabilized. The reward on each trial was then reduced to 1 pellet, and training was continued for 3 days. Immediately after completion of the first six trials with the 1-pellet reward, the animals received intra-amygdala infusions of a buffer solution or lidocaine. The results are shown in Fig. 2.2. As was expected, on the day that the reward was reduced to 1 pellet, the animals' running latencies increased. On the day after the reduction in reward, the running latencies of the group given intra-amygdala infusions of lidocaine were markedly lower than those of the buffer control group. Moreover, the latencies were only slightly longer than those of animals given the same reward each day. The finding that posttraining inactivation of the amygdala with lidocaine attenuated the response to reward reduction is consistent with the evidence summarized above (Bucherelli et al., 1992; Parent & McGaugh, 1994) indicating that posttraining infusions of lidocaine impair retention of inhibitory avoidance training and provides additional support for the view that the amygdala is involved in regulating memory storage.

FIG. 2.2. Effects of posttraining intra-amygdala infusions of lidocaine on retention of a reduction in reward magnitude. Inactivation of the amygdala by lidocaine after the reward reduction on Day 10 impaired memory for change in reward magnitude as indicated by latencies on Days 11 and 12 (from Salinas et al., 1993).

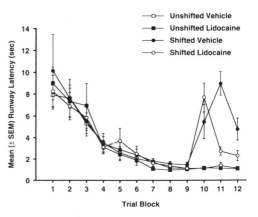

NEUROMODULATORY INFLUENCES
ON MEMORY STORAGE

Extensive evidence indicating that retention can be enhanced by posttraining administration of stimulant drugs (McGaugh, 1973) suggests that memory storage may be modulated by the actions of endogenous neurotransmitters and hormones released by emotionally arousing stimulation (Gold & McGaugh, 1975). In the initial experiments investigating this hypothesis, Gold and van Buskirk (1975) found that retention of inhibitory avoidance training was enhanced by posttraining systemic injections of the adrenergic hormone, epinephrine. Subsequent experiments in many laboratories demonstrated that comparable effects can be obtained in experiments using different kinds of training tasks (McGaugh & Gold, 1989). Furthermore, other stress-related hormones, including vasopressin, ACTH, and corticosterone have also been found to enhance retention when administered posttraining (Izquierdo & Dias, 1983; McGaugh, 1989; McGaugh & Gold, 1989).

Involvement of the Amygdala

Emotionally arousing stimulation of the kinds typically used in learning experiments activates stress-related hormonal systems and alters the release of neurotransmitters in the amygdala (Tanaka et al., 1982). The findings of many experiments indicate that the memory- modulating effects of a number of systemically administered drugs and hormones are mediated by influences involving the amygdala. For example, in Table 2.1, the findings indicating that the memory-modulating effects of systemically administered epinephrine are blocked by lesions of the amygdala or lesions of the stria terminalis (ST), a major amygdala pathway, clearly suggest that the epinephrine effects are mediated by the amygdala (Cahill & McGaugh, 1991; Liang & McGaugh, 1983b). ST lesions also block the memory-enhancing effects of systemic injections of the β-adrenergic agonist, clenbuterol (Introini-Collison, Miyazaki, & McGaugh, 1991). The evidence indicating that epinephrine's effects on memory are attenuated by intra-amygdala infusions of the β-adrenergic antagonist, propranolol (Liang, Juler, & McGaugh, 1986), as well as the opioid peptide, β-endorphin (Flood, Garland, & Morley, 1992) suggest that the effects involve both adrenergic and opioid peptidergic systems within the amygdala. Because opiates and opioid peptides are known to inhibit the release of norepinephrine (NE) (Werling, McMahon, Portoghese, Takemori, & Cox, 1989), these findings suggest that epinephrine's effects on memory are mediated by the release of NE within the amygdala. That is, propranolol and β-endorphin, according to this view, have a common effect in reducing the activation of β-adrenergic receptors in the amygdala. Recent findings from our laboratory support this hypothesis: Posttraining intra-amygdala infusions of doses of propranolol and β-endorphin that are ineffective when

21

TABLE 2.1
Amygdala Treatments Block the Memory-Modulating Effects
of Systemically Administered Hormones and Drugs

Systemic Treatment	Amygdala Treatment	Effect	Reference
Epinephrine	Excitotoxic Lesions (NMDA)	Blocks Enhancement	Cahill & McGaugh, 1991
	Stria Terminalis Lesions	Blocks Enhancement	Liang & McGaugh, 1983b
	Intra-Amygdala β-endorphin	Blocks Enhancement	Flood et al., 1992
	Intra-Amygdala propranolol	Blocks Enhancement	Liang et al., 1986
Clenbuterol	Stria Terminalis Lesions	Blocks Enhancement	Introini-Collison et al., 1991
Naloxone	Stria Terminalis Lesions	Blocks Enhancement	McGaugh et al, 1986
	Intra-Amygdala β-endorphin	Blocks Enhancement	Flood et al., 1992
	Intra-Amygdala propranolol	Blocks Enhancement	McGaugh et al., 1988
β-endorphin	Stria Terminalis Lesions	Blocks Impairment	McGaugh et al, 1986
Muscimol	Electrolytic Lesions	Blocks Impairment	Ammassari-Teule et al., 1991
Bicuculline	Electrolytic Lesions	Blocks Enhancement	Ammassari-Teule et al., 1991
Diazepam	Excitotoxic Lesions (NMDA)	Blocks Impairment	Tomaz et al., 1992
	Excitotoxic Lesions of Basolateral Nucleus (Ibotenic Acid)	Blocks Impairment	Tomaz et al., 1993
Midazolam	Intra-Amygdala Bicuculline	Blocks Impairment	Dickinson-Anson et al., 1993
CCK	Intra-Amygdala β-endorphin	Blocks Enhancement	Flood et al., 1992

administered alone significantly impair retention when administered together (Introini-Collision, Ford, & McGaugh, 1994).

These findings are consistent with extensive evidence indicating that retention is enhanced by posttraining systemic injections of opiate antagonists (Gallagher, Kapp, Pascoe, & Rapp, 1981; McGaugh, Introini-Collison, & Castellano, 1993) and that the enhancement is blocked by propranolol (Izquierdo & Graudenz, 1980). Furthermore, the results of several experiments indicate that the memory-enhancing effect of opiate antagonists, like that of epinephrine, is mediated by the amygdala. Naloxone's effects on memory are blocked by lesions of the ST (McGaugh, Introini-Collison, Juler, & Izquierdo, 1986), as well as by intra-amygdala infusions of β-endorphin (Flood et al., 1992) or propranolol (Introini-Collison, Nagahara, & McGaugh, 1989; McGaugh, Introini-Collison, & Nagahara, 1988).

It is also well established that retention is modulated by systemic administration of γ-amino-butyric-acid–related (GABAergic) drugs. Generally, when administered posttraining, GABAergic agonists impair retention and GABAergic antagonists enhance retention (Castellano, Brioni, & McGaugh, 1990). GABAergic influences on memory appear to be mediated by the amygdala. As is shown in Fig. 2.3, lesions of the amygdala block the memory-impairing effects, as-

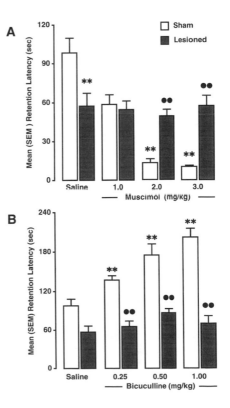

FIG. 2.3. Effects of posttraining administration of muscimol (A) and bicuculline (B) on inhibitory avoidance retention in animals with lesions of the amygdala. Retention was tested 24 hr after training. Amygdala lesions blocked muscimol-induced impairment of memory, as well as bicuculline-induced enhancement of memory (from Ammassari-Teule et al., 1991). **$p < .01$, compared with the saline-injected control group. ●● $p < .01$, compared with the sham group receiving the same drug treatment.

sessed in an inhibitory avoidance task, of the $GABA_A$ agonist, muscimol, as well as the memory-enhancing effects of the $GABA_A$ antagonist, bicuculline (Ammassari-Teule, Pavone, Castellano, & McGaugh, 1991). Extensive evidence indicates that benzodiazepines induce anterograde amnesia in humans, as well as in animals, in doses commonly used for anxiolytic effects (Izquierdo, Da Cunha, & Medina, 1990; Izquierdo, Medina, Netto, & Pereira, 1991; Lister, 1985). Because benzodiazepines are known to act by enhancing $GABA_A$-mediated synaptic inhibition, these findings provide additional evidence that memory storage is regulated by GABAergic influences.

Our findings indicating that the amygdala mediates the memory-modulating effects of GABAergic drugs suggested that the amygdala might also be involved in mediating the influences of peripherally administered benzodiazepines on memory. The results of several experiments provide strong support for this hypothesis (Tomaz et al., 1993). In rats trained in an inhibitory avoidance task, lesions of the amygdala block the memory-impairing effects of diazepam administered systemically prior to training (Tomaz, Dickinson-Anson, & McGaugh, 1991, 1992). The finding that intra-amygdala infusions of the GABAergic antagonist, bicuculline, block the amnestic effects of systemic injections of a benzodiazepine (midazolam; Dickinson-Anson, Mesches, Coleman, & McGaugh, 1993) provides additional evidence that the benzodiazepine effect is mediated by GABAergic influences within the amygdala (see Fig. 2.4).

It is of particular interest that, although lesions restricted to the basolateral complex of the amygdala did not impair retention, the lesions did block the effects of diazepam on retention (Tomaz et al., 1993). Such findings suggest that a functioning basolateral nucleus may not be required for either the acquisition or the expression of memory. However, as was already summarized, retention is impaired by posttraining inactivation of the basolateral complex of the amygdala (Parent & McGaugh, 1994). Thus, although an intact amygdala is not required

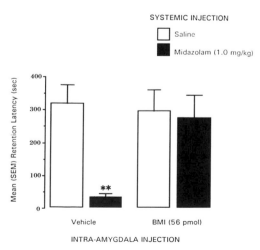

FIG. 2.4. Effects of pretraining intra-amygdala administration of bicuculline methiodide (BMI) and systemic administration of midazolam on inhibitory avoidance retention. Retention was tested 48 hr after training. Intra-amygdala infusion of BMI blocked midazolam-induced impairment of memory (from Dickinson-Anson et al., 1993). $**p < .01$, compared to all other groups.

for learning, posttraining alterations of amygdala functioning alter memory. Such findings support the view that the amygdala is involved in modulating memory storage.

The findings we have summarized so far provide strong and consistent evidence suggesting that the memory-modulating effects of hormones and drugs affecting several transmitter systems—including noradrenergic, opioid peptidergic, and GABAergic systems—are mediated by influences within the amygdala. Furthermore, they suggest that the memory-modulating influences of these several systems are based on the converging effects on noradrenergic activity in the amygdala. Findings of many other experiments examining the effects of intra-amygdala infusions of noradrenergic, opiate, and GABAergic agonists and antagonists provide additional support for these conclusions.

As shown in Table 2.2, memory is enhanced by intra-amygdala infusions of adrenergic agonists, including NE and clenbuterol (Introini-Collison et al., 1991; Liang et al., 1986), naloxone (Gallagher et al., 1981; Introini-Collison et al., 1989), and bicuculline (Brioni, Nagahara, & McGaugh, 1989). Retention is impaired by intra-amygdala infusions of propranolol (Gallagher et al., 1981),

TABLE 2.2
Effects, on Memory, of Intra-Amygdala Infusions of Drugs
and Neurotransmitters Administered Alone or Concurrently

Administered Alone	Concurrent Administration	Effect	Reference
Norepinephrine		Enhances	Liang et al., 1986
Norepinephrine	Propranolol	Blocks Enhancement	Liang et al., 1986
Clenbuterol		Enhances	Introini-Collison et al., 1989
Naloxone		Enhances	Gallagher et al., 1981; Introini-Collison et al., 1989
Naloxone	Propranolol	Blocks Enhancement	Introini-Collison et al., 1989
Bicuculline		Enhances	Brioni et al., 1989
Bicuculline	Propranolol	Blocks Enhancement	unpublished findings
Muscimol		Impairs	Brioni et al., 1989; Izquierdo et al., 1990
β-endorphin		Impairs	Flood et al., 1992; Introini-Collison et al., 1994
β-endorphin	Clenbuterol	Blocks Impairment	Introini-Collison et al., 1994
β-endorphin (low dose)	Propranolol (low dose)	Impairs	Introini-Collison et al., 1994
Midazolam		Impairs	Dickinson-Anson & McGaugh, 1993
Flumazenil		Enhances	Wolfman et al., 1991

β-endorphin (Introini-Collison et al., 1994), and muscimol (Brioni et al., 1989). Furthermore, intra-amygdala infusions of propranolol block the memory-enhancing effects of concurrently administered NE (Liang et al., 1986), naloxone (Introini-Collison et al., 1989), and bicuculline (unpublished findings).

Furthermore, as was indicated above, propranolol and β-endorphin infused together into the amygdala, in doses that are ineffective when administered alone, significantly impair retention. Additionally, when injected into the amygdala concurrently, the adrenergic agonist, clenbuterol, attenuates the retention impairment induced by β-endorphin (Introini-Collison et al., 1994). These findings thus provide additional evidence supporting the hypothesis that the influence of noradrenergic, opioid peptidergic, and GABAergic systems on memory storage involves noradrenergic activation within the amygdala. Retention is also impaired by intra-amygdala infusions of the benzodiazepine, midazolam (Dickinson-Anson & McGaugh, 1993) and enhanced by the benzodiazepine antagonist, flumazenil (Wolfman et al., 1991).

Other findings from our laboratory suggest that the intra-amygdala noradrenergic influence on memory storage involves subsequent activation of cholinergic receptors within the amygdala. Intra-amygdala infusions of atropine block the memory-enhancing effects of clenbuterol administered concurrently (Introini-Collison, Dalmaz & McGaugh, submitted). Furthermore, intra-amygdala infusions of propranolol do not attenuate the memory-enhancing effects of systemic injections of the muscarinic cholinergic agonist, oxotremorine. Thus, as the cholinergic influence overrides the noradrenergic influences on memory, it appears that noradrenergic effects are mediated through cholinergic activation.

LOCUS OF MODULATORY INFLUENCES

As is summarized above, the results of studies of the effects of hormones and drugs affecting several neurotransmitter systems provide strong support for the hypothesis that the amygdala is a critical site for integrating the interactions of these systems in regulating memory storage. Those findings, considered alone, do not identify the locus of the influence of the amygdala. It is possible, of course, that the neural change underlying the memory effects is located within the amygdala. The evidence that long-term potentiation (LTP) can be induced in the amygdala (Clugnet & LeDoux, 1990), as well as the findings indicating that drugs that block LTP attenuate fear-based learning when administered into the amygdala prior to training (Falls, Miserendino, & Davis, 1992; Fanselow, Kim, & Landeira-Fernandez, 1991; Kim & McGaugh, 1992; LeDoux, 1992; Miserendino, Sananes, Melia, & Davis, 1990), support this view.

However, other findings suggest that the amygdala is not the site of memory storage, but, that the amygdala influences retention by modulating memory storage processes occurring in other brain regions. This view is supported by studies examining the effects of: ST lesions, posttraining lesions, and reversible inactivation of the amygdala.

Effects of ST Lesions

The ST is a major amygdala pathway that carries both afferent and efferent projections. The finding that lesions of the ST block the memory-enhancing effects of posttraining systemic injections of epinephrine (Liang & McGaugh, 1983b) was one of the early findings suggesting that epinephrine effects on memory involved the amygdala. Still, it was not clear from that experiment whether the lesion effect was due to the disruption of projections *to* the amygdala or *from* the amygdala. Other findings indicated that ST lesions also block the effects, on memory, of posttraining electrical stimulation of the amygdala (Liang & McGaugh, 1983a). These results clearly suggested that modulatory influences on memory involving the amygdala are not based on alteration of memory storage processes within the amygdala, but, rather, appear to be due to influences mediated by amygdala efferents. In support of this interpretation, the findings of other experiments indicated that ST lesions blocked the memory enhancement induced by posttraining systemic injections of the β-adrenergic agonist, clenbuterol (Introini-Collison et al., 1991), which readily enters the brain, as well as posttraining intra-amygdala infusions of NE (Liang, McGaugh, & Yao, 1990; see Fig. 2.5). These findings clearly indicate that alteration of amygdala functioning is not a sufficient condition for modulating memory storage; an intact ST is required. Such findings strongly suggest that the memory modulating influences involve amygdala efferents mediated by the ST and, by implication, modulatory influences on memory storage in brain regions activated by the amygdala.

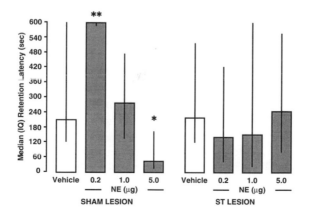

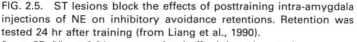

FIG. 2.5. ST lesions block the effects of posttraining intra-amygdala injections of NE on inhibitory avoidance retentions. Retention was tested 24 hr after training (from Liang et al., 1990).
*$p < .05$, **$p < 0.01$, compared to buffer-injected control group.

Effects of Posttraining Lesions of the Amygdala

Experiments in which the amygdala is lesioned after training would seem to provide a direct test of whether the amygdala is a critical site of the neural changes underlying learning. As noted in the introduction, there is extensive evidence indicating that lesions of the amygdala impair retention of fear-motivated learning tasks. However, because amygdala lesions might affect many processes influencing retention performance, it is not clear that the impaired retention induced by the lesions is due specifically to disruption of presumed neural changes located within the amygdala. Findings of several studies from our laboratory suggest that the amygdala lesions may induce other effects that alter retention performance and that, when these other effects are considered, amygdala-lesioned animals clearly demonstrate that they retain memory acquired during prior training.

Our experiments investigating this issue examined the effects of amygdala lesions on the retention of animals given different amounts of footshock-motivated training prior to induction of the lesions. If it is assumed that retention of the training is based solely on neural changes within the amygdala, lesions of the amygdala induced after training should abolish memory of the training. Evidence from several prior studies questions this assumption: These findings suggested that the retention-impairing effects of posttraining amygdala lesions can be attenuated by increasing the amount of training given prior to the lesions (Brady, Schreiner, Geller, & Kling, 1954; Horvath, 1963; Peinado-Manzano, 1987; Thatcher & Kimble, 1966). To examine this issue further (Parent, Tomaz, & McGaugh, 1992), rats received either 1, 10 or 20 escape training trials in a straight-alley. Controls received 1 trial without footshock. Bilateral excitotoxic (N-methyl-D-aspartate; NMDA) amygdala lesions (or sham control lesions) were induced 7 days after the training. Four days later, retention was tested using inhibitory avoidance testing procedures: The rats were placed in the safe compartment of the alley and their latencies to enter the compartment where they had received shock during the escape training were recorded.

In both the amygdala-lesioned groups and the sham control groups, retention was influenced by the amount of training given prior to the lesion, confirming the findings of previous studies. However, the lesions significantly impaired retention performance: Although the degree of sparing of retention was influenced by the amount of prior escape training, the retention performance demonstrated by the amygdala-lesioned rats was modest, at best, in comparison with that of sham-lesioned controls. Two days later, a subset of the rats was tested again. On this second retention test, the animals received footshock each time they entered the shock compartment, and they were retained in the apparatus until they remained in the safe compartment for 100 consecutive seconds. We refer to this procedure as continuous multi-trial inhibitory avoidance (CMIA) training. In comparison with rats that received no footshock on the original training, rats given 20 escape training trials required fewer trials (i.e., entries into the shock compartment) to reach the 100-second criterion. These findings provide additional evidence that the learning occurring in footshock-motivated training is not completely blocked by posttraining amygdala lesions.

Because of previous findings indicating that the effects of posttraining lesions on inhibitory avoidance retention decrease as the interval between training and induction of the lesions is increased (Liang et al., 1982), a second experiment was conducted using essentially the same procedures, except that the groups received 1 or 10 escape training trials and the bilateral amygdala lesions were induced 30 days after training (Parent, West, & McGaugh, 1994). Additionally, CMIA test procedures, as described above, were used for the retention test. The results are shown in Fig. 2.6. As can be seen (Fig. 2.6A), the amount of escape training influenced retention. As in the first experiment, in lesioned animals the degree of training effect, as indicated by initial latencies to enter the shock compartment, was modest. Thus, the effects of posttraining lesions on inhibitory avoidance retention performance were not decreased by increasing the interval between training and induction of the lesion.

However, as is shown in Fig. 2.6B, performance on the CMIA test clearly reflected the amount of prior training. Furthermore, the amygdala lesions significantly impaired the CMIA performance of the controls that were given no shock on the original training: In comparison with the sham controls, the lesioned

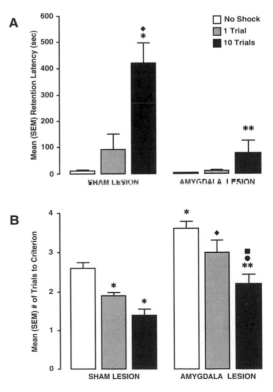

FIG. 2.6. The effects of (A) degree of training in an escape task latency to enter the dark, shock compartment on the initial retention test, and (B) number of trials required to reach the CMIA acquisition criterion 2 days after the initial retention test. Neurotoxic lesions were induced 30 days after escape training (from Parent, West, & McGaugh, 1994).
*$p < .05$, compared to Sham-No-Shock group. ♦ $p < .05$, compared to Sham-1 Trial group. **$p < .05$, compared to Sham-10 TRIAL group. ■ $p < .05$, compared to Amygdala Lesion-No Shock group. ● $p < .05$, compared to Amygdala Lesion-1 Trial group.

animals made more entries into the shock compartment before reaching the criterion of 100 seconds. When we take into account the magnitude of this lesion effect on the CMIA performance of the controls that were not given prior escape training, it appears that the lesions did not impair retention of the escape training. That is, on the CMIA test, the differences between sham- and amygdala-lesion groups given the same amount of prior escape training appear to be due solely to the nonspecific lesion effects on CMIA performance. The issue concerning the bases of the "non-specific" effects is addressed below.

A third experiment (Parent, Avila, & McGaugh, 1995), using procedures essentially the same as those in the first two, examined the effects of lesions restricted primarily to the complex nucleus of the amygdala. The findings of this experiment were comparable to those of the previous experiments. Retention on the first CMIA test trial, as well as the trials-to-criterion on the CMIA, varied with the amount of prior escape training. Furthermore, amygdala lesions impaired CMIA performance in animals that were given no footshock on the original training.

Effects of Inactivation of the Amygdala With Lidocaine

A subsequent experiment using training and testing procedures similar to those used in the experiments just described examined the effects of intra-amygdala infusions of lidocaine administered prior to the retention test. In this experiment (Coleman-Mesches, West, & McGaugh, in preparation), rats were given 0 (i.e., no shock), 2, or 10 escape training trials; 48 hours later, lidocaine or a buffer solution was infused into either the left or right amygdala 5 minutes before CMIA training. In the buffer control groups the initial latencies to enter the shock compartment varied directly with the number of escape training trials the animals had received. The lidocaine infusions administered into either the left or right amygdala significantly impaired retention performance, as indicated by the initial latencies to enter the dark compartment: That is, in the lidocaine-treated animals, the latencies did not reflect the degree of prior training. However, the lidocaine infusions did not impair CMIA performance and did not block the effects of prior training on CMIA performance. Two days after the CMIA training, the animals were given a single-trial inhibitory avoidance test. On this test, performance varied directly with the degree of prior escape training.

Considered together, these studies indicate that lesions of the amygdala induced after training and intra-amygdala infusions of lidocaine administered prior to the retention test impair inhibitory avoidance performance (i.e., reduce initial latencies to enter the shock compartment), but do not block the effects of degree of prior escape training on retention, as indicated by CMIA performance. These findings strongly suggest that the effects of these treatments on the initial inhibitory avoidance response latencies are not due to the disruption of memory of the training, but, rather, are due to some other effect(s) of impaired amygdala functioning.

Effects of Intra-Amygdala CNQX

These findings are of interest in interpreting the results of experiments investigating the effects of intra-amygdala infusions of the AMPA-receptor antagonist, CNQX. As already noted, the evidence that LTP can be induced in the amygdala (Clugnet & LeDoux, 1990) and that NMDA antagonists infused into the amygdala prior to training attenuate aversively motivated learning (Falls et al., 1992; Fanselow et al., 1991; Kim & McGaugh, 1992; LeDoux, 1992; Miserendino et al., 1990) suggests that fear-based learning may be based on LTP within the amygdala. LTP expression is known to involve the activation of AMPA glutamatergic receptors (Collingridge et al., 1990). Recent experiments have reported that intra-amygdala infusion of the AMPA receptor antagonist, CNQX, prior to the retention test impairs inhibitory avoidance performance (Bianchin et al., 1993; Izquierdo, this volume, chapter 3; Izquierdo et al., 1993; Liang, 1991) and fear-potentiated startle (Kim et al., 1993). These findings are consistent with the hypothesis that fear-based learning is mediated by LTP in the amygdala.

To investigate this issue further, recent experiments in our laboratory (Mesches, Bianchin, & McGaugh, in preparation) examined the effects of intra-amygdala infusions of CNQX on inhibitory avoidance and CMIA performance, using training and testing procedures similar to those already described. Rats were first given 0 (no shock), 1, or 10 escape training trials in the straight alley. Eight days later, buffer or CNQX solutions were infused bilaterally 10 minutes before inhibitory avoidance testing and CMIA training. The results are shown in Fig. 2.7. The CNQX clearly attenuated, but did not block, the effect of prior escape training on the initial retention latency (Fig. 2.7A). These findings are consistent with those of previous studies of intra-amygdala CNQX effects on inhibitory avoidance performance. However, in both the CNQX-treated and the buffer controls, the amount of prior escape training clearly affected CMIA performance (Fig. 2.7B). Additionally, as we previously found with amygdala lesions, CNQX tended to impair the CMIA performance of animals that did not receive footshock escape training. Thus, as with the effects of posttraining lesions, the effects of CNQX infusions or retention performance do not appear to result from the blocking of memory of the escape training. Accordingly, the findings do not support the view that the learning of fear-motivated escape is mediated by LTP in the amygdala.

The findings of other experiments (Mesches et al., in preparation) indicated that intra-amygdala infusions of CNQX increased rats' locomotor activity and decreased sensitivity to footshock. The locomotor effect might account, at least in part, for the low response latencies seen in the inhibitory avoidance test. Furthermore, it seems likely that the increased locomotor activity and reduced shock sensitivity induced by intra-amygdala infusions of CNQX are at least

FIG. 2.7. The effects of pre-test, intra-amygdala infusions of CNQX, and degree of training in an escape task on Mean(SEM) latency to enter the dark shock compartment (A) and Mean(SEM) number of tri-als required to reach the CMIA acquisition criterion immediately after the initial retention test (B). CNQX infused into the amygdala 10 min before the retention test impaired performance as mea-sured by the initial step-through latency and the increased num-ber of trials to reach criterion. However, CNQX did not block the influence on CMIA perfor-mance of the initial degree of training (from Mesches, Bi-anchin & McGaugh, 1994).
♦ $p < .05$, compared to all other groups. *$p < .05$, compared to VEH-NO SHOCK group. ●$p < .05$, compared to CNQX-NO SHOCK group. **$p < .05$, com-pared to VEH-1 TRIAL group. ■ $p < .05$, compared to VEH-10 TRIAL group.

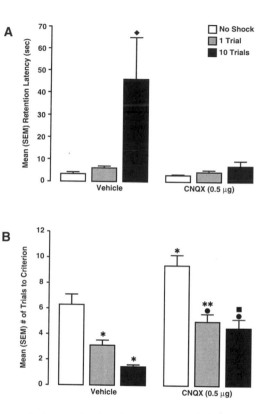

partially responsible for the difference between the buffer controls and CNQX-treated animals in number of trials (shocks received) in the CMIA task. Intra-amygdala infusions of CNQX also reduced anxiety assessed in a "+" maze, a task that is sensitive to benzodiazepines. Thus, the effects of CNQX on inhibi-tory avoidance performance may be due, at least in part, to a non-specific attenuation of fear.

What is Lost and What is Spared?

The findings of our studies of the effects of intra-amygdala infusions of CNQX and lidocaine as well as our findings of studies of the effects of posttraining lesions of the amygdala quite clearly indicate that an intact amygdala is required for normal expression of inhibitory avoidance performance. Furthermore, the findings suggest that these treatments have a common effect in attenuating emo-tional arousal associated with aversive stimulation. From this perspective our findings are consistent with the view that the amygdala is involved in the expres-sion of learned fear (Davis, 1992a; LeDoux, 1992; Izquierdo, et al., 1993). However, the posttraining amygdala lesions and intra-amygdala drug injections clearly did not block the effects of prior escape training and did not block responsiveness to the footshock stimulation received in the CMIA testing: All animals learned the CMIA task. Thus, an intact amygdala does not seem to be required either for the retention of fear-based learning or for the fear-based learning that is assessed in the CMIA task.

These results contrast with findings indicating that posttraining lesions of the amygdala induced after extensive training block the expression of fear-potentiated startle (Kim & Davis, 1993). In our experiments, as in those of Izquierdo and his colleagues (Izquierdo, this volume, chapter 3), the amygdala treatments typically attenuated, but did not completely block, inhibitory avoidance performance. However, our findings are consistent with the evidence that rats given extensive training prior to induction of lesions readily relearn the fear-potentiated response (Kim & Davis, 1993). These findings clearly indicate that an intact amygdala is not essential for the expression of fear-based learning.

Although escape and inhibitory avoidance training procedures clearly induce fear, it is also evident that the animals given such training learn much about the specific conditions of the training. They learn when and where the footshock is delivered, and they learn that they can escape from the punishment. Lesions and drug infusions that disrupt amygdala functioning do not appear to block memory of these conditions of training. In fact, as we have emphasized, the impairment, when seen, may be due to influences of the treatments on perceptual, motivational, and motor processes, in addition to attenuation of fear-based responses.

Recent studies from our laboratory investigating the involvement of the amygdala in retention of training in water maze tasks provide additional insights into the role of the amygdala in memory (Packard, Cahill, & McGaugh, 1994). Although the motivation in these tasks is aversive (i.e., escape from water by swimming to a platform), retention is not based on the expression of fear. In these experiments, rats were trained in one of two water maze tasks, a spatial task and a visually cued task. In the spatial task, a submerged escape platform was positioned in a constant location in the water tank. In the visually cued task, a visible escape platform was positioned at different locations on each trial. Latency to mount the platform was used as the measure of learning and subsequent retention. In the first experiment, amphetamine or a control solution was infused unilaterally into the amygdala, hippocampus, or caudate nucleus immediately after the training session. When they were tested the following day, animals given the intra-hippocampal injections showed selective enhancement of the retention of memory for the spatial task, and animals given intra-caudate injections showed selective enhancement of retention of the cued task. The hippocampal and caudate injections specifically influenced retention of the task that is known, from the results of double-dissociation experiments, to be differentially impaired by lesions of the hippocampus and caudate, respectively. In contrast, animals given posttraining intra-amygdala infusion of amphetamine showed enhanced retention on both tasks. In a second experiment, rats received intra-amygdala infusions of amphetamine or a control solution immediately after training, and lidocaine was infused into the amygdala prior to the retention test. As in the first experiment, the amphetamine infusions enhanced retention on both tasks. Most importantly, the lidocaine infusions into the amygdala prior to the retention tests did not block the memory-enhancing effects of the intra-amygdala amphetamine infusions.

These results provide additional support for the view that the amygdala plays a general role in modulating the storage of recently acquired information. In addition, the findings provide further evidence that inactivation of the amygdala does not block the expression of learning based on aversive motivation. The attenuation of memory induced by amygdala inactivation, when observed, may be restricted to the expression of the emotion (e.g., fear) associated with the training stimulation. In this regard, it is of interest that, although intra-amygdala infusions of CNQX administered prior to retention tests only partially attenuated inhibitory avoidance performance, concurrent infusion of CNQX into the hippocampus produced severe retention impairment (Izquierdo, this volume, chapter 3; Izquierdo et al., 1993). These findings are consistent with extensive evidence (Eichenbaum, Young, & Bunsey this volume, chapter 9) suggesting that the hippocampus is involved in mediating retention of information concerning the training conditions.

CONCLUDING COMMENTS

Several conclusions can be drawn from the experimental findings summarized in this chapter. First, there is strong evidence supporting the hypothesis that the amygdala is involved in regulating the storage of recently acquired information. Second, the effects of many treatments affecting hormonal and neurotransmitter systems appear to be mediated by converging influences involving the amygdala. Third, the findings suggest that the amygdala is not the site of lasting neural changes underlying the memory-modulating influences of treatments affecting amygdala functioning. Fourth, although the findings are consistent with the hypothesis that the amygdala is involved in the expression of learned fear, they strongly suggest that the amygdala is not a critical locus of memory storage resulting from aversively motivated training. Overall, the findings provide strong support for the hypothesis that the amygdala regulates the storage of recently acquired information by modulating memory storage processes occurring in brain regions activated by the amygdala.

ACKNOWLEDGMENTS

This work was supported by USPHS Grant MH-12526 from NIMH and NIDA (to J. L. M.), by NIA AG00096 (to L. C.), by NIMH Training Grant MH14599 (to M. H. M. and K. C.-M.), by 1967 Natural Science and Engineering Research

Council of Canada (to M. B. P.), and by NSF Graduate Fellowship RCD-9054728 and APA Minority Research Fellowship 2-T32 MH18882 (to J.A.S.).

REFERENCES

Aggleton, J. P., & Passingham, R. E. (1982). An assessment of the reinforcing properties of foods after amygdaloid lesions in rhesus monkeys. *Journal of Comparative Physiological Psychology*, *96*, 71–77.

Ammassari-Teule, M., Pavone, F., Castellano, C., & McGaugh, J. (1991). Amygdala and dorsal hippocampus lesions block the effects of GABAergic drugs on memory storage. *Brain Research*, *551*, 104–109.

Amsel, A. (1962). Frustrative nonreward in partial reinforcement and discrimination learning. *Psychological Review*, *69*, 306–328.

Bennett, C., Liang, K. C., & McGaugh, J. L. (1985). Depletion of adrenal catecholamines alters the amnestic effect of amygdala stimulation. *Behavioural Brain Research*, *15*, 83–91.

Bianchin, M., Walz, R., Ruschel, A. C., Zanatta, M. S., Da Silva, R. C., Bueno e Silva, M., Paczko, N., Medina, J. H., & Izquierdo, I. (1993). Memory expression is blocked by the infusion of CNQX into the hippocampus and/or the amygdala up to 20 days after training. *Behavioral and Neural Biology*, *59*, 83–86.

Brady, J. V., Schreiner, L., Geller, I., & Kling, A. (1954). Subcortical mechanisms in emotional behavior: The effect of rhinencephalic injury upon the acquisition and retention of a conditioned avoidance response in cats. *Journal of Comparative and Physiological Psychology*, *47*, 178–186.

Brioni, J. D., Nagahara, A. H., & McGaugh, J. L. (1989). Involvement of the amygdala GABAergic system in the modulation of memory storage. *Brain Research*, *487*, 105–112.

Bucherelli, C., Tassoni, G., & Bures, J. (1992). Time-dependent disruption of passive avoidance acquisition by post-training intra-amygdala injection of tetrodotoxin in rats. *Neuroscience Letters*, *140*, 231–234.

Cahill, L., & McGaugh, J. L. (1991). NMDA-induced lesions of the amygdaloid complex block the retention enhancing effect of posttraining epinephrine. *Psychobiology*, *19*, 206–210.

Castellano, C., Brioni, J. D., & McGaugh, J. L. (1990). GABAergic modulation of memory. In L. Squire & E. Lindenlaub (Eds.), *The biology of memory* (pp. 361–378). Stuttgart: F. K. Schattauer Verlag.

Clugnet, M. C., & LeDoux, J. E. (1990). Synaptic plasticity in fear conditioning circuits: Induction of LTP in the lateral nucleus of the amygdala by stimulation of the medial geniculate body. *Journal of Neuroscience*, *10*, 2818–2824.

Coleman-Mesches, K., West, M. A. & McGaugh, J. L. (in preparation). *Overtraining in an escape task attenuates differential involvement of the right and left amygdalae in retrieval of inhibitory avoidance training*.

Collingridge, G. L., Bashir, Z. I., Blake, J. F., Davies, C. H., Davies, S. N., Irving, A. J., Randall, A. D., & Schofield, J. G. (1990). Amino acid receptors and LTP in area CA1 of the hippocampus. In L. R. Squire & E. Lindenlaub (Eds.), *The biology of memory* (pp. 233–250). Stuttgart: F. K. Schattauer Verlag.

Crespi, L. (1942). Quantitative variation in incentive and performance in the white rat. *American Journal of Psychology*, *55*, 467–515.

Davis, M. (1992a). The role of the amygdala in conditioned fear. In J. Aggleton (Eds.), *The amygdala* (pp. 255–306). New York: Wiley-Liss.

Davis, M. (1992b). The role of the amygdala in fear and anxiety. *Annual Review of Neuroscience*, *15*, 353–375.

Dickinson-Anson, H., & McGaugh, J. L. (1993). Midazolam administered into the amygdala impairs retention of an inhibitory avoidance task. *Behavioral and Neural Biology*, *60*, 84–87.

Dickinson-Anson, H., Mesches, M. H., Coleman, K., & McGaugh, J. L. (1993). Bicuculline administered into the amygdala blocks benzodiazepine-induced amnesia. *Behavioral and Neural Biology, 60*, 1–4.

Everitt, B. J., & Robbins, T. W. (1992). *Amygdala–ventral striatal interactions and reward-related processes.* In J. P. Aggleton (Ed.), The amygdala (pp. 401–430) New York: Wiley-Liss.

Falls, W. A., Miserendino, M. J. D., & Davis, M. (1992). Extinction of fear-potentiated startle: Blockade by infusion of an NMDA antagonist into the amygdala. *Journal of Neuroscience, 12*, 854–863.

Fanselow, M. S., Kim, J. J., & Landeira-Fernandez, J. (1991). Anatomically selective blockade of Pavlovian fear conditioning by application of an NMDA antagonist to the amygdala and periaqueductal gray. *Society for Neuroscience Abstracts,17*659

Flood, J., Garland, J., & Morley, J. (1992). Evidence that cholecystokinin-enhanced retention is mediated by changes in opioid activity in the amygdala. *Brain Research, 585*, 94–104.

Gaffan, D. (1992). Amygdala and the memory of reward. In J. Aggleton (Ed.), *The amygdala* (pp. 471–484). New York: Wiley-Liss.

Gallagher, M., Kapp, B. S., Pascoe, J. P., & Rapp, P. R. (1981). A neuropharmacology of amygdaloid systems which contribute to learning and memory. In Y. Ben-Ari (Eds.), *The amygdaloid complex* (pp. 343–354). Amsterdam: Elsevier North Holland.

Gold, P. E., Hankins, L., Edwards, R. M., Chester, J., & McGaugh, J. L. (1975). Memory interference and facilitation with posttrial amygdala stimulation: Effect on memory varies with footshock level. *Brain Research, 86*, 509–513.

Gold, P. E., & McGaugh, J. L. (1975). A single-trace, two-process view of memory storage processes. In D. Deutsch & J. A. Deutsch (Eds.), *Short-term memory* (pp. 355–378). New York: Academic Press.

Gold, P. E., & van Buskirk, R. (1975). Facilitation of time-dependent memory processes with posttrial epinephrine injections. *Behavioral Biology, 13*, 247–260.

Hiroi, N., & White, N. M. (1991). The lateral nucleus of the amygdala mediates expression of the amphetamine-produced conditioned place preference. *Journal of Neuroscience, 11*, 2107–2116.

Horvath, F. E. (1963). Effects of basolateral amygdalectomy on three types of avoidance behavior in cats. *Journal of Comparative and Physiological Psychology, 56*, 380–389.

Introini-Collison, I. B., Dalmaz, C., & McGaugh, J. L. (submitted) Amygdala β-noradrenergic influences on memory storage involve cholinergic activation.

Introini-Collison, I., Ford, L., & McGaugh, J. L. (1994). Memory impairment induced by intra-amygdala b-endorphin is mediated by noradrenergic influences. *Neurobiology of Learning and Memory.*

Introini-Collison, I. B., Miyazaki, B., & McGaugh, J. (1991). Involvement of the amygdala in the memory-enhancing effects of clenbuterol. *Psychopharmacology, 104*, 541–544.

Introini-Collison, I. B., Nagahara, A. H., & McGaugh, J. L. (1989). Memory-enhancement with intra-amygdala posttraining naloxone is blocked by concurrent administration of propranolol. *Brain Research, 476*, 94–101.

Izquierdo, I., Bianchin, M., Silva, M., Zanatta, M., Walz, R., Ruschel, A., Silva, R., Paczko, N., & Medina, J. (1993). CNQX infused into rat hippocampus or amygdala disrupts the expression of memory of two different tasks. *Behavioral and Neural Biology, 59*, 104.

Izquierdo, I., Da Cunha, C., & Medina, J. (1990). Endogenous benzodiazepine modulation of memory processes. *Neuroscience and Biobehavioral Reviews, 14*, 419–424.

Izquierdo, I., & Dias, R. D. (1983). Effect of ACTH, epinephrine, b-endorphin, naloxone, and of the combination of naloxone or b-endorphin with ACTH or epinephrine on memory consolidation. *Psychoneuroendocrinology, 8*, 81–87.

Izquierdo, I., & Graudenz, M. (1980). Memory facilitation by naloxone is due to release of dopaminergic and beta-adrenergic systems from tonic inhibition. *Psychopharmacology, 67*, 265–268.

Izquierdo, I., Medina, J. H., Netto, C. A., & Pereira, M. E. (1991). Peripheral and central effects on memory of peripherally and centrally administered opioids and benzodiazepines. In R. C. A.

Frederickson, J. L. McGaugh, & D. L. Felten (Eds.), *Peripheral signalling of the brain: Role of neural–immune interactions in learning and memory.* (pp. 419–424). Toronto: Hogrefe and Huber.

Jones, B., & Mishkin, M. (1972). Limbic lesions and the problem of stimulus–reinforcement associations. *Experimental Neurology, 36,* 362–377.

Kesner, R. P. (1992). Learning and memory in rats with an emphasis on the role of the amygdala. In J. P. Aggleton (Ed.), *The amygdala: Neurobiological aspects of emotion, memory, and mental dysfunction* (pp. 379–399). New York: Wiley-Liss.

Kesner, R. P., & Wilburn, M. (1974). A review of electrical stimulation of the brain in the context of learning and retention. *Behavioral Biology, 10,* 259–293.

Kim, M., Campeau, S., Falls, W. A., & Davis, M. (1993). Intra-amygdala infusion of the non-NMDA receptor antagonist CNQX blocks the expression of fear-potentiated startle. *Behavioral and Neural Biology, 59,* 5–8.

Kim, M., & Davis, M. (1993). Electrolytic lesions of the amygdala block acquisition and expression of fear-potentiated startle even with extensive training but do not prevent reacquisition. *Behavioral Neuroscience, 107,* 580–595.

Kim, M., & McGaugh, J. L. (1992). Effects of intra-amygdala injections of NMDA receptor antagonists on acquisition and retention of inhibitory avoidance. *Brain Research, 585,* 35–48.

LeDoux, J. (1992). Emotion as memory: Anatomical systems underlying indelible neural traces. In S.-A. Christianson (Ed.), *The handbook of emotion and memory: Research and Theory* (pp. 269–288). Hillsdale, NJ: Lawrence Erlbaum Associates.

Liang, K. C. (1991). Pretest intra-amygdala injection of lidocaine or glutamate antagonists impairs retention performance in an inhibitory avoidance response. *Society for Neuroscience Abstracts, 17,* 486.

Liang, K. C., Bennett, C., & McGaugh, J. L. (1985). Peripheral epinephrine modulates the effects of posttraining amygdala stimulation on memory. *Behavioural Brain Research, 15,* 93–100.

Liang, K. C., Juler, R., & McGaugh, J. L. (1986). Modulating effects of posttraining epinephrine on memory: Involvement of the amygdala noradrenergic system. *Brain Research, 368,* 125–133.

Liang, K. C., & McGaugh, J. L. (1983a). Lesions of the stria terminalis attenuate the amnestic effect of amygdaloid stimulation on avoidance responses. *Brain Research, 274,* 309–318.

Liang, K. C., & McGaugh, J. L. (1983b). Lesions of the stria terminalis attenuate the enhancing effect of posttraining epinephrine on retention of an inhibitory avoidance response. *Behavioural Brain Research, 9,* 49–58.

Liang, K. C., McGaugh, J. L., Martinez, J. L. J., Jensen, R. A., Vasquez, B. J., & Messing, R. B. (1982). Post-training amygdaloid lesions impair retention of an inhibitory avoidance response. *Behavioral Brain Research, 4,* 237–249.

Liang, K. C., McGaugh, J. L., & Yao, H. (1990). Involvement of amygdala pathways in the influence of posttraining amygdala norepinephrine and peripheral epinephrine on memory storage. *Brain Research, 508,* 225–233.

Lister, R. G. (1985). The amnestic action of benzodiazepines in man. *Neuroscience and Biobehavioral Review, 9,* 87–93.

McGaugh, J. L. (1973). Drug facilitation of learning and memory. *Annual Review of Pharmacology, 13,* 229–241.

McGaugh, J. L. (1989). Involvement of hormonal and neuromodulatory systems in the regulation of memory storage. *Annual Review of Neuroscience, 12,* 255–287.

McGaugh, J.L. (1990) Significance and remembrance: The role of neuromodulatory systems. *Psychological Science, 1,* 15–25.

McGaugh, J. L. (1992). Affect, neuromodulatory systems, and memory storage. In S.-A. Christianson (Ed.), *The handbook of emotion and memory: research and theory* (pp. 245–268). Hillsdale, NJ: Lawrence Erlbaum Associates.

McGaugh, J. L., & Gold, P. E. (1976). Modulation of memory by electrical stimulation of the brain. In M. R. Rosenzweig & E. L. Bennett (Eds.), *Neural mechanisms of learning and memory* (pp. 549–560). Cambridge, MA: MIT Press.

McGaugh, J. L., & Gold, P. E. (1989). Hormonal modulation of memory. In R. B. Brush & S. Levine (Eds.), *Psychoendocrinology* (pp. 305–339). New York: Academic Press.

McGaugh, J. L., & Herz, M. J. (1972). *Memory consolidation*. San Francisco: Albion.

McGaugh, J., Introini-Collison, I., & Castellano, C. (1993). Involvement of opioid peptides in learning and memory. In A. Herz, H. Akil, & E. Simon (Eds.), *Handbook of experimental pharmacology: Opioids. Part II* (pp. 429–447). Heidelberg: Springer-Verlag.

McGaugh, J. L., Introini-Collison, I. B., Juler, R. G., & Izquierdo, I. (1986). Stria terminalis lesions attenuate the effects of posttraining naloxone and β-endorphin on retention. *Behavioral Neuroscience, 100*, 839–844.

McGaugh, J. L., Introini-Collison, I. B., & Nagahara, A. H. (1988). Memory-enhancing effects of posttraining naloxone: Involvement of β-noradrenergic influences in the amygdaloid complex. *Brain Research, 446*, 37–49.

Mesches, M. H., Bianchin, M., & McGaugh, J. L. (in preparation). *Intra-amygdala CNQX does not block retention of escape training*.

Miserendino, M. J. D., Sananes, C. B., Melia, K. R., & Davis, M. (1990). Blocking of acquisition but not expression of conditioned fear-potentiated startle by NMDA antagonists in the amygdala. *Nature, 345*, 716–718.

Packard, M., Cahill, L., & McGaugh, J. L. (1995). Amygdala modulation of hippocampal-dependent and caudate nucleus-dependent memory processes. *Proceedings of the National Academy of Sciences, 91*, 8477–8481.

Packard, M., Williams, C. L., Cahill, L., & McGaugh, J. L. (in press). The anatomy of a memory modulatory system: From periphery to brain. In N. Spear, L. Spear, & M. Woodruff (Eds.), *Neurobehavioral plasticity: Learning, development and response to brain insults* (pp. 149–184). Hillsdale, NJ: Lawrence Erlbaum Associates.

Parent, M. B., Avila, E., & McGaugh, J. L. (1995). Increased training in a footshock-motivated task attenuates the memory-impairing effects of posttraining amygdala basolateral complex lesions. *Brain Research*.

Parent, M. B., & McGaugh, J. L. (1994). Posttraining infusion of lidocaine into the amygdala basolateral complex impairs retention of inhibitory avoidance training. *Brain Research, 661*, 97–103.

Parent, M., Tomaz, C., & McGaugh, J. (1992). Increased training in an aversively motivated task attenuates the memory impairing effects of posttraining N-Methyl-D-Aspartate-induced amygdala lesions. *Behavioral Neuroscience, 106*, 791–799.

Parent, M. B., West, M., & McGaugh, J. L. (1994). Retention of rats with amygdala lesions induced 30 days after footshock-motivated escape training reflects degree of original training. *Behavioral Neuroscience, 6*, 1080–1087.

Peinado-Manzano, M. A. (1987). Intervention of the basolateral amygdala on the retention of one trial versus multiple trial passive avoidance learning. *Medical Science Research, 15*, 245–246.

Salinas, J. A., Packard, M. G., & McGaugh, J. L. (1993). Amygdala modulates memory for changes in reward magnitude: Reversible post-training inactivation with lidocaine attenuates the response to a reduction in reward. *Behavioral Brain Research, 59*, 153–159.

Sarter, M., & Markowitsch, H. J. (1985). Involvement of the amygdala in learning and memory: A critical review, with emphasis on anatomical relations. *Behavioral Neuroscience, 99*, 342–380.

Tanaka, M., Kohno, Y., Nakagawa, R., Ida, Y., Takeda, S., & Nagasaki, N. (1982). Time-related differences in noradrenaline turnover in rat brain regions by stress. *Pharmacology, Biochemistry and Behavior, 16*, 315–319.

Thatcher, R. W., & Kimble, D. P. (1966). Effect of amygdaloid lesions on retention of an avoidance response in overtrained and non-overtrained rats. *Psychonomic Science, 6*, 9-10.

Tomaz, C., Dickinson-Anson, H., & McGaugh, J. L. (1991). Amygdala lesions block the amnestic effects of diazepam. *Brain Research, 568*, 85–91.

Tomaz, C., Dickinson-Anson, H., & McGaugh, J. L. (1992). Basolateral amygdala lesions block diazepam-induced anterograde amnesia in an inhibitory avoidance task. *Proceedings of the National Academy of Sciences (USA)*, *89*, 3615–3619.

Tomaz, C. T., Dickinson-Anson, H., McGaugh, J. L., Souza-Silva, M. B., Viana, M. B., & Graeff, F. G. (1993). Localization in the amygdala of the amnestic action of diazepam on emotional memory. *Behavioural Brain Research*, *58*, 99–105.

Werling, L., McMahon, P., Portoghese, P., Takemori, A., & Cox, B. (1989). Selective opioid antagonist effects on opioid-induced inhibition of release of norepinephrine in guinea pig cortex. *Neuropharmacology*, *28*, 103–107.

Williams, C., & McGaugh, J. (1993). Reversible lesions of the nucleus of the solitary tract attenuate the memory-modulating effects of posttraining epinephrine. *Behavioral Neuroscience*, *107*, 1–8.

Wolfman, C., DaCunha, C., Jerusalinsky, D., Levi de Stein, M., Viola, H., Izquierdo, I., & Medina, J. H. (1991). Habituation and inhibitory avoidance training alter brain regional levels of benzodiazepine-like molecules and are affected by intracerebral flumazenil microinjection. *Brain Research*, *548*, 74–80.

3

Role of the Hippocampus, Amygdala, and Entorhinal Cortex in Memory Storage and Expression

Ivan Izquierdo
Universidade Federal do Rio Grande do Sul

SUMMARY

Recent evidence suggests that the hippocampus, amygdala, medial septum and entorhinal cortex participate in memory through long-term potentiation (LTP). This is induced at the time of training in the former three structures and in the entorhinal cortex 90–180 minutes later. Memories can be blocked by the immediate posttraining infusion into one or other of these structures of D-amino-5-phosphono pentanoate (AP5), of the GABA-A receptor antagonist, muscimol, or of blockers of the synthesis or action of various putative retrograde messenger substances, by the delayed post-training infusion of inhibitors of calcium calmodulin kinase II or of protein kinase C, and by the infusion of 6-cyano-7-nitroquinoxaline-2,3-dione (CNQX) at the time of memory expression. Post-training drug effects are seen 90–180 minutes later in the entorhinal cortex than in hippocampus, amygdala or medial septum, suggesting that memory-relevant LTP is initiated in that structure later than in the others. In addition, the early intrahippocampal posttraining infusion of an antagonist of glutamate metabotropic receptors blocks memory, and protein kinase C activity and the binding of D,L-alpha-amino-3-hydroxy-5-methyl-4-isoxazole propionate (AMPA) to its receptors increases in hippocampus for 2 h after training. The nature and the time course of the drug effects and biochemical findings is closely similar to those reported by other authors for hippocampal LTP.

Long-term potentiation (LTP) is by itself a form of memory measurable at the synaptic level (Bliss & Collingridge, 1993; Izquierdo, 1994; Lynch & Granger, 1992). Accordingly, it has often been viewed as a mechanism of memory at the whole animal level, since its discovery in 1973 (see Bliss & Collingridge, 1993).

Suggestions that LTP can actually be a basis of memory processes come from four sources:

1. Similarities between LTP and memory: Evidence comes from input specificity, associativity, the existence of a labile period during and after induction, the long maintenance without the need for expression (Lynch & Granger, 1992; Müller, Arai, & Lynch, 1992), and the rapid expression in response to a reiteration of the stimuli that had been used for their acquisition (Bianchin et al., 1993; M. Davis, 1992; Izquierdo, Da Silva, et al., 1993; Quillfeldt et al., 1993).

2. Correlational experiments: Roman, Stäubli, and Lynch (1987), and Roman, Chaillan, and Soumireu-Mourat (1993) measured LTP in the piriform cortex simultaneously with learning of olfactory tasks that use the same stimulus that triggers the LTP as a behavioral cue.

3. Mutant mice with specific deletion of metabotropic glutamate receptor subunits (Conquet et al., 1994), of various protein kinases (Grant & Silva, 1994), or with a targeted mutation of proteins involved in the transcription process (Bourtchuladze et al., 1994) show an impaired capacity to make both hippocampal LTP and hippocampus-based memories, which suggests a correlation between both processes. However, the learning impairment is seldom as complete as that of LTP, and the possibility of developmental abmormalities and compensatory changes forbids a clear-cut conclusion from experiments of this sort (Malenka, 1994).

4. Pharmacologic experiments: These have provided, by far, the best evidence that LTP in discrete regions of the brain can actually underlie, or at least be the basis of important aspects of, memory. Recent experiments have shown a great similarity of action of a large number and variety of drugs on both LTP and memory, and point to a role of LTP in hippocampus, amygdala, medial septum and entorhinal cortex in memory storage and retrieval (see Izquierdo, 1994; Izquierdo & Medina, 1995; Izquierdo, Medina et al., 1993). The present chapter reviews these findings.

THE ROLE OF THE HIPPOCAMPUS, AMYGDALA
AND ENTORHINAL CORTEX IN MEMORY:
LESION VERSUS INFUSION STUDIES

Lesion studies have shown that the amygdala specializes in the processing of alerting (Cahill & McGaugh, 1990) and/or aversive information (M. Davis, 1992; Gray, 1982). The hippocampus handles spatial information, which in monkeys and humans is mainly visual and in the rat is mostly olfactory (Izquierdo & Medina, 1991, 1995; Izquierdo, Medina et al., 1993; Morris, Anderson, Lynch, & Baudry, 1986). The medial septum shares a role in the processing of spatial memory with the hippocampus and a role in aversive memories with the amygdala (Gray, 1982; Izquierdo, Medina et al., 1993).

The entorhinal cortex processes aversive, spatial, and other types of information (Ferreira, Da Silva, et al., 1992; R. Thompson, 1976; Zola-Morgan, Squire, Amaral, & Suzuki, 1989; Zola-Morgan, Squire, Clower & Rempel, 1993). This correlates with the fact that the entorhinal cortex has two-way monosynaptic and polysynaptic connections with the amygdala, hippocampus and medial septum (Arriagada, Marzloff & Hyman, 1992; Hyman, Van Hoesen, & Damasio, 1990; Witter et al., 1989). Further, the entorhinal cortex is intimately linked with the neighboring perirhinal cortex, and through it connects with most sensory and associative cortical areas (Witter, Groenewegen, Lopes da Silva, & Lohman, 1989).

In view of all these connections, it is not surprising that the combined lesion of hippocampus and amygdala, or hippocampus and septum, can cause severe anterograde amnesia; but the bilateral lesion of the entorhinal cortex is more amnestic than the former (Squire, 1987; Zola-Morgan et al., 1989, 1993). The amnesia caused by lesions of these structures spares memories acquired some time before the lesions. Patient H.M., who underwent bilateral temporal lobectomy in 1953 and has been basically unable to form new memories since, can remember memories acquired until a few weeks prior to his surgery (see Squire, 1987).

One problem with lesion studies is that the areas to which the injured regions project suffer extensive rearrangements that may modify their physiology. An illustrative case is that of the thorough rearrangement of hippocampal synapses following lesions of the entorhinal cortex or the perforant path (Cotman, Nieto-Sampedro, & Harris, 1981; Reeves & Smith, 1987). Alternative circuits that are normally inoperative may take over the function of the injured region (see Izquierdo, 1989, 1993).

For these reasons, some laboratories prefer to study the reversible effects of infusions into discrete brain areas of specific agonists and antagonists of neurotransmitter receptors, or enzyme inhibitors, dissolved in volumes usually not larger than 0.5 μl. The effects of such treatments are limited in time (<60 minutes) and space (<8–10 cu. mm), as shown by Martin (1991) using radiolabeled lidocaine and muscimol. These two substances produce inhibition of neural activity within these space and time constraints, measurable by a decline of the uptake of 2-deoxyglucose in the tissue surrounding the tip of the infusion cannula. Because no differences are seen in this response between lidocaine and muscimol, it is to be presumed that other polar substances dissolved in water or saline would present diffusion constants similar to those of these two substances. Our observations on the spread of 2% or 4% methylene blue or India ink infused into brain tissue (Ferreira, Da Silva, et al., 1992; Jerusalinsky et al., 1992) are consistent with those of Martin (1991) on lidocaine and muscimol.

The use of localized infusions of muscimol allowed Krupa, J. K. Thompson, & R. F. Thompson (1993) to determine that the memory trace of eye-blink conditioning in rabbits is formed and stored in the cerebellum and is expressed through the red nucleus. It also allowed Jerusalinsky, Quillfeldt et al. (1994a) to determine that, in the posttraining period, memory-relevant information does not flow from the entorhinal cortex to the amygdala and hippocampus.

MEMORY STORAGE: INVOLVEMENT OF GLUTAMATE RECEPTORS IN THE HIPPOCAMPUS, AMYGDALA AND MEDIAL SEPTUM

As in most other regions of the brain, in the amygdala, hippocampus, medial septum and entorhinal cortex excitatory transmission is mainly mediated by glutamate, and inhibitory transmission is mediated by gamma-amino butyric acid (GABA) (see Nieuwenhuys, 1989). There are three major glutamate receptor families: the NMDA and AMPA/kainate receptors, which are ionotropic, and the metabotropic receptors (mGluRs) (Bliss & Collingridge, 1993). NMDA stands for N-methyl-D-aspartate, and AMPA for D,L-alpha-amino-3-hydroxy-5-methyl-4-isoxazolone propionate, two artificial selective agonists at each of these receptors. Cholinergic muscarinic and β-noradrenergic receptors probably play important modulatory roles in all of these structures (Cheun & Yen, 1992; Leranth & Frotscher, 1989; Milner & Bacon, 1989; see Izquierdo, 1992).

In 1986, Morris, Anderson, Lynch and Baudry showed that the intracerebroventricular infusion of a specific antagonist at NMDA receptors, AP5 (D-amino-5-phosphono pentanoate) at doses that block hippocampal LTP hindered learning in the water maze, a spatial task that relies heavily on the hippocampus. In 1989, Stäubli, Thibault, De Lorenzo and Lynch reported that infusion of AP5 into one lateral ventricle hindered an olfactory discrimination task in rats. The importance of these findings relied on the fact that LTP induction in the hippocampus CA1 region and elsewhere is mediated by NMDA receptors (Bliss & Collingridge, 1993). Therefore, the findings of Morris et al. and of Stäubli et al. were taken to suggest that memory depended or relied on LTP, and were very heuristic.

In the following years, it was shown that intra-amygdala infusion of AP5 or of its heptanoic acid analog, AP7, blocks fear-potentiated startle (Miserendino, Sananes, Meliá, & Davis, 1990) and different forms of inhibitory avoidance in the rat (Izquierdo et al., 1992; Kim & McGaugh, 1992). This task, like others of an alerting or aversive nature, depends on the functional integrity of the amygdala (Cahill & McGaugh, 1990; Davis, 1992). It also depends, however, on the hippocampus and the medial septum (Izquierdo et al., 1993; Wolfman et al., 1991). Accordingly, it was observed that the immediate posttraining infusion of AP5 into the hippocampus or medial septum is also amnestic for inhibitory avoidance (Izquierdo et al., 1992). The amnestic effect of AP5 is not seen when the drug was administered into the hippocampus, amygdala or septum 90 min after training (Jerusalinsky et al., 1992; Walz, Da Silva, Bueno e Silva, Medina, & Izquierdo, 1992).

The immediate posttraining infusion of AP5 into the hippocampus, but not into the amygdala or medial septum, disrupts retention of habituation to a novel environment in rats (Izquierdo et al., 1992). This task is largely olfactory and spatial, and not alerting or aversive; it had previously been found to depend on the hippocampus but not the amygdala or medial septum (Izquierdo & Medina, 1991; Wolfman et al., 1991).

NMDA receptor function, and very particularly LTP induction, has been suggested to depend on diverse retrograde messenger substances released by the postsynaptic cell which enhance glutamate release (Bliss & Collingridge, 1993). Two gases, nitric oxide (NO) and carbon monoxide (CO), and two lipids, arachidonic acid and the platelet-activating factor (PAF) have been proposed as retrograde messengers (see Izquierdo, 1994; Izquierdo & Medina, 1995). In hippocampal slices, administration of a blocker of the synthesis of NO (Nitro-arginine), or of the synthesis of CO (Zinc protoporphyrin 9), or of the presynaptic membrane receptors to PAF (the gingkolide, BN52021) blocks CA1 LTP; the addition of NO, CO or methylcarbamyl-PAF to the bath produces a long-lasting potentiation on its own (see Izquierdo & Medina, 1995). Pretraining or immediate posttraining intrahippocampal infusion of Nitroarginine (Fin, Da Cunha, et al., 1995), Zinc protoporphirin 9 (Fin, Schmitz et al., 1995), or BN52051 (Izquierdo et al., 1995; Jerusalinsky, Fin et al., 1994) blocks the memory of inhibitory avoidance and of spatial habituation. Inhibitory avoidance training in the rat is followed by a rapid but transitory increase of the activity of heme oxygenase, the enzyme that produces CO, in hippocampus but not neocortex (Bernabeu, Levi de Stein, et al., 1995). Posttraining intrahippocampal infusion of the NO donor, S-Nitroso-N-acetylpenicillamine (Fin, Da Cunha, et al., 1995), or of methylcarbamyl-PAF (Izquierdo et al., 1995) enhances retention of the inhibitory avoidance task.

In the hippocampal CA1 region and perhaps elsewhere, mGluRs are also involved in the genesis of LTP (Bortolotto & Collingridge, 1993). The immediate posttraining infusion in this region of the mGluR agonist, 1S,2R-aminocyclopentane dicarboxylate (ACPD), enhances memory of the inhibitory avoidance task in rats. Infusion of the mGLUR antagonist, [RS]-α-methyl 4 carboxyphenyl glycine (MCPG), is amnestic and is able to antagonize the effect of ACPD (Bianchin et al., 1994). Conquet et al. (1994) recently described impaired spatial learning and impaired LTP in transgenic mice lacking the mGluR1 subtype

CNQX (6-cyano-7-nitroquinoxaline-2,3-dione) is a specific antagonist at AMPA receptors. These are involved in the depolarization needed to activate NMDA receptors in the induction of LTP (Bliss & Collingridge, 1993), as well as in regular glutamatergic transmission and, in particular, in the expression of LTP (Müller, Arai & Lynch, 1992). Obviously, AMPA receptors are also involved in the initiation of LTP at synapses in which this does not rely on NMDA receptors, such as in the CA3 region of the hippocampus (Bliss & Collingridge, 1993). CNQX administered into the hippocampus, amygdala or medial septum

0, 90 or 180 minutes after training disrupts memory of inhibitory avoidance in the rat (Jerusalinsky et al., 1992; Walz et al., 1992). This is accompanied by enhanced binding of ^{3}H-AMPA to AMPA receptors in all subregions of the rat hippocampus (Cammarota et al., 1995), which is remindful of the enhanced responsiveness of AMPA receptors to AMPA in the first 2 hours of LTP observed by Sergueeva, Fedorov, and Reymann (1993) in the CA1 region. The findings suggest that LTP initiated at the time of training in these structures must be expressed in the next 3 hours in order for memory to become established.

Taken together, all these findings strongly suggest that LTP in the hippocampus, the amygdala and the medial septum is necessary for the formation or consolidation of memories. Thus, they endorse the hypothesis raised by Morris and his coworkers in 1986 on a role of hippocampal LTP in spatial memory, and extend it to other forms of memory and to other brain regions.

MEMORY STORAGE: THE ROLE OF GABAERGIC AND OTHER RECEPTORS IN HIPPOCAMPUS, AMYGDALA, AND MEDIAL SEPTUM

As in LTP, the early phase of memory is highly sensitive to inhibition by GABA type A receptor agonists. Muscimol infused into the hippocampus, amygdala or medial septum hinders consolidation of the inhibitory avoidance task; intrahippocampal but not intra-amygdala or intra-septal muscimol administration hindered the memory of habituation (Izquierdo et al., 1992). In the avoidance task, posttraining intra-amygdala infusion of the GABA-A receptor antagonist, biculline (Brioni, Nagahara & McGaugh, 1989), or posttraining intrahippocampal, intra-amygdala or intraseptal administration of the chloride channel blocker, picrotoxin (Da Cunha et al., 1991; Izquierdo et al., 1992), enhance memory consolidation. These findings suggest that GABA-A receptors are important modulators of memory formation in the hippocampus, amygdala and septum, as they are of LTP induction.

The effect of picrotoxin is not seen when timolol is coadministered, which suggests that, in these structures, GABAergic transmission is modulated by B-noradrenergic synapses (Izquierdo et al., 1992), which is consistent with previous neuroanatomical and electrophysiological data (Cheun & Yen, 1992; Leranth & Frotscher, 1989; Milner & Bacon, 1989; Nieuwenhuys, 1985).

The binding of GABA or muscimol to GABA-A receptors is modulated by benzodiazepines acting at a specific site within the GABA-A receptor complex. Benzodiazepines inhibit both LTP induction (Del Cerro, Jung & Lynch, 1992) and various forms of learning (see Izquierdo & Medina, 1991). Recently, naturally occurring benzodiazepines, probably of endogenous origin, have been described in brain (see De Blas, 1993; Medina et al., 1992). They are found mainly in synaptic vesicles, occur in high concentration in medial septum, amygdala and hippocampus, and appear to be released from these structures following habituation or inhibitory avoidance training (Medina, Peña, Piva, Paladini & De Robertis, 1988; Medina et al., 1992; Wolfman et al., 1991). Systemic administration of the benzodiazepine receptor antagonist, flumazenil enhances several forms of learning in the rat (see Izquierdo & Medina, 1991), and reduces sensitivity of the amygdala to the amnestic effect of muscimol (Izquierdo et al., 1990). Posttraining intrahippocampal, intra-amygdala or intraseptal infusion of flumazenil enhances retention of the inhibitory avoidance task; the intrahippocampal infusion of flumazenil also enhances retention of the habituation task (Wolfman et al., 1991). These findings suggest that brain benzodiazepine-like molecules are involved in the modulatory effect of GABAergic transmission on memory processes (Izquierdo & Medina, 1991). It is possible that this may be related to the anxiogenic content of each task, and to a role of brain benzodiazepine-like molecules in the regulation of anxiety (Da Cunha, Wolfman, Izquierdo, & Medina, 1993; Izquierdo & Medina, 1991). In addition to their role in memory, the medial septum, hippocampus and amygdala are involved in the regulation of anxiety (Gray, 1982).

The immediate posttraining infusion of norepinephrine or oxotremorine into the hippocampus, amygdala or medial septum enhances retention of inhibitory avoidance in rats, while timolol has no effect and scopolamine is amnestic (Izquierdo et al., 1992). Timolol, like other β-blockers (McGaugh, 1988) is capable, however, of antagonizing the effect of norepinephrine. In the habituation task, the effects are seen only when the drugs are given into the hippocampus (Izquierdo et al., 1992; Izquierdo & Medina, 1995; Izquierdo, Medina, et al., 1993). These data endorse previous suggestions that muscarinic cholinergic and β-noradrenergic transmission play important modulatory roles in memory (see McGaugh, 1988). Abundant evidence indicates that β-noradrenergic (Hopkins & Johnston, 1988) and cholinergic muscarinic (Markram & Segal, 1992) receptors modulate glutamatergic transmission, particularly the induction of LTP (Katsuki, Saito, & Satoh, 1992; and see Izquierdo, 1994; Izquierdo & Medina, 1995).

MEMORY CONSOLIDATION: THE LATE ROLE OF THE ENTORHINAL CORTEX

As mentioned above, the entorhinal cortex is interconnected with the hippocampus, amygdala and medial septum by monosynaptic pathways, and, via the perirhinal area, with the rest of the neocortex (Witter et al., 1989). Thus, it is strategically located to link early memory processing by the hippocampus, amygdala and medial septum with areas of the cortex presumed to be involved in permanent memory storage (Mishkin, Malamut & Bachevalier, 1984; Zola-Morgan et al., 1989). Lesions of the entorhinal-perirhinal region cause severe amnesia in rats (R. Thompson, 1976) and primates (Zola-Morgan et al., 1989) and, in the latter, exacerbate the memory impairment caused by hippocampal lesions (Zola-Morgan et al., 1993). Entorhinal, CA1 and subicular amyloid plaques and neurofibrillary tangles are seen in normal elderly individuals (Arriagada et al., 1992) and, to a much larger extent, in victims of Alzheimer's disease (Hyman et al., 1990; Jellinger, H. Braak, E. Braak, & Fisher, 1991).

We have recently observed that the entorhinal cortex also plays a NMDA receptor-dependent, GABA-modulated role in memory, but 90–180 minutes after the memories had been initially processed by the hippocampus, amygdala and medial septum (Ferreira, Da Silva, et al., 1992; Ferreira, Wolfman, et al., 1992; Willner et al., 1993). The infusion of AP5 or muscimol into the entorhinal cortex 90 or 100 minutes after training causes full retrograde amnesia for both inhibitory avoidance and habituation. The treatments are ineffective when given immediately or 360 minutes after training. Activation of the entorhinal cortex during training appears necessary for the late intervention of this structure in memory: Pre-training intra-entorhinal muscimol administration prevents the late posttraining amnestic effect of this substance (Willner et al., 1993). Activation of the entorhinal cortex during training is not necessary for the posttraining influence of the hippocampus or the amygdala on retention: Pre-training intra-entorhinal muscimol administration does not hinder the posttraining effect of the intrahippocampal or intra-amygdala administration of the same substance (Jerusalinsky, Quillfeldt, et al., 1994a). Thus, information flux in the posttraining period is from the hippocampus, amygdala (and probably medial septum) to the entorhinal cortex and not viceversa (Izquierdo & Medina, 1995; Jerusalinsky, Quillfeldt, et al., 1994a). It has been suggested that hippocampal, amygdaloid and septal LTP in the posttraining priod mediates the late activation of the entorhinal cortex (see Jerusalinsky et al., 1992).

ROLE OF PROTEIN KINASES IN MEMORY

The induction of LTP occurs in seconds and is followed by a series of events probably triggered by a build-up of intracellular calcium, among which the sequential activation of calcium calmodulin kinase II (CamII) (Fukunaga, Stoppini, Miyamoto, & Müller, 1993) and of at least two isoforms of protein kinase C (Y.-Y. Huang, Colley, & Routtenberg, 1992). Other phosphorylating enzymes, such as protein kinase A and tyrosine kinases are also activated at this time (see Izquierdo & Medina, 1994). It is believed that the early post-induction phosphorylation of glutamate or other receptors, or the late phosphorylation of structural proteins (see Rodnight & Wofchuk, 1992), or of the cyclic adenosine monophosphate responsive element binding protein (CREB) (Y.-Y. Huang, Li, & Kandel, 1994; Nguyen, Abel, & Kandel, 1994) are critical for the initial and late phases of LTP maintenance, respectively (see Izquierdo & Medina, 1995). Transgenic mice lacking protein kinase C or CaM II (Grant & Silva, 1994), or with a targeted mutation of CREB (Bourtchuladze et al., 1994) show deficits in hippocampal LTP and in the performance of spatial tasks. Inhibitors of Cam II, protein kinase C, or other protein kinases abort LTP (Bliss & Collingridge, 1993; Huang et al., 1992, 1994; Izquierdo, 1994).

Inhibitory avoidance training in the rat is followed by a marked (60–80%) but transient (<2 hours) increase of protein kinase C activity in all subregions of the rat hippocampus (Bernabeu, Izquierdo, et al., 1995). The infusion of KN62, an inhibitor of calcium calmodulin kinase II (Wolfman et al., 1994), or of CGP41231 or staurosporin, two inhibitors of protein kinase C (Jerusalinsky, Quillfeldt, et al., 1994b), into the hippocampus or the amygdala immediately or 30 minutes after training causes amnesia for the inhibitory avoidance task in rats. At later periods (i.e., 120–150 minutes), the drugs become ineffective in these structures but may induce amnesia if administered into the entorhinal cortex (see Izquierdo, 1994; Izquierdo & Medina, 1995). The findings suggest that activity of these enzymes in the hippocampus, amygdala and entorhinal cortex is as essential for memory as it is for LTP, and, further, that these brain structures indeed participate sequentially and by processes involving LTP in memory consolidation (Izquierdo & Medina, 1994).

PHARMACOLOGICAL EXPERIMENTS LINKING MEMORY EXPRESSION WITH LTP EXPRESSION

LTP is expressed through AMPA receptors. A permanent change of these receptors has been suggested as a basis for the maintenance of LTP (see Hollmann & Heinemann, 1994). Indeed, LTP expression is accompanied by a hyperresponsiveness of AMPA receptors to AMPA, at least in the first few hours (Sergueeva, Fedorov & Reymann, 1993). Blockade of AMPA receptors by CNQX blocks LTP expression; AP5 has no effect (Müller, Arai, & Lynch, 1992). Therefore, if memory indeed relies on LTP in hippocampus, amygdala and entorhinal cortex, its expression should also be blocked by CNQX infused into these structures at the time of testing.

Liang (1991) blocked memory expression of inhibitory avoidance in rats with CNQX or lidocaine infused into the amygdala prior to testing, 1 or 2, but not 20, days after training. Memory of this task, however, depends not only on the amygdala but also on the hippocampus, medial septum and entorhinal cortex (see above, and Izquierdo et al., 1992; Izquierdo & Medina, 1991, 1995). Since the medial septum has a much smaller number of cells than the other structures (Niewenhuys, 1985), if memories were stored by a mechanism involving LTP maintenance in these brain regions, it is very likely that the vast majority of the synapses involved would be in the hippocampus, amygdala and entorhinal cortex.

My colleagues and I recently observed that CNQX given into either the amygdala or hippocampus prior to inhibitory avoidance testing inhibited expression of this behavior only partially, even at a dose of 1.25 μg per structure; however, when given into both the amygdala and the hippocampus, CNQX completely blocked the expression of inhibitory avoidance at a dose 2.5 times lower, either 1 day (Izquierdo, Bianchin, et al., 1993) or 6, 13, or 20 days after training (Bianchin et al., 1993).

As already mentioned, memory of fear-potentiated startle appears to depend exclusively on the amygdala (M. Davis, 1992), and memory of habituation to a novel environment depends on the hippocampus (Izquierdo et al., 1992). Accordingly, the expression of fear-potentiated startle is blocked by bilateral infusions of CNQX into the amygdala (Kim et al., 1993), and the expression of habituation is blocked by intrahippocampal, but not intra-amygdala, CNQX given 1 or 20 days after training (Bianchin et al., 1993; Izquierdo, Bianchin, et al., 1993). CNQX infused into the entorhinal cortex blocks expression of both inhibitory avoidance and habituation 1 and 26 after training (Izquierdo, Da Silva, et al., 1993; Jerusalinsky, Quillfeldt, et al., 1994a); its effect is reversed by AMPA (Quillfeldt et al., 1993). In all cases, the effect of CNQX on memory expression disappears within 90 or 120 min, at which time the drug probably diffuses away from the infusion site (Bianchin et al., 1993; Izquierdo, Bianchin, et al., 1993.

These findings support the idea that memory is stored by a mechanism involving LTP in the hippocampus, amygdala and entorhinal cortex (see above).

THE LOCALIZATION OF MEMORY

The findings so far discussed suggest that, in rats, memories are made and stored in and retrieved (at least up to the 20th or 26th day) from the hippocampus, amygdala, medial septum and entorhinal cortex, depending on the task, and that the basic mechanism involved in all cases is LTP (Izquierdo & Medina, 1995; Izquierdo, Medina et al., 1993). Clearly, the synapse specificity of LTP (Lynch & Granger, 1992) and the well-known polysensory convergence on these structures (Izquierdo & Medina, 1994) makes it possible for an exceedingly large number of memories to be stored in these places.

The data provide no indication, however, that these are the only areas or that LTP is the only mechanism involved in memory formation and retrieval. The preservation of memory (albeit impaired) in transgenic mice with severe deficits of hippocampal LTP suggests that other mechanisms in addition to LTP must exist (Grant & Silva, 1994) or at least develop in these animals in order to compensate for the lack of appropriate LTP (see Malenka, 1994).

The detailed study of patient H.M. by a number of investigators over 40 years (see Squire, 1987) suggests that temporal lobe structures are essential for the formation of so-called explicit or declarative memories and for their storage over a period of 30 or so days. (The memories of the tasks studied in rats and reviewed above might to a large extent fall into this category; see Izquierdo & Medina,

1991, 1995). Patient H.M. underwent the bilateral removal of both temporal lobes in 1953. He subsequently lost permanently the memories he had acquired in the few weeks prior to the operation, and has been unable to form any new explicit or declarative memories. However, H.M. has retained older memories, and has been able to learn a variety of motor or perceptual skills (what Squire and others call implicit or procedural memories; see Squire, 1987; Zola-Morgan et al., 1989, 1993). A striatum-based memory system exists, separate and independent from the temporal lobe system(s) (Packard & McGaugh, 1992), and lesion studies strongly suggest that implicit or procedural memories are processed by the striatum (Mishkin et al., 1984). A variety of data suggest that after the first few weeks, explicit or declarative memories are stored in the neocortex outside the temporal lobe, perhaps redundantly (see Izquierdo, 1989; Squire, 1987). Whether this long-term storage involves LTP or not is a matter of debate; the point has not been addressed experimentally so far.

Finally, most (some would say all) memories include an affective or emotional component, which involves hormonal and neuromodulatory changes, both at the time of acquisition and at the time of expression (Izquierdo, 1989; Markowitsch, 1994; McGaugh, 1988). In fact, many memories can only be retrieved when that particular emotional and neurohumoral state is reestablished, a phenomenon that is known as "state dependency" (Izquierdo, 1989). The systems involved in the processing of affective and emotional states overlap in part with those that participate in the construction and retrieval of memories (Da Cunha et al., 1993; Gray, 1982), but include many other regions of the brain as well; and most of the hormones and neuromodulators involved in the operation of those systems are fairly well known (Izquierdo, 1989; Izquierdo & Medina, 1995). The interaction of the systems and substances that "tinge" memories, often irreversibly, with those that process synaptic-specific information should be an important subject for future research (Izquierdo, 1994; Izquierdo & Medina, 1995).

ACKNOWLEDGEMENT

I am indebted to Jorge Medina, Rudy Bernabeu, Martín Cammarota (Buenos Aires), Maria Beatriz Ferreira, Jorge Quillfeldt and Marino Bianchin (Porto Alegre) for many valuable dicusions. Work supported by Fundação de Amparo à Pesquisa do Estado do Rio Grande do Sul (FAPERGS) and Financiadora de Estudos e Projetos (FINEP) (Brazil), and by Fundación Antorchas (Argentina).

REFERENCES

Arriagada, P. V., Marzloff, K., & Hyman, B. T. (1992). Distribution of Alzheimer-type pathologic changes in nondemented elderly individuals matches the pattern in Alzheimer's disease. *Neurology, 42,* 1681–1688.
Bernabeu, R., Izquierdo, I., Cammarota, M., Jerusalinsky, D., & Medina, J. H. (1995). Learning-

specific, time-dependent increase in ^{3}H-phorbol dibutyrate binding to protein kinase C in selected regions of the rat brain. *Brain Research*, in press.

Bernabeu, R., Levi de Stein, M., Princ, F., Fin, C., Juknat, A. A., Batlle, A., Izquierdo, I., & Medina, J. H. (1995). Evidence for the involvement of hippocampal CO production in the acquisition and consolidation of inhibitory avoidance learning. *NeuroReport, 6,* 516–518.

Bianchin, M., Da Silva, R. C., Schmitz, P. K., Medina, J. H., & Izquierdo, I. (1994). Memory of inhibitory avoidance in the rat is regulated by glutamate metabotropic receptors in the hippocampus. *Behavioural Pharmacology, 5,* 356–359.

Bianchin, M., Walz, R., Ruschel, A., Zanatta, M. S., Da Silva, R. C., Bueno e Silva, M., Paczko, N., Medina, J. H., & Izquierdo, I. (1993). Memory expression is blocked by CNQX infused into the hippocampus and/or amygdala up to 20 days after training. *Behavioral and Neural Biology, 59,* 83–86.

Bliss, T. V. P., & Collingridge, G. L. (1993). A synaptic model of memory: Long-term potentiation in the hippocampus. *Nature, 361,* 31–39.

Bortolotto, Z. A., & Collingridge, G. L. (1993). Characterization of LTP induced by the activation of glutamate metabotropuc receptors in area CA1 of the hippocampus. *Neuropharmacology, 32,* 1–9.

Bourtchuladze, R., Frenguelli, B., Blendy, J., Cioffi, D., Schultz, G. & Silva, A. J. (1994). Deficient long-term memory in mice with a targeted mutation of the cAMP-responsive element-binding protein. *Cell, 79,* 59–68.

Brioni, J. D., Nagahara, A., & McGaugh, J. L. (1989). Involvement of the amygdala GABAergic system in the modulation of memory storage. *Brain Research, 47,* 105–112.

Cahill, L., & McGaugh, J. L. (1990). Amygdaloid complex lesions diferently affect retention of tasks using appetitive and aversive reinforcement. *Behavioral Neuroscience, 104,* 532–543.

Cammarota, M., Izquierdo, I., Wolfman, C., Levi de Stein, M., Bernabeu, R., Jerusalinsky, D., & Medina, J. H. (1995). Inhibitory avoidance training induces rapid and selective changes in ^{3}[H]-AMPA receptor binding in rat hippocampal formation. *Neurobiology of Learning and Memory*, in press.

Cheun, J. E., & Yen, H. H. (1992). Modulation of GABA receptor-activated current bynorepinephrine in cerebellar Purkinje cells. *Neuroscience, 51,* 951–960.

Conquet, F., Bashir, Z. I., Davies, C. H., Daniel, H., Ferraguti, F., Bordi, F., Franz-Bacon, K., Reggiani, A., Matarese, V., Condé, F., Collingridge, G. L., & Crépel, F. (1994). Motor deficit and impairment of synaptic plasticity in mice lacking mGluR1. *Nature, 372,* 237–243.

Cotman, C. W., Nieto-Sampedro, M., & Harris, W. (1981). Synapse replacement in the central nervous system of vertebrates. *Physiological Reviews, 61,* 684–784.

Da Cunha, C., Huang, C. H., Walz, R., Dias, M., Koya, R., Bianchin, M., Pereira, M. E., Izquierdo, I., & Medina, J. H. (1991). Memory facilitation by post-training intraperitoneal, intraventricular and intra-amygdala injection of Ro5–4864. *Brain Research, 544,* 133–136.

Da Cunha, C., Wolfman, C., Izquierdo, I., & Medina, J. H. (1993). Anxiety and brain benzodiazepine-like molecules. In I. Izquierdo & J.H. Medina (Eds.), *Naturally occurring benzodiazepines: Structure, distribution and function* (pp. 81–88). London: Ellis Horwood.

Davis, M. (1992). The role of the amygdala in fear-potentiated strtle: Implications for animal models of anxiety. *Trends in Pharmacological Sciences, 13,* 35–41.

De Blas, A. (1993). Benzodiazepines and benzodiazepine-like molecules are pent in brain. In I. Izquierdo & J.H. Medina (Eds.), *Naturally Occurring Benzodiazepines: Structure, Distribution and Function* (pp. 1–27). London: Ellis Horwood.

Del Cerro, S., Jung, M., & Lynch, G. (1992). Benzodiazepines block long-term potentiation in slices of hippocampus and pyriform cortex. *Neuroscience, 49,* 1–6.

Ferreira, M. B. C., Da Silva, R. C., Medina, J. H., & Izquierdo, I. (1992). Late post-training memory processing by entorhinal cortex: Role of NMDA and GABA-A receptors. *Pharmacology, Biochemistry and Behavior, 41,* 767–771.

Ferreira, M. B. C., Wolfman, C., Walz, R., Da Silva, R. C., Zanatta, M. S., Medina, J. H., & Izquierdo, I. (1992). NMDA-dependent, GABA-A-sensitive role of the entorhinal cortex in post-training memory processing. *Behavioural Pharmacology*, *3*, 387–394.

Fin, C., Da Cunha, C., Bromberg, E., Schmitz, P. K., Bianchin, M., Medina, J. H., & Izquierdo, I. (1995). Experiments suggesting a role for nitric oxide in the hippocampus in memory. *Neurobiology of Learning and Memory*, *63*, 113–115.

Fin, C., Schmitz, P. K., Da Silva, R. C., Bernabeu, R., Medina, J. H., & Izquierdo, I. (1995). Intrahippocampal but not intra-amygdala infusion of an inhibitor of Heme-oxygenase causes amnesia in the rat. *European Journal of Pharmacology*, *271*, 227–229.

Fukunaga, K., Stoppini, L., Miyamoto, E., & Müller, D. (1993). Long-term potentiation is associated with an increased activity of Ca^{2+}/Calmodulin-dependent protein kinase II. *Journal of Biological Chemistry*, *268*, 7863–7867.

Grant, S. G. N., & Silva, A. J. (1994). Targeting learning. *Trends in Neurosciences*, *17*, 71–75.

Gray, J. A. (1982). *The Neuropsychology of Anxiety: An Enquiry into the Septohippocampal System*. Oxford: Oxford University Press.

Hollmann, M., & Heinemann, S. (1994). Cloned glutamate receptors. *Annual Review of Neuroscience*, *17*, 31–108.

Hopkins, W. F., & Johnston, D. (1988). Noradrenergic enhancement of long-term potentiation at mossy fiber synapses in the hippocampus. *Journal of Neurophysiology*, *59*, 667–687.

Huang, Y.-Y., Colley, P. A., & Routtenberg, A. (1992). Postsynaptic then presynaptic protein kinase C activity may be necessary for long-term potentiation. *Neuroscience*, *44*, 819–827.

Huang, Y.-Y., Li, X.-C., & Kandel, E. R. (1994). cAMP contributes to mossy fiber LTP by initiating both a covalently mediated early phase and macromolecular synthesis-dependent late phase. *Cell*, *79*, 69–79.

Hyman, B. T., Van Hoesen, G. W., & Damasio, A. R. (1990). Memory-related neural systems in Alzheimer's disease: An anatomic study. *Neurology*, *40*, 1721–1730.

Izquierdo, I. (1989). Different forms of post-training memory processing. *Behavioral and Neural Biology*, *51*, 171–202.

Izquierdo, I. (1994). Pharmacological evidence for a role of long-term potentiation in memory. *FASEB Journal*, *8*, 1139–1145.

Izquierdo, I., Bianchin, M., Bueno e Silva, M., Zanatta, M. S., Walz, R., Da Silva, R. C., Ruschel, A., Paczko, N., & Medina, J. H. (1993). CNQX infused into rat hippocampus or amygdala disrupts the expression of memory of two different tasks. *Behavioral and Neural Biology*, *59*, 1–4.

Izquierdo, I., Da Cunha, C., Huang, C. H., Walz, R., Wolfman, C., & Medina, J. H. (1990). Post-training down-regulation by a GABA-A mechanism in the amygdala modulated by endogenous benzodiazepines. *Behavioral and Neural Biology*, *54*, 105–109.

Izquierdo, I., Da Cunha, C., Rosat, R., Jerusalinsky, D., Ferreira, M. B. C., & Medina, J. H. (1992). Neurotransmitter receptors involved in memory processing by the amygdala, medial septum and hippocampus of rats. *Behavioral and Neural Biology*, *58*, 16–26.

Izquierdo, I., Da Silva, R. C., Bueno e Silva, M., Quillfeldt, J. A., & Medina, J. H. (1993). Memory expression of habituation and of inhibitory avoidance is blocked by CNQX infused into the entorhinal cortex. *Behavioral and Neural Biology*, *60*, 5–8.

Izquierdo, I., Fin, C., Schmitz, P. K., Da Silva, R. C., Jerusalinsky, D., Quillfeldt, J. A., Ferreira, M. B. C., Medina, J. H., & Bazan, N. G. (1995). Memory enhancement by intrahippocampal, intra-amygdala or intra-entorhinal infusion of the platelet-activating factor. *Proceedings of the National Academy of Sciences, U.S.A.*, in press.

Izquierdo, I., & Medina, J. H. (1991). GABA-A receptor modulation of memory: The role of endogenous benzodiazepines. *Trends in Pharmacological Sciences*, *12*, 260–265.

Izquierdo, I., & Medina, J. H. (1995). Correlation between the pharmacology of long-term potentiation and the pharmacology of memory. *Neurobiology of Learning and Memory*, *63*, 19–32.

Izquierdo, I., Medina, J. H., Bianchin, M., Walz, R., Zanatta, M. S., Da Silva, R. C., Bueno e Silva, M., Ruschel, A. C., & Paczko, N. (1993). Memory processing by the limbic system: Role of specific neurotransmitter systems. *Behavioral Brain Research*, *58*, 91–98.

Jellinger, K., Braak, H., Braak, E., & Fisher, P. (1991). Alzheimer lesions in the entorhinal region and isocortex in Parkinson's and Alzheimer's disease. *Annals of the New York Academy of Sciences*, *640*, 203–209.

Jerusalinsky, D., Ferreira, M. B. C., Walz, R., Da Silva, R. C., Bianchin M., Ruschel, A., Medina, J. H., & Izquierdo, I. (1992). Amnesia by infusion of glutamate receptor blockers into the amygdala, hippocampus and entorhinal cortex. *Behavioral and Neural Biology*, *58*, 76–80.

Jerusalinsky, D., Fin, C., Quillfeldt, J. A., Ferreira, M. B. C., Schmitz, P. K., Da Silva, R. C., Walz, R., Bazan, N. G., Medina, J. H., & Izquierdo, I. (1994). Effect of antagonists of platelet-activating factor receptors on memory of inhibitory avoidance in rats. *Behavioral and Neural Biology*, *62*, 1-7

Jerusalinsky, D., Quillfeldt, J. A., Walz, R., Da Silva, R. C., Bueno e Silva, M., Bianchin, M., Zanatta, M. S., Ruschel, A. C., Schmitz, R., Paczko, N., Medina, J. H., & Izquierdo, I. (1994a). Effect of the infusion of the GABA-A receptor agonist, muscimol, on the role of the entorhinal cortex, amygdala and hippocampus in memory processes. *Behavioral and Neural Biology*, *61*, 132–138.

Jerusalinsky, D., Quillfeldt, J. H., Walz, R., Da Silva, R. C., Medina, J. H., & Izquierdo, I. (1994b). Post-training intrahippocampal infusion of protein kinase C inhibitors causes retrograde amnesia in rats. *Behavioral and Neural Biology*, *61*, 107–109.

Katsuki, H., Saito, H., & Satoh, M. (1992). The involvement of muscarinic, β-adrenergic and metabotropic glutamate receptors in long-term potentiation in the fimbria-CA3 pathway of the hippocampus. *Neuroscience Letters*, *142*, 249–252.

Kim, M., Campeau, S., Falls, W. A., & Davis, M. (1993). Intra-amygdala infusion of the non-NMDA receptor antagonist CNQX blocks the expression of fear-potentiated startle. *Behavioral and Neural Biology*, *59*, 5–8.

Kim, M., & McGaugh, J. L. (1992). Effects of intra-amygdala injections of NMDA receptor antagonists on acquisition and retention of inhibitory avoidance. *Brain Research*, *585*, 35–48.

Krupa, D. J., Thompson, J. K., & Thompson, R. F. (1993). Localization of a memory trace in the mammalian brain. *Science*, *260*, 989–991.

Leranth, C., & Frotscher, M. (1989). Organization of the septal region in the rat brain: Cholinergic-GABAergic interconnections and the termination of hippocampo-septal fibers. *Journal of Comparative Neurology*, *289*, 304–314.

Liang, K. C. (1991). Pretest intra-amygdala injection of lidocaine or glutamate antagonists impairs retention performance in an inhibitory avoidance task. *Society for Neuroscience Abstracts*, *17*, 486.

Lynch, G., & Granger, R. (1992). Variations in synaptic plasticity and types of memory in corticohippocampal networks. *Journal of Cognitive Neuroscience*, *4*, 189–199.

Malenka, R. (1994). Mucking up movements. *Nature*, *372*, 218–219.

Markowitsch, H. (1994). Effects of emotion and arousal on memory processing in the brain. In J. Delacour (Ed.), *The memory system of the brain* (pp. 210–240). Singapore: World Scientific.

Markram, H., & Segal, M. (1992). The inositol 1,4,5-triphosphate pathway mediates cholinergic potentiation of rat hippocampal neuronal responses to NMDA. *Journal of Physiology*, *447*, 513–533.

Martin, J. H. (1991). Autoradiographic estimation of the extent of reversible inactivation produced by microinjection of lidocaine and muscimol in the rat. *Neuroscience Letters*, *127*, 160–164.

McGaugh, J. L. (1988). Modulation of memory storage processes. In P. R. Solomon, G. R. Goethals, C. M. Kelley, & B. R. Stephens (Eds.), *Perspectives of memory research* (pp. 33–64). New York: Springer.

Medina, J. H., Peña, C., Piva, M., Paladini, A. C., & De Robertis, E. (1988). Presence of benzodiazepine-like molecules in mammalian brain and milk. *Biochemical and Biophysical Research Communications*, *165*, 547–553.

Medina, J. H., Peña, C., Piva, M., Wolfman, C., Levi de Stein, M., Wasowski, C., Da Cunha, C., Izquierdo, I., & Paladini, A. C. (1992). Benzodiazepines in the brain: Their origin and possible biological roles. *Molecular Neurobiology*, *6*, 1–10.

Milner, T. A., & Bacon, C. E. (1989). GABAergic neurons in the rat hippocampal formation: Ultrastructure and synaptic relationship with catecholaminergic terminals. *Journal of Neuroscience*, *9*, 3410–3427.

Miserendino, M. J. D., Sananes, C. B., Meliá, K. R., & Davis, M. (1990). Blocking of acquisition but not expression of conditioned fear-potentiated startle by NMDA antagonists in the amygdala. *Nature*, *345*, 716–718.

Mishkin, M., Malamut, N., & Bachevalier, J. (1984). Memories and habits: Two neural systems. In G. Lynch, N. M. Weingerger, & J. L. McGaugh (Eds.), *Neurobiology of learning and memory* (pp. 65–77). New York: Guilford.

Morris R. G. M., Anderson, E., Lynch, G. S., & Baudry, M. (1986). Selective impairment of learning and blockade of long-term potentiation by an N-methyl-D-aspartate receptor antagonist, Ap-5. *Nature*, *319*, 774–776.

Müller, D., Arai, A., & Lynch, G. S. (1992). Factors governing the potentiation of NMDA-receptor mediated responses in hippocampus. *Hippocampus*, *2*, 29–38.

Nieuwenhuys, R. (1985). *Chemoarchitecture of the brain*. Berlin: Springer.

Nguyen, P. T., Abel, T., & Kandel, E. R. (1994). Requirement of a critical period of transcription for induction of a late phase of LTP. *Science*, *265*, 1104–1107.

Packard, M. G., & McGaugh, J. L. (1992). Double dissociation of fornix and caudate nucleus lesions on acquisition of two water maze tasks: Further evidence for multiple memory systems. *Behavioral Neuroscience*, *106*, 439–446.

Quillfeldt, J. A., Schmitz, P. K., Walz, R., Bianchin, M., Zanatta, M. S., Medina, J. H., & Izquierdo, I. (1994). CNQX infused into entorhinal cortex blocks memory expression; AMPA reverses the effect. *Pharmacology, Biochemistry and Behavior*, *48*, 437–440.

Reeves, T. M., & Smith, D. C. (1987). Reinervation of the dentate gyrus and recovery of alternation behavior following entorhinal cortex lesions. *Behavioral Neuroscience*, *101*, 179–186.

Rodnight, R., & Wofchuk, S. T. (1992). Roles for protein phosphorylation in synaptic transmission. *Essays in Biochemistry*, *27*, 91–102.

Roman, F. S., Chaillan, F. A., & Soumireu-Mourat B. (1993). Long-term potentiation in rat piriform cortex following discrimination learning. *Brain Research*, *601*, 265–272.

Roman, F., Stäubli, U., & Lynch, G. (1987). Evidence for synaptic potentiation in a cortical network during learning. *Brain Research*, *418*, 221–226.

Sergueeva, O. A., Fedorov, N. B., & Reymann, K. G. (1993). An antagonist of glutamate metabotropic receptors, (R) α-methyl-4-carboxyphenyl glycine, prevents the LTP-related increase in postsynaptic AMPA sensitivity in hippocampal slices. *Neuropharmacology*, *32*, 933–935.

Squire, L. R. (1987). *Memory and brain*. Oxford: Oxford University Press.

Stäubil, U., Thibault, O., De Lorenzo, M., Lynch, G. (1989). Antagonism of NMDA receptors impairs acquisition but not retention of olfactory memory. *Behavioral Neuroscience, 103*, 54–60.

Thompson, R. (1976). Entorhinal-subicular lesions: Amnestic effects on an assortment of learned responses in the white rat. *Bulletin of the Psychological Society*, *8*, 433–434.

Walz, R., Da Silva, R. C., Bueno e Silva, M., Medina, J. H., & Izquierdo, I. (1992). Post-training infusion of glutamate receptor antagonists into the medial septum of rats causes amnesia. *Ciencia e Cultura (Sao Paulo)*, *44*, 339–341.

Willner, P., Bianchin, M., Walz, R., Bueno e Silva, M., Zanatta, M. S., & Izquierdo, I. (1993). Muscimol infused into the entorhinal cortex prior to training blocksthe involvement of this area in posttraining memory processing. *Behavioral Pharmacology*, *4*, 95–100.

Witter, M. P., Groenewegen, H. J., Lopes da Silva, F. H., & Lohmann, A. H. M. (1989). Functional organization of the extrinsic and intrinsic circuitry of the rat parahippocampal region. *Progress in Neurobiology, 33*, 161–253.

Wolfman, C., Da Cunha, C., Jerusalinsky, D., Levi de Stein, M., Viola, H., Izquierdo, I., & Medina, J. H. (1991). Habituation and inhibitory avoidance training alter brain regional levels of benzodiazepine-like molecules and are afected by intracerebral flumazenil microinjectionm. *Brain Research, 548*, 74–80.

Wolfman, C., Fin, C., Dias, M., Bianchin, M., Da Silva, R. C., Schmitz, P. K., Medina, J. H. & Izquierdo, I. (1994). Intrahippocampal or intra-amygdala infusion of KN62, a specific inhibitor of calcium/calmodulin dependent protein kinase II, causes retrograde amnesia in the rat. *Behavioral and Neural Biology, 61*, 203–205.

Zola-Morgan, S., Squire, L. R., Amaral, D. G., & Suzuki, W. (1989). Lesions of perirhinal and parahippocampal cortex that spare the amygdala and hippocampal formation produce severe memory impairment. *Journal of Neuroscience, 9*, 4355–4370.

Zola-Morgan, S., Squire, L. R., Clower, R. P., & Rempel, N. L. (1993). Damage to the perirhinal cortex exacerbates memory impairment following lesions to the hippocampal formation. *Journal of Neuroscience, 13*, 251–265.

4 Serial and Parallel Processing During Memory Consolidation

Roberto A. Prado-Alcalá
National University of México

Despite the great amount of research devoted to the search for the *engram*, the set of changes in the nervous system that represents stored memory (Squire, 1987), this endeavor has proven unsuccessful. We have only a few instances where there seem to be particular cerebral structures that mediate very specific—relatively simple—types of learned behaviors (e.g., Cohen, 1980; Thompson, Berger & Madden, 1983; but see Russell, 1993). Other scientists have postulated that the engram is diffusely distributed in many areas of the brain, such that many neurons may participate, in a probabilistic manner, in memory for specific events (e.g., John, 1972). This proposition, although sound, leaves little room for determining the whereabouts of a possible plastic change that represents memory.

There are many experimental results, however, that show that the physiological activity of several brain regions are necessary for memory consolidation of instrumental tasks. For example, lesions to the cerebral cortex (Kolb, 1984), hippocampus (Schmajuk, 1984), amygdala (Sarter & Markowitsch, 1985), or neostriatum (Divac & Oberg, 1979) produce marked deficits in a wide variety of conditioned behaviors. These findings indicate that these areas participate in learning and memory, but they do not reveal the location of the engram.

We are thus faced with a methodological problem: How are we going to search for an engram that might be located in different places at different times? Furthermore, how can we explain the fact that several structures are necessary for memory consolidation, yet none of them has proven to be the seat of memory?

Since the 1970s, there have been occasional, but consistent, reports that may shed some light on these problems, and that have allowed us to propose a possible mechanism to explain how memory consolidation for instrumental learning occurs. Most of these reports deal with the participation of cholinergic activity of the neostriatum in different aspects of learning. Experimental modifications of acetylcholine (ACh) neurotransmission in the neostriatum bring about changes in conditioned behaviors, which are congruent with the view that striatal ACh is involved in memory functions.

Regarding positively reinforced tasks, muscarinic blockade of the striatum disrupts the acquisition (Bermúdez-Rattoni, Mujica-Gonzalez, & Prado-Alcalá, 1986) and performance (Prado-Alcalá et al., 1972; Prado-Alcalá, Kaufmann, & Moscona, 1980) of lever pressing and of spatial alternation (Prado-Alcalá, Bermúdez-Rattoni, Velázquez-Martínez, & Bacha, 1978). Conversely, an improvement in the acquisition and performance of these conditioned behaviors is seen when cholinergic striatal synaptic activity is facilitated with local injections of choline or ACh (Brust-Carmona, Prado-Alcalá, Grinberg-Zylberbaum, Alvarez-Leefmans, & Zarco-Coronado, 1974; Díaz del Guante et al., 1993; Prado-Alcalá & Cobos-Zapiaín, 1979a).

With respect to negatively reinforced behaviors, when antimuscarinic drugs are delivered to the striatum after training of active avoidance, animals show a slowing in the acquisition of the task (Neill & Grossman, 1970; Prado-Alcalá, Cepeda, Verduzco, Jiménez, & Vargas-Ortega, 1984), whereas choline administration to this structure has the opposite effect (Prado-Alcalá et al., 1984). There is also a marked retrograde amnesia of passive avoidance after striatal cholinergic blockade (Haycock, Deadwyler, Sideroff, & McGaugh, 1973; Prado-Alcalá, Cruz-Morales, & López-Miro, 1980), which is both dose- and time-dependent (Prado-Alcalá, Fernández-Samblancat, & Solodkin-Herrera, 1985; Prado-Alcalá, Signoret, & Figueroa, 1981). Compatible results have been reported by Sandberg, Sanberg, Hanin, Fisher, and Coyle (1984) and by Barker, Glick, Green, and Khandelwal (1982). In the case of Sandberg et al., when AF64A (a drug that causes permanent damage to cholinergic neurons) was injected into the striatum, there was a profound deficit in the acquisition and retention of passive avoidance; in Barker et al., it was shown that ACh synthesis was enhanced right after training on the same task. It has also been reported that the amnesic effect of scopolamine on this conditioned behavior could be prevented by the administration of choline into the striatum (Solana-Figueroa & Prado-Alcalá, 1990).

In sum, the data lend strong support to the hypothesis that striatal cholinergic activity is necessary for memory consolidation. Evidence is starting to accumulate, however, that indicates that this hypothesis is only partially correct. It seems that cholinergic neurons of the striatum may be involved only in the memory of instrumental behaviors that were acquired through a relatively small number of training sessions (albeit sufficient to reach asymptotic performance) or through low intensities of footshock, as in the cases just presented. When these parameters of training are modified, a totally different picture emerges.

In 1975, we started a research program in which animals were exposed to systematic variations in amount of training and were then submitted to treatments that interfere with cholinergic synaptic activity. First, we replicated the reported amnestic effect of intrastriatal injections of atropine (Prado-Alcalá et al., 1972) in cats that were trained to lever press for 15 sessions. The performance of these animals before treatment could not be distinguished from that of animals trained for 30 sessions. Notably, these overtrained cats did not show any modification in responding when injected with the anticholinergic drug (Prado-Alcalá & Cobos-Zapiaín, 1977).

To test the generality of the protective effect of overtraining, rats were given 5, 15, or 25 sessions of the lever-pressing task, after which scopolamine was injected into the striatum. Again, there was a significant deficit in retention in the 5- and 15-session groups, and a sparing of the conditioned response in the 25-session group (Prado-Alcalá, Kaufmann, et al., 1980). Equivalent effects had been found when spatial alternation was studied (Prado-Alcalá et al., 1978).

Concerning one-trial passive avoidance, retrograde amnesia is produced by intrastriatal administration of atropine after training with moderate footshock intensities; if footshock intensity is increased twofold or threefold (overreinforcement), however, animals show perfect retention in spite of the atropine injection (Giordano & Prado-Alcalá, 1986). In a follow-up study, scopolamine injection to the striatum was also ineffective in producing amnesia when relatively high footshock intensities were used for training (Díaz del Guante, Rivas-Arancibia, Quirarte & Prado-Alcalá, 1990).

Thus, we have a particular set of neurons (cholinergic interneurons), within a particular cerebral nucleus (neostriatum), that is essential for the memory consolidation of both positively and negatively reinforced behaviors. When we increase the learning experience through overtraining or overreinforcement, the normal activity of this set of neurons is no longer necessary for memory consolidation.

Is the striatum, as a whole, then, involved in consolidation and performance of overtrained and overreinforced conditioning? To answer this question, we tested the effects of generalized interference and blockade of neural activity of the striatum on regular and enhanced learning. Rats were trained to lever press for 5, 15, or 25 sessions and then injected, intrastriatally, with a high concentration of potassium chloride (Prado-Alcalá et al., 1978); the same treatment was given to cats that had been trained in the same task for 15, 30, 45, or 60 sessions (Prado-Alcalá & Cobos-Zapiaín, 1979b). In both instances, an amnesic state was evident in the low-training groups, and no significant deficits were seen in the overtrained animals.

A similar outcome was obtained in passive avoidance: Intrastriatal application of lidocaine shortly after training induced retrograde amnesia when low footshock intensities were used during training, but not when the noxious stimulation was increased (Pérez-Ruiz & Prado-Alcalá, 1989).

This evidence, although not abundant, allows us to postulate that the normal activity of the neostriatum is necessary for memory consolidation and for the maintenance of instrumental learning, but that it is not necessary for the development of these functions after extended training or overreinforcement.

There are other illustrations of the protective effect of enhanced learning experiences. It is well known that systemic administration of antimuscarinic drugs produce amnesia in a wide variety of behavioral tests (for reviews, see Bartus, Dean, Pontecorvo, & Flicker, 1985; Fibiger, 1991; Prado-Alcalá, Fernández-Ruiz, & Quirarte, 1993), including passive avoidance (Bammer, 1982, but see Lewis & Bregman, 1972; Myers, 1965). Thus, it was of interest to determine whether a generalized blockade of ACh-receptors would also induce amnesia in conditions of overreinforcement. As expected, there was a deficit in the consolidation of passive avoidance after scopolamine administration to rats trained with mild electric footshocks, but no behavioral changes when the drug was given to animals that had been trained with footshocks of relatively high intensities (Durán-Arévalo, Cruz-Morales, & Prado-Alcalá, 1990). It was subsequently found that the protective effect of overreinforcement is not established in a gradual fashion, but in an all-or-nothing manner, with a minute increase of less than 5% of the intensity of footshock with which scopolamine produced amnesia (Cruz-Morales, Durán-Arévalo, Díaz del Guante, Quirarte, & Prado-Alcalá, 1992).

Myhre (1975) trained rats in active avoidance under unilateral cortical spreading depression. She reported that there was no transfer of training in animals that had been trained to 90% performance; in contrast, a significant amount of transfer was achieved in rats with 100% performance (i.e., overtraining). It has also been shown that extended training ameliorates behavioral deficits in the active avoidance produced by peripheral depletion of noradrenaline (Oei & King, 1978), and that animals submitted to pretraining of one-way active avoidance, were significantly less impaired by pimozide with as little as two sessions, compared to animals that were not pretrained (Beninger, Phillips, & Fibiger, 1983).

It has also been reported that lesions of the amygdala (Parent, Quirarte, & McGaugh, 1993; Parent, Tomaz, & McGaugh, 1992; Thatcher & Kimble, 1966) and thalamus (Markowitsch, Kessler, & Streicher, 1985), and injections of picrotoxin into the substantia nigra (Cobos-Zapiaín & Prado-Alcalá, 1986) produced memory deficiencies, that are surmounted by an enhanced training experience.

How can we integrate all this information in the context of the localization of the engram? I think that the consistency of the experimental results I have described allows for the proposition of a hypothetical model that can explain some of the events that probably occur in the central nervous system during memory consolidation of instrumental tasks learned in conditions of regular and strengthened training.

I postulate that the functional integrity of a number of structures (e.g., cerebral cortex, hippocampus, amygdala, neostriatum, and substantia nigra) is necessary for memory consolidation of instrumental behaviors that have been acquired through a limited number of trials (which can be sufficient to reach asymptotic performance) or with a low level of aversive stimulation. Lesions of any of these structures produce marked impairments in memory in a wide variety of learning situations. This reflects an arrangement in which all of these structures are functionally interconnected *in series*, in such a way that lesions or other types of interference with the activity of *any* one of them will bring about an inability to establish the permanent storage of information. According to this model, different aspects of the experience are processed by different structures involved in the storage of information.

As the learning experience is increased (through overtraining or overreinforcement), these same structures (and probably additional structures) also participate in the process of consolidation; however, under these circumstances, no particular structure is essential for this mnemonic process, because the activation of just some of them would be sufficient for consolidation. In other words, when a subject goes through an enhanced learning experience, the cerebral regions involved in consolidation undergo a rearrangement whereby they become functionally connected *in parallel*. Thus, even if one or more of these nuclei becomes dysfunctional, the information derived from the learning experience will reach the other nuclei, which will still be capable of performing memory functions. A diagrammatic representation of the model is offered in Fig. 4.1.

This figure provides a schematic representation of the proposed model, which explains the way in which functional pathways convey information derived from a learning experience. In A, during acquisition, those structures or areas (empty

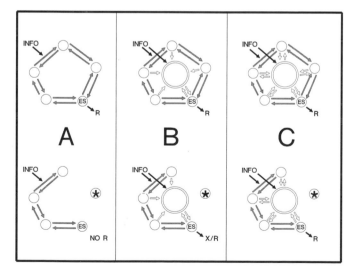

FIG. 4.1.   Hypothetical functional changes during memory consolidation during a low (A), medium (B), or high (C) learning experience.

circles) involved in the processing and/or storage of the information (INFO) are connected *in series*, and feed back to one another; particular structures are in charge of processing different aspects of the learning situation. Thus, the participation of every one of them is necessary for this process to take place, and for the activation of the effector systems (ES) that mediate the conditioned response (R). When there is an interference with the activity of any one of these structures (*), the flow of information necessary for consolidation and for activation of ES is interrupted, rendering the animal incapable of performing the response (NO R).

In B, as the learning experience is strengthened, the information follows two routes: the original one (through the structures that are connected in series) and, by virtue of a functional reorganization, an additional path (ring), *in parallel* with the former. In order for consolidation to take place, both routes must be activated. When the activity of one, or several, of the structures of this system is impaired, the serial arrangement will be disrupted and the information will only be processed by the new functional parallel connection. This situation will allow for only partial storage of memory and a concomitant deficit in responding (X/R).

Finally, when learning conditions are optimal (e.g., with overtraining or overreinforcement), as shown in C, there is feedback of communication among all elements. If there is a disturbance in the activity of any of the structures, the rest of the structures will have access to the information, and memory consolidation, as well as performance, will take place, just as in conditions of normality. In this situation, even though all, or most, of the elements of the system are involved in the mnemonic process, no one is indispensable.

ACKNOWLEDGMENT

Work supported by DGAPA-UNAM.

REFERENCES

Bammer, G. (1982). Pharmacological investigations of neurotransmitter involvement in passive avoidance responding: A review and some new results. *Neuroscience and Biobehavioral Reviews*, 6, 247–296.

Barker, L. A., Glick, S. A., Green, J. P., & Khandelwal, J. (1982). Acetylcholine metabolism in the rat hippocampus and striatum following one-trial passive training. *Neuropharmacology*, 21, 183–185.

Bartus, R. T., Dean, R. L., Pontecorvo, M. J., & Flicker, C. (1985). The cholinergic hypothesis: A historical overview, current perspectives, and future directions. *Annals of the New York Academy of Sciences*, 44, 332–358.

Beninger, R. J., Phillips, A. G., & Fibiger, H. C. (1983). Prior training and intermittent retraining attenuate pimozide-induced avoidance deficits. *Pharmacology, Biochemistry and Behavior*, 18, 619–624.

Bermúdez-Rattoni, F., Mujica-Gonzalez, M., & Prado-Alcalá, R. A. (1986). Is cholinergic activity of the striatum involved in the acquisition of positively-motivated behaviors? *Pharmacology, Biochemistry and Behavior*, *24*, 715–719.

Brust-Carmona, H., Prado-Alcalá, R., Grinberg-Zylberbaum, J., Alvarez-Leefmans, J., & Zarco-Coronado, I. (1974). Modulatory effects of acetylcholine and catecholamines in the caudate nucleus during motor conditioning. In R. D. Myers & R. R. Drucker-Colín (Eds.), *Neurohumoral coding of brain function* (171–187). New York: Plenum.

Cobos-Zapiaín, G. G., & Prado-Alcalá, R. A. (1986, August). *Aplicación de picrotoxina en la substancia nigra reticulada: efectos sobre la memoria de largo plazo, en una tarea sobrentrenada* [Application of picrotoxin to the substantia nigra reticulata: Effects on long-term memory of an overreinforced task.] Presented at the Annual Meeting of the Sociedad Mexicana de Ciencias Fisiológicas, Guanajuato, México.

Cohen, D. H. (1980). The functional neuroanatomy of a conditioned response. In R. F. Thompson, L. H. Hicks, & V. B. Shvyrkov (Eds.), *Neural mechanisms of goal-directed behavior and learning* (pp. 283–302). New York: Academic Press.

Cruz-Morales, S. E., Durán-Arévalo, M., Díaz del Guante, M. A., Quirarte, G., & Prado-Alcalá, R. A. (1992). A threshold for the protective effect of over-reinforced passive avoidance against scopolamine-induced amnesia. *Behavioral and Neural Biology*, *57*, 256–259.

Díaz del Guante, M. A., Carbonell-Hernández, C., Quirarte, G., Cruz-Morales, S. E., Rivas-Arancibia, S., & Prado-Alcalá, R. A. (1993). Intrastriatal injections of choline accelerates the acquisition of positively rewarded behaviors. *Brain Research Bulletin*, *30*, 671–675.

Díaz del Guante, M. A., Rivas-Arancibia, S., Quirarte, G., & Prado-Alcalá, R. A. (1990). Over-reinforcement protects against memory deficits induced by muscarinic blockade of the striatum. *Boletín de Estudios Médicos y Biológicos* (Mexico), *38*, 49–53.

Divac, I., & Oberg, R. G. E. (1979). *The neostriatum*. Oxford: Pergamon.

Durán-Arévalo, M., Cruz-Morales, S. E., & Prado-Alcalá, R. A. (1990). Is acetylcholine involved in memory consolidation of over-reinforced learning? *Brain Research Bulletin*, *24*, 725–727.

Fibiger, H. C. (1991). Cholinergic mechanisms in learning, memory and dementia: A review of recent evidence *Trends in Neurosciences*, *14*, 220–223.

Giordano, M., & Prado-Alcalá, R. A. (1986). Retrograde amnesia produced by post-trial injection of atropine into the caudate–putamen: Protective effect of the negative reinforcer. *Pharmacology, Biochemistry and Behavior*, *24*, 905–909.

Haycock, J. W., Deadwyler, S. A., Sideroff, S. I., & McGaugh, J. L. (1973). Retrograde amnesia and cholinergic systems in the caudate–putamen complex and dorsal hippocampus. *Experimental Neurology*, *41*, 201–213.

John, E. R. (1972). Switchboard versus statistical theories of learning and memory. *Science*, *177*, 850–864.

Kolb, B. (1984). Functions of the frontal cortex of the rat: A comparative review. *Brain Research Reviews*, *8*, 65–98.

Lewis, D. J., & Bregman, N. J. (1972). The cholinergic system, amnesia and memory. *Physiology and Behavior*, *8*, 511–514.

Markowitsch, H. J., Kessler, J., & Streicher, M. (1985). Consequences of serial cortical, hippocampal, and thalamic lesions or of different lengths of overtraining on the acquisition and retention of learning tasks. *Behavioral Neuroscience*, *99*, 233–256.

Myers, B. (1965). Some effects of scopolamine on passive avoidance response in rats. *Psychopharmacologia*, *8*, 111–119.

Myhre, G. (1975). Overtraining in hooded rats under unilateral spreading depression. *Physiology and Behavior*, *14*, 363–366.

Neill, D. B., & Grossman, P. S. (1970). Behavioral effects of lesions or cholinergic blockade of dorsal and ventral caudate of rats. *Journal of Comparative and Physiological Psychology*, *71*, 311–317.

Oei, T. P. S., & King, M. G. (1978). Effects of extended training on rats depleted of central and/or peripheral catecholamines. *Pharmacology, Biochemistry and Behavior, 9*, 243–247.

Parent, M. B., Quirarte, G. L., & McGaugh, J. L. (1993, August). *Inhibitory avoidance retention impairment produced by posttraining amygdala lesions: Effects of variations in footshock intensity.* Paper presented at the Annual Meeting of the Sociedad Mexicana de Ciencias Fisiológicas, Acapulco, Mexico.

Parent, M. B., Tomaz, C., & McGaugh, J. L. (1992). Increased training in an aversively motivated task attenuates the memory-impairing effects of posttraining N-Methyl-D-Aspartate–induced amygdala lesions. *Behavioral Neuroscience, 106*, 789–797.

Pérez-Ruiz, C., & Prado-Alcalá, R. A. (1989). Retrograde amnesia induced by lidocaine injection into the striatum: Protective effect of the negative reinforcer. *Brain Research Bulletin, 22*, 599–603.

Prado-Alcalá, R. A., Bermúdez-Rattoni, F., Velázquez-Martínez, D., & Bacha, M. G. (1978). Cholinergic blockade of the caudate nucleus and spatial alternation performance in rats: Overtraining-induced protection against behavioral deficits. *Life Sciences, 23*, 889–896.

Prado-Alcalá, R. A., Cepeda, G., Verduzco, L., Jiménez, A., & Vargas-Ortega, E. (1984). Effects of cholinergic stimulation of the caudate nucleus on active avoidance. *Neuroscience Letters, 51*, 31–36.

Prado-Alcalá, R. A., & Cobos-Zapiaín, G. G. (1977). Learning deficits induced by cholinergic blockade of the caudate nucleus as a function of experience. *Brain Research, 138*, 190–196.

Prado-Alcalá, R. A., & Cobos-Zapiaín, G. G. (1979a). Improvement of learned behavior through cholinergic stimulation of the caudate nucleus. *Neuroscience Letters, 14*, 253–258.

Prado-Alcalá, R. A., & Cobos-Zapiaín, G. G. (1979b). Interference with caudate nucleus activity by potassium chloride: Evidence for a "moving" engram. *Brain Research, 172*, 577–583.

Prado-Alcalá, R. A., Cruz-Morales, S. E., & López-Miro, F. A. (1980). Differential effects of cholinergic blockade of anterior and posterior caudate nucleus on avoidance behaviors. *Neuroscience Letters, 18*, 339–345.

Prado-Alcalá, R. A., Fernández-Ruiz, J., & Quirate, G. (1993). Cholinergic neurons and memory. In T. W. Stone (Ed.), *Synaptic transmission 2* (pp. 57–69). London: Taylor & Francis.

Prado-Alcalá, R. A., Fernández-Samblancat, M., & Solodkin-Herrera, M. (1985). Injections of atropine into the caudate nucleus impair the acquisition and the maintenance of passive avoidance. *Pharmacology, Biochemistry and Behavior, 22*, 243–247.

Prado-Alcalá, R. A., Grinberg, Z. J., Alvarez-Leefmans, F. J., Gómez, A., Singer, S., & Brust-Carmona, H. (1972). A possible caudate-cholinergic mechanism in two instrumental conditioned responses. *Psychopharmacologia, 25*, 339–346.

Prado-Alcalá, R. A., Kaufmann, P., & Moscona, R. (1980). Scopolamine and KCl injections into the caudate-putamen. Overtraining-induced protection against deficits of learning. *Pharmacology, Biochemistry and Behavior, 12*, 249–253.

Prado-Alcalá, R. A., Signoret, L., & Figueroa, M. (1981). Time-dependent retention deficits induced by post-training injections of atropine into the caudate nucleus. *Pharmacology, Biochemistry and Behavior, 15*, 633–636.

Russell, I. E. (1993, April). *The cerebellum is not the site of Pavlovian conditioning of the NM response in rabbits.* Paper presented at the meeting of the International Behavioral Neuroscience Society, Clearwater, Florida.

Sandberg, K., Sanberg, P. R., Hanin, I., Fisher, A., & Coyle, J. T. (1984). Cholinergic lesion of striatum impairs acquisition and retention of a passive avoidance response. *Behavioral Neuroscience, 98*, 162–165.

Sarter, M., & Markowitsch, H. J. (1985). Involvement of the amygdala in learning and memory: A critical review, with emphasis on anatomical relations. *Behavioral Neuroscience, 99*, 342–380.

Schmajuk, N. A. (1984). Psychological theories of hippocampal function. *Physiological Psychology, 12*, 166–183.

Solana-Figueroa, R., & Prado-Alcalá, R. A. (1990). Retrograde amnesia produced by intrastriatal atropine and its reversal by choline. *Life Sciences*, *46*, 679–686.

Squire, L. R. (1987). *Memory and the brain*. Oxford: Oxford University Press.

Thatcher, R. W., & Kimble, D. P. (1966). Effect of amygdaloid lesions on retention of an avoidance response in overtrained and non-overtrained rats. *Psychonomic Science*, *6*, 9–10.

Thompson, R. F., Berger, T. W., & Madden, J. (1983). Cellular processes of learning and memory in the mammalian CNS. *Annual Review of Neuroscience*, *6*, 447–491.

5

The Role of the Insular Cortex in the Acquisition and Long Lasting Memory for Aversively Motivated Behavior

Federico Bermúdez-Rattoni
Christopher E. Ormsby
Martha L. Escobar
Elizabeth Hernández-Echeagaray
Instituto de Fisiología Celular Universidad Nacional Autónoma de México

Research in our laboratory has focused on the role of the insular cortex (IC) on the acquisition and retention of different learning tasks. In the first part of this chapter, we discuss the influence of brain grafts on the recovery of learning ability in cortically lesioned animals. The findings suggest that graft maturation and/or acetylcholine (ACh) activity may play an important role in graft-mediated behavioral recovery following brain lesions. In the second part, we discuss how the IC, a brain region previously thought to be involved in only one kind of motivated learning (visceral aversive), is also involved in spatial memory. Finally, we have investigated IC in the long term storage of visceral externally and spatially motivated learning.

CONDITIONED TASTE AVERSION

In our laboratory, we have used the conditioned taste aversions (CTA) paradigm to examine the effects of lesions of the IC on learning and memory. CTA is a simple learning model in which animals acquire aversion to flavors by experiencing a taste as a conditioned stimulus (CS), followed by illness (gastric irritation) as an unconditioned stimulus (US). Taste is readily associated with illness and can be observed after a single taste illness experience (for review, see Garcia, Lasiter, Bermúdez-Rattoni, & Deems, 1985). Flavor illness association has been demonstrated in many laboratories and with many different species of animals. A major advantage of this model in the study of the neurobiology of learning and memory is the knowledge of the neural pathways involved. The pathways for CTA have been established with the use of anatomical, electrophysiological, and behavioral methods (Garcia et al., 1985; Garcia, Rusiniak, Kiefer, & Bermúdez-Rattoni, 1982).

THE IC

The anatomical connections of the IC clearly suggest that this brain region may play a role in integrating, and possibly in storing, visceral information. The nucleus solitarius (NTS, the first gustatory relay) receives heavy visceral input from the hepatic branch of the vagus nerve (which is sensitive to stomach-irritating toxins), as well as input from the area postrema (which is sensitive to blood-irritating toxins), and the vestibular system (which is sensitive to nausea-causing motion). The NTS also receives primary taste afferents from the entire tongue, via nerves VII and IX, and from the larynx and pharynx, via nerve X. Neurons responding to both gustatory and visceral stimuli are found in the pontine taste area of the parabrachial complex (second gustatory relay). There are two main projections from the parabrachial nucleus. One major projection of fibers ends in ventral forebrain structures, including the amygdala, the lateral hypothalamus, and the substantia innominata. The second projection ascends ipsilaterally in the central tegmental bundle and projects to the posterior ventromedial and ventromedial nuclei of the thalamus, a zone identified as a relay site for gustatory and lingual afferents (Kiefer, 1985). From the thalamic nuclei, there are projections to the IC, a region 1 mm wide and 3 mm long located along the rhinal sulcus in the rat. The IC has been referred to as the *visceral cortex* because it receives taste and visceral information from the thalamus. These anatomical connections suggest that the IC plays an integral role in the mediation of visceral reactions. Moreover, it has been postulated that the IC receives convergences of limbic input with primary sensory inputs this is not seen within any other sensory areas in the cortex (Krushel & van der Kooy, 1988).

Among the IC connections that may be important for memorial processing are those of the limbic system the amygdala, the dorsomedial nucleus of the thalamus, and the prefrontal cortex (Krushel & van der Kooy, 1988). Extensive evidence suggests that among the limbic structures, the amygdala is particularly involved in the modulatory influences on aversive memory (McGaugh, Intrioni-Collison, Nagahara, Cahill, Brioni and Castellano, 1990). There is evidence that the amygdala and the IC are functionally and reciprocally interconnected (Escobar, Fernández, Guevara-Aguilar, & Bermúdez-Rattoni, 1989; Lasiter & Glanzman, 1985). A direct projection between the amygdala and the IC via the internal capsule has been described (Kiefer, 1985; Norgren & Wolf, 1975). It has been suggested that cortical projections to the amygdala, including those from the IC, convey processed cognitive information which is then integrated with emotional and motivational processes (Pascoe & Kapp, 1987).

Several studies have shown that the IC area is involved in mediating the associative aspects of taste responding, but is not involved in the hedonic responses to taste. Rats lacking an IC are impaired in acquiring and retaining taste aversion. That is, when IC lesions are made, either before or after acquisition of the CTA, animals do not show taste aversion. However, the hedonic responses of lesioned IC rats appear to be normal: Like normal rats, IC lesioned animals prefer sucrose, as well as low concentrations of sodium chloride, over water and reject quinine and acid solutions. Also, taste responsiveness remains intact, even in decerebrate rats (Kiefer, 1985).

RECOVERY OF FUNCTIONS BY FETAL BRAIN GRAFTS

The fetal brain transplant technique has been widely used to produce functional behavioral recovery from brain injury in adult mammal brains. Thus, it has been established that the transplanted neurons can differentiate and make connections with the host brain (see Björklund & Stenevi, 1985, Dunnet & Richards, 1990). We have shown that fetal brain transplants can produce a significant recovery in the ability of IC-lesioned rats to acquire a CTA (Bermúdez-Rattoni, Fernández, Sánchez, Aguilar-Roblero, & Drucker-Colin, 1987). The possibility of spontaneous recovery was excluded, because the animals with IC lesions that did not receive transplants were unable to acquire the CTA 8 weeks after the transplant even after two acquisition trials (Bermúdez-Rattoni et al., 1987). In contrast, animals with lesions in the amygdala showed spontaneous recovery eight weeks after the lesion was induced. Similar spontaneous recovery of performance in an alternation task has been found in animals tested 6 weeks after receiving large cortical ablations (Dunnett & Björklund, 1987). Elsewhere, we have discussed in detail these functional differences between the amygdala and the IC (Bermúdez-Rattoni et al., 1987). One possible explanation is that, for taste aversion learning, the IC may be a permanent memory storage site, whereas the amygdala may only serve to influence an initial step in the storage of CTA (Bermúdez-Rattoni et al., 1987). This is supported by the fact that chemical lesions induced by N-methyl-D-aspartate (NMDA) in the amygda, but sparing the "fibers of passage," did not affect the acquisition of CTA, whereas similar lesions of the IC have strong disruptive effects on CTA (Aggleton, Petrides & Iversen, 1981; Bermúdez-Rattoni & McGaugh, 1991. Moreover, it has been demonstrated that NMDA-induced lesions, when applied to the basolateral nucleus of the amygdala, alter potentiation of odor by a concurrent taste aversion, but do not alter taste aversion learning itself (Hatfield, Phillips, & Gallagher, 1992).

The first conclusion we drew from these findings was that the recovery of function seen in animals with cortical grafts might be due to the formation of connections between the graft tissue and the host brain; several experiments showed the existence of reciprocal connections between the thalamus and cortical grafts (Sharp & Gonzalez, 1986). Therefore, we decided to test the hypothesis of reconnectivity between IC grafts and the host tissue. A series of experiments carried out in our laboratory showed that the degree of functional recovery induced by fetal brain tissue grafts depends on the place from which the graft tissue was taken. The animals that received homotopic, but not occipital, cortical tissue recovered the CTA; the animals that received either tectal heterotopic tissue or no transplant showed no behavioral recovery. Results based on horseradish peroxidase (HRP) histochemistry revealed that cortical, but not brain stem, grafts established connections with the amygdala and with the ventromedial nucleus of the thalamus (Escobar et al., 1989).

All the experiments discussed so far were made with long (60-day) waiting times between the grafting and the retraining post graft period. Therefore, we decided to find out which were the best post graft times at which to observe functional recovery. For that purpose, we used rats with IC lesions showing disrupted taste aversion the animals received cortical transplants and were retrained at 15, 30, 45, and 60 days after transplantation. The behavioral results showed almost complete functional recovery at 60 days, slight recovery at 45 and 30 days, and poor recovery at 15 days post graft. HRP histochemistry revealed that, at 15 days, there were no HRP labeled cells in the ventromedial nucleus or in the amygdala. At 30, 45, and 60 days post graft, there were increasing numbers of connections almost as many as seen in the controls with the thalamus and with the amygdala. The behavioral recovery was correlated with increased acetylcholinesterase activity, detected histochemically, and with morphological maturation, revealed by Golgi staining. These results suggest that some morphological recovery was necessary for the acquisition of taste aversion. It has been suggested by other investigators, however, that the structural and morphological integrity of fetal brain grafts may not be essential for behavioral recovery after cortical brain injury (Dunnett & Björklund, 1987; Kesslak, Brown, Steichen, & Cotman, 1986). These investigators have speculated that both brain injury and brain grafts induce a release of neurotrophic factors that can reactivate neural function and/or prevent injury-induced degeneration in the damaged host brain (Dunnet & Björklund, 1987; Kesslak et al., 1986). Moreover, Dunnet and Björklund (1987) have reported that neocortical grafts produce short term improvement in the T-maze alternation performance. These authors concluded that the short term effects were attributable to diffuse influences of the embryonic tissue on the lesioned host brain, rather than a reconnection of the damaged circuits.

Regarding the functional activity of the brain grafts, we decided to look first at some of the neurochemical elements that could be responsible for the functional recovery. We started by making biochemical assays of the cholinergic activity that is present in the brain grafts and compared them with control levels. In a series of experiments, we demonstrated that slices taken from the IC are able to release labeled gamma-amino-butiric acid (GABA), ACh, and glutamate, but not dopamine. Additionally, significant amounts of glutamic acid decarboxylase, choline acetyltransferase, and acetylcholinesterase activity were found in IC homogenates (López-García, Bermúdez-Rattoni, & Tapia, 1990). Biochemical analyses revealed that IC fetal grafts released GABA, ACh, and glutamate in response to K$^+$ depolarization. In contrast, occipital grafts released labeled GABA and glutamate, but not ACh (López-García, Fernández-Ruíz, Bermúdez-Rattoni, & Tapia, 1990). These results suggest that cholinergic transmission is important for CTA and that ACh may play a role in graft mediated behavioral recovery.

THE ROLE OF NERVE GROWTH FACTOR
ON RECOVERY

The implication of these series of grafting experiments, was that, for the IC and CTA, functional recovery is related to the morphological maturation and/or cholinergic activity of the graft. At this point in our research, several alternative hypotheses needed to be examined, such as the role of pharmacological agents that are known to facilitate behavioral recovery after brain injury, neurotrophic factors, gangliosides, etc. Several experiments have shown that nerve growth factor (NGF) produces significant regeneration, regrowth and penetration of cholinergic axons in the hippocampal formation (Gage, 1990; Hagg, Vahlsing, Manthorpe, & Varon, 1990). Constant infusion of NGF in fimbria fornix lesioned animals with severe learning deficits, has produced functional and anatomical recovery (Varon, Hagg, Vahlsing, & Manthorpe, 1989), and aged rats with functional impairments that received constant intracerebral infusions of NGF, improved enormously after several weeks of treatment (Gage & Björklund, 1986).

Recently, we evaluated the role of NGF in the recovery of the ability to acquire CTA induced by IC grafts at 15, 30, and 60 days after transplantation. In this experiment, several groups of rats showing disrupted taste aversions due to IC electrolytic lesions, were grafted as follows: one group received gelfoam plus NGF, another received fetal cortical graft plus NGF, the third group received gelfoam plus vehicle and the fourth group received only fetal cortical grafts. An additional group of animals was used as an unoperated control. All the groups were subdivided into three subgroups that were retrained for CTA at 15, 30, and 60 days post graft, respectively. The control groups had strong taste aversions at all the three post graft times. The IC graft + NGF group showed a significantly recovered ability to acquire the taste aversions at the three post graft times when compared with the control group. The IC-graft groups showed a disrupted taste aversion at 15 days post-graft, and recovered the ability to acquire the taste aversion by 30 and 60 days postgraft. The groups that received gelfoam plus NGF or gelfoam plus vehicle remained significantly impaired at the three postgraft times tested, compared with the control group. The results indicate that the administration of NGF to animals with cortical grafts accelerates the ability to acquire the CTA at 15 days postgraft (Bermúdez-Rattoni, Escobar, Piña, Tapia, López-García, & Hiriart, 1992).

Taken together, these results clearly show that the application of NGF with IC grafts accelerates recovery in the ability to acquire CTA learning. It is important to note that previous studies showed that, in the absence of NGF, IC grafts only start to induce the functional recovery 30 days after implantation, so the effects of NGF appear to accelerate recovery. In other studies, we tested the possibility that the combination of NGF with other fetal brain tissue could produce similar functional recovery in cortically lesioned animals. Thus, groups of IC-lesioned animals showing disrupted taste aversions received insular or occipital cortical grafts plus NGF, IC grafts plus vehicle, or remained lesioned as a control group. The results showed that the combination of NGF with insular, but not with occipital, cortical grafts produced recovery in the ability to acquire CTA at 15 days postgraft (Escobar, Jiménez, López-García, Tapia, & Bermúdez-Rattoni, 1993; Escobar, Russell, Booth, & Bermúdez-Rattoni, 1994).

CHOLINERGIC INVOLVEMENT
IN FUNCTIONAL RECOVERY

The cholinergic neurotransmitter system has been involved in learning and memory processes for a long time (Decker & McGaugh, 1991). Several studies have demonstrated that lesions affecting cholinergic innervation of the fimbria fornix produce severe impairments on different learning tasks (Varon et al., 1989). Using this model, several authors have demonstrated that the exogenous application of NGF can enhance and accelerate the regrowth and penetration of cholinergic axons into a lesioned area (Hagg, Vahlsing, Manthorpe & Varon, 1990; Vahlsing, Hagg, Spencer, Conner, Manthorpe & Varon, 1991), restore rhythmic theta activity in the denervated hippocampus (Buzsaki, Gage, Czopf, & Björklund, 1987), and stimulate the recovery of cholinergic functions (Lapchak, Jenden, & Hefti, 1991). As mentioned, biochemical analyses reveal that IC, but not occipital fetal, grafts released ACh in response to K^+ depolarization (López-García, Fernández-Ruíz, et. al., 1990). These results suggest that cholinergic transmission may play a role in graft-mediated behavioral recovery. In a later study, we have been able to demonstrate that choline acetyltransferase (ChAT) activity in the IC grafts with, but not without, NGF was similar to the normal IC activity of unoperated controls at 15 days post graft (Escobar et al., 1993). In addition, measurements of glutamic acid descarboxilase (GAD) activity in the same groups of animals remained similar. In that study, we concluded that the NGF associated with IC grafts induced recovery of learning abilities that correlate with the reestablishment of ChAT activity (Escobar et al., 1993). Recent experiments were designed to investigate the involvement of the cholinergic neurotransmitter system in behavioral recovery by the fetal brain grafts in combination with NGF. For that purpose, we used in vivo assays of ACh turnover in the IC of rats subjected to lesion and implant treatments similar to those already described: IC + NGF, IC + vehicle, occipital graft + NGF, NGF alone, and lesioned animals. The biochemical results showed that IC implants combined with NGF were at nonlesioned-control ACh levels. In contrast, those animals that received heterotopical occipital grafts with NGF or received the factor alone showed significantly higher levels of ACh and deficits in learning and memory when compared with controls (Russell, Escobar, Booth, & Bermúdez-Rattoni, 1994). The results suggested that there was some up regulation of the cholinergic function that accompanies IC lesions, and that this can be reversed, as can the behavioral deficits, by the IC implants supplemented with NGF (Russell et al., 1994).

ROLE OF THE IC IN EXTERO-NOCICEPTIVE MOTIVATED BEHAVIOR

Until recently, studies investigating the role of the IC in learning and memory processes focused primarily on taste-visceral memorial representation (Bermúdez-Rattoni, Sánchez, & Prado-Alcalá, 1989; Garcia et al., 1985; Lasiter & Glanzman, 1985). In a recent series of experiments, we have examined the effects of NMDA induced lesions in either the amygdala or the IC on the acquisition of inhibitory avoidance behavior and on CTA. The results showed that IC lesions, but not amygdala lesions, disrupted the acquisition of CTA. Surprisingly, IC-lesioned animals were also unable to acquire the inhibitory avoidance response, which, as expected, was disrupted by the amygdala lesions. These results constitute the first demonstration that the IC is involved in mediating the memorial representation of both extero-nociceptive stimuli visceral stimuli. Such effects may be mediated by the reciprocal connections of the IC with the amygdala (Bermúdez-Rattoni & McGaugh, 1991).

A majority of the studies examining the involvement of certain areas in learning and memory have used extensive lesions, applications of electrical current, or chemical substances whose effects spread throughout the cortex. Such experimental approaches preclude conclusive results concerning the role of specific cortical areas in learning and memory. In recent studies, we have applied a reversible neural blocker to the IC before or after the animals were trained on different learning tasks. In these experiments, we examined the effects of tetrodotoxin (TTX, a voltage-sensitive sodium channel blocker injected into the IC, the frontal cortex, the parietal cortex, or the caudate nucleus of rats (either before or after) they were trained in an inhibitory avoidance task, and in a Morris water maze spatial task. For the inhibitory avoidance task we used repeated acquisition trials. Thus, all the animals were trained on a step-through inhibitory avoidance apparatus (McGaugh, Introini-Collison, & Nagahara, 1988). On the training trial, each rat was placed in the lighted compartment when the rat turned around, the door leading to the dark compartment was opened. After the rat stepped through the door into the dark compartment, the door was closed, and a foot-shock was delivered through floor plates. On the retention test, the rat was placed in the lighted compartment (as in the training session), and the step-through latency (a maximum of 600 seconds) was recorded. For the water maze, the animals were trained in a circular galvanized-steel watering tank divided into four equal quadrants (see, Decker, Introini-Collison, & McGaugh, 1989). Located in the center of one of the quadrants was a rectangular clear Plexiglas® platform. On each trial the rat was allowed to swim until it located and climbed onto the platform. The rats received 10 trials in one day, with an intertrial interval of 5 to 10 seconds, twenty-four hours later, each rat received a single free-swim probe trial; the rat was allowed to swim for 60 seconds with the escape platform removed. The performance of the rat was recorded and analyzed to determine the time it took the rat to reach the place where the platform had been located and the number of times the rat crossed it (Bermúdez-Rattoni, Introini-Collison, & McGaugh, 1991).

Both pretraining and posttraining injections of TTX into the IC, but not into the frontal or parietal cortices, impaired retention in both tasks. These results clearly show that functional deactivation of the IC produces retrograde and anterograde amnesia in two aversively motivated learning tasks: inhibitory avoid-ance and water maze spatial learning (Bermúdez-Rattoni et al., 1991). These findings constitute the first demonstration that the IC is involved in the acquisi-tion and consolidation of memory for spatial and external aversively motivated learning. Spatial memory disruption has been reported previously only with large lesions of the parietal cortex or the dorsal hippocampus (DiMattia & Kesner, 1988; Kesner, 1991).

The next step was to assess the effects of the fetal brain grafts on the acquisi-tion of inhibitory avoidance. Several groups of rats received electrolytic or sham lesions before training on CTA. Two weeks after recovery, the animals were trained and tested. One week later, they received cortical grafts supplemented with NGF or vehicle. Each group was retrained and tested at 15 days for CTA; 4 days later all the animals received training for inhibitory avoidance in a shuttle box. At the end of the experiment, the animals were sacrificed and their brains were examined to determine enzymatic activities for ChAT and GAD (Escobar et al., 1993). The behavioral results for CTA have been described elsewhere (Es-cobar et al., 1993). The results for the inhibitory avoidance task showed that the control and IC-NGF groups learned the task with the highest latencies; the group with the IC graft supplemented with vehicle and the group that remained lesioned showed significatively lower latencies, indicating that the latest two groups did not learn the task (see Fig. 5.1).

In order to further assess the role of the cholinergic activity of the IC grafts, additional experiments were run. Several rats showing disrupted taste aversions

FIG. 5.1. Effects of 15 day-old IC fetal grafts with NGF on inhibitory avoidance training. Bars show step-through latency into the dark (punishment) chamber. The first bar of each pair (a) is the value for the aquisition day, the second bar of each pair (t) is the value for the tast day. **CON,** control group; **LX,** IC-lesioned group; **IC-NGF,** IC graft with NGF; **IC-VEH,** IC graft with vehicle. *$p < 0.05$, compared to **CON** group.

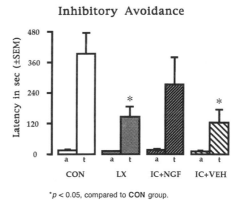

Inhibitory Avoidance

*$p < 0.05$, compared to **CON** group.

due to IC lesions were grafted with homotopic IC grafts supplemented with NGF. Eight days later, all animals were implanted with a cannula above the IC. After 15 days of recovery, the animals were subdivided into two groups: One received a microinjection of scopolamine 15 minutes before acquisition of CTA, and the other group received a microinjection of saline as a control. One week later, the groups' treatments were reversed, and the rats received either scopolamine or

FIG. 5.2. Effects of scopolamine on IC grafts supplemented with NGF. The top graph (**2A**) represents the effects on CTA training expressed in volume consumption of the saline solution. The bottom graph (**2B**) shows the results of the aquisition of a Morris water maze task, expressed in latency to reach the hidden platform on the aquisition trials (**Tn**). CON, control, grafted with no pretraining infusion; **SAL,** group received saline solution infused into the graft before training; **SCOP,** group receiving scopolamine solution into the graft before training. *$p < 0.05$, compared to **CON** group.

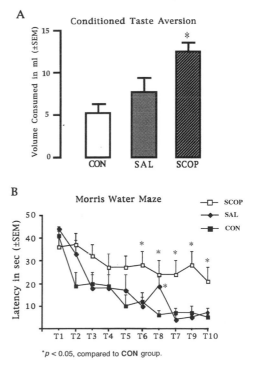

*$p < 0.05$, compared to **CON** group.

saline before the acquisition of a Morris water maze task. The results showed that scopolamine, but not saline significantly disrupted learning for whichever task was performed immediately after administration, whether CTA or the water maze (see Fig. 5.2). These results confirm that a functional a cholinergic blockade of the IC grafts produces disruptive effects in the acquisition of two learning tasks.

IS THE IC A STORAGE SITE FOR SEVERAL KINDS OF MEMORY?

The results just described clearly show that the IC is involved in the acquisition and retention of different learning tasks. Nevertheless, in a series of experiments, we challenged the hypothesis that the IC is a permanent memory store for different kinds of aversively motived learning; that is, CTA, spatial water maze learning, and inhibitory avoidance. In addition, we used the fetal brain grafts as a "reversible lesion" technique, to further assess the role of the IC in the evocation of a learned CTA task.

Our question was whether the IC is involved only in the learning aspects of CTA and inhibitory avoidance (acquisition and consolidation), or whether it plays a role in long-term memory (retention and retrieval), as well, we therefore designed an experiment to test the long-term memory hypothesis. We used three groups of intact rats that were trained in CTA and subsequently in inhibitory avoidance. One group received bilateral elecrolytic IC lesions 4 days after CTA training (2 days after inhibitory avoidance training) to allow consolidation. The other two groups received sham operations or remained unoperated, as controls. After a week of recovery the animals were given the test trials for taste aversion and for the step-through inhibitory avoidance. The results showed that the IC lesions induced a significant impairment in the retrieval of both tasks, indicating that the IC is involved in long-term memory, as well as in learning processes (Ormsby, Piña, & Bermúdez-Rattoni, 1991).

Long-term memory processes can be divided into two phases, retention and retrieval, which are also called storage and evocation. To further assess the role that the IC might play in either or both of the phases of CTA memory, we performed another series of studies. Taking into account the findings of (Escobar et al., 1994), in which homotopic fetal IC grafts supplemented with NGF induced recovery of the ability to learn CTA 15 days after transplantation we decided to use this model to examine the possibility that the grafts could also produce recovery of the memory processes. To achieve this, we trained five groups of intact rats on CTA; 4 days later we gave the animals in four groups NMDA induced lesions, using bilateral microinjections of NMDA. This procedure impairs acquisitions of CTA and inhibitory avoidance, as already described (Bermúdez-Rattoni & McGaugh, 1991). The fifth experimental group remained unlesioned, as a control. Eight days after lesioning, one group received grafts

FIG. 5.3. Effects of posttraining IC grafts on CTA. The top
graph (**A**) represents the effects
on the evocation of a prelesion-
trained CTA. Saccharin consumption is expressed as the
percentage of each group's previous day water baseline. The
bottom graph (**B**) represents the
effects on the retraining of a different CTA (to saline solution)
with two acquisition (**Acq**) sessions. **CON,** intact control
group; **IC + NGF,** IC-grafted,
supplemented with NGF; IC+V-
EH; IC-grafted with vehicle;
Glfm + NGF, gelfoam implanted with NGF; **Glfm + VEH,**
gelfoam implanted with vehicle.
*$p < 0.05$, compared to **CON**
group.
◇$p < 0.05$ compared to all other groups.

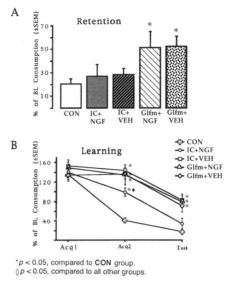

*$p < 0.05$, compared to **CON** group.
◇$p < 0.05$, compared to all other groups.

containing NGF, one group received grafts with vehicle, one group received an
implant of gelfoam embedded in NGF, and the last group received an implant of
gelfoam embedded in vehicle. As expected, the controls had a good recall of the
CTA, but, surprisingly, both grafted groups (those with and without NGF) recovered the ability to recall (see Fig. 5.3). None of the gelfoam-implanted groups
showed recall of the task. It is noteworthy that, although the rats in the group
grafted with vehicle did recall, they did not recover the ability to acquire a new
CTA using a different taste stimulus. The group grafted with NGF recovered the
ability to acquire this last task, but none of the gelfoam-implanted groups did.
These results corroborate the notion that the IC is involved in the learning and
evocation of CTA, but probably not in its long term storage.

DISCUSSION

In the first series of experiments, we showed that it is possible to produce
recovery of the acquisition of CTA using cortical fetal brain grafts. Moreover, it
is clear from our results that the heterotopic fetal brain grafts did not produce the
recovery of function seen with the use of homotopic grafts. In other models of
cortical lesions, it has been shown that recovery from learning deficits can be
produced with the use of heterotopic grafts or even with glial elements produced
by cortical lesions (Nieto-Sampedro, & Cotman 1986). In our model, the best

time to start seeing recovery is 30 to 40 days after the brain grafts that is also the time when more clear maturity of the grafts was observed in morphology and in biochemical assays (Escobar et al., 1989; Fernández-Ruíz, Escobar, Pina, Díaz-Cintra, Cintra-McGlone, & Bermúdez-Rattoni, R., 1991). In other studies we demonstrated that IC, but not occipital fetal grafts, release ACh in response to K^+ depolarization, suggesting that cholinergic transmission may play a role in graft-mediated behavioral recovery (López-García, Fernández-Ruíz, et al., 1990). It is noteworthy that, to observe functional recovery in IC lesioned animals, it is necessary to do homotopic grafting, because heterotopic grafts, even with occipital cortex, do not produce functional recuperation (Bermúdez-Rattoni, Fernández, & Escobar, 1989; Escobar et al., 1994). It is also noteworthy that the tissue taken at various times after fetal brain transplants without NGF supplementation were at different stages of maturation. That is, at 15 days there was little development of neurons and blood vessels in the implanted tissue. By 60 days, a greater neuronal density had developed: With abundant vascularization, proliferation of glial cells was very apparent, and fibers increasingly crossed the border between the graft and the host tissue (Fernández et al., 1991). Together, these results suggest that the behavioral effects are related to the integration and maturity of the implanted tissue.

The application of NGF with IC grafts accelerates recovery in the ability to acquire CTA. Thus, it appears that the combination of NGF with insular, but not with occipital, cortical grafts produces recovery in the ability to acquire CTA at 15 days post graft. The cholinergic graft activity is related somehow to the observed behavioral recuperation (Bermúdez-Rattoni, Fernández, et al., 1989; Escobar et al., 1989; López-García, Fernández-Ruíz, 1990). The combination of NGF and IC graft induces recovery of learning abilities that correlate with the ChAT activity, and in vivo assays corroborate that cholinergic activity is reestablished to control levels with the combination of NGF with IC-grafts (Escobar et al., 1994; Russell et al., 1994).

Finally, microinjections of scopolamine, a muscarinic cholinergic antagonist, also produces blockade in the recovery effects of brain grafts supplemented with NGF. The blockade effects were seen in two different learning tasks; CTA and the Morris spatial water maze. These results confirm that normal cholinergic activity is necessary to produce the observed recovery effects of fetal brain grafts, although it remains to be determined whether there is a possible dual role for cholinergic activity: in the morphological recovery and in the behavioral recovery. In this regard, it has been shown that there is transient expression of acetylcholinesterase activity during early development in some thalamocortical projection systems (Robertson, Hanes, & Yu, 1988; Robertson, Mostamand, Kageyama, Gallardo, & Yu, 1991). These results suggest that the cholinergic system may play a role in normal neural development and in the differentiation of the thalamocortical projections, which could also be applied to the development of connectivity the cortical grafts.

Regarding the role of the IC in recall, we have used the fetal brain grafts as a "reversible lesion" during recall processes. As already mentioned, it appears that under normal circumstances the IC is important for the acquisition and consolidation of aversively motivated learning tasks. However, it seems to be less important for the long term recall of taste aversion. With the use of fetal brain grafts as "reversible long-lasting lesions," it is possible to see if the studied structure is a real storage place or if it is only a place through which stored information from somewhere else in the brain exits. Other research has demonstrated that it is necessary to have an interaction between one side of the cortex and the ipsilateral subcortical parabrachial nucleus for the formation of CTA (Gallo & Bures, 1991). Combining our results with those of Bures and his colleagues, it is possible that the IC is an important structure for the acquisition and consolidation of CTA, and that for the retrieval the cortical and subcortical structures must participate. In other words, it is possible that a functional loop is established between the IC and the parabrachial nucleus which is responsible for the retrieval of CTA. More research is necessary to clarify the role of the IC as a permanent storage place for other aversively motivated learning tasks (i.e., spatial and inhibitory avoidance learning).

ACKNOWLEDGMENTS

This research was supported by grants N201893 from DGAPA-UNAM and grant 0178-N9107 CONACYT.

REFERENCES

Aggleton, J. P., Petrides, M., & Iversen, S. D. (1981). Differential effects of amygdaloid lesion on conditioned taste aversion learning by rats. *Physiology and Behavior*, 27, 397–403.

Bermúdez-Rattoni, F., Escobar, M. L., Piña, A. L., Tapia, T., López-García, J. C., & Hiriart, M. (1992). Effects of NGF on the recovery of conditioned taste aversion in insular cortex lesioned rats. In R. L. Doty (Ed.), *Chemical signals in vertebrates* (Vol. 4, pp. 297–303). New York: Plenum Press.

Bermúdez-Rattoni, F., Fernández, J., & Escobar, M. L. (1989). Fetal brain transplants induce recovery of morphological and learning deficits of cortical lesioned rats. In L. E. Canedo, L. E. Todd, L. Packer, & J. Jaz (Eds.), *C Cell function and disease* (pp. 261–273). New York: Plenum Press.

Bermúdez-Rattoni, F., Fernández, J., Sánchez, M. A., Aguilar-Roblero, R., & Drucker-Colin, R. (1987). Fetal brain transplants induce recuperation of taste aversion learning. *Brain Research*, 416, 147–152.

Bermúdez-Rattoni, F., Introini-Collison, I. B., & McGaugh, J. L. (1991). Reversible inactivation of the insular cortex by tetrodotoxin produces retrograde and anterograde amnesia for inhibitory avoidance and spatial learning. *Proceedings of the National Academy of Sciences (USA)*, 88, 5379–5382.

Bermúdez-Rattoni, F., & McGaugh, J. L. (1991). Insular cortex and amygdala lesions differentially affect acquisition of inhibitory avoidance and conditioned taste aversion. *Brain Research, 549,* 165–170.

Bermúdez-Rattoni, F., Sánchez, M. A., & Prado-Alcalá, R. A. (1989). Learning of external and visceral cue consequences may be subserved by different neuroanatomical substrates. In T. Archer & N. Lars-Goran (Eds.), *Aversion avoidance and anxiety* (pp. 121–138). Hillsdale, NJ: Lawrence Erlbaum Associates.

Björklund, A., & Stenevi, U. (Eds.). (1985). *Neural grafting in the mammalian CNS.* Amsterdam: Elsevier.

Buzsaki, G., Gage, F. H., Czopf, J., & Björklund, A. (1987). Restoration of rhythmic slow activity (theta) in the subcortically denervated hippocampus by fetal CNS transplants. *Brain Research, 400,* 334–347.

Decker, M. W., Introini-Collison, I. B., & McGaugh, J. L. (1989). Effects of naloxone on Morris water maze learning in the rat: Enhanced acquisition with pretraining but not posttraining administration. *Psychobiology, 17,* 270–275.

Decker, M. W., & McGaugh, J. L. (1991). The role of interactions between the cholinergic and other neuromodulatory systems in learning and memory. *Synapse, 7,* 151–168.

DiMattia, B. D., & Kesner, R. P. (1988). Spatial cognitive maps: Differential role of parietal cortex and hippocampal formation. *Behavioral Neuroscience, 102,* 471–480.

Dunnett, S. B., & Björklund, A. (1987). Mechanisms of function of neural grafts in the adult mammalian brain. *Journal of Experimental Biology, 132,* 256–289.

Dunnet, S. B., & Richards, S. J. (Eds.). (1990). *Neural transplantation: from molecular basis to clinical applications. Progress in brain research. Vol. 82.* Oxford Elsevier Press.

Escobar, M. L., Fernández, J., Guevara-Aguilar, R., & Bermúdez-Rattoni, F. (1989). Fetal brain grafts induce recovery of learning deficits and connectivity in rats with gustatory neocortex lesion. *Brain Research, 478,* 368–374.

Escobar, M. L., Jiménez, N., López-García, J. C., Tapia, R., & Bermúdez-Rattoni, F. (1993). Nerve growth factor with insular cortical grafts induces recovery of learning and reestablishes graft choline acetyltransferase activity. *Journal of Neural Transplantation and Plasticity* (Vol. 2, pp. 167–172).

Escobar, M. L., Russell, R. W., Booth, R. A., & Bermúdez-Rattoni, F. (1994). Accelerating behavioral recovery after cortical lesions: I. Homotopic implants plus NGF. *Behavioral and Neural Biology.* Vol. *61,* pp. 73–80.

Fernández-Ruiz, J., Escobar, M. L., Piña, A. L., Díaz-Cintra, S., Cintra-McGlone, F. L., & Bermúdez-Rattoni, F. (1991). Time-dependent recovery of taste aversion learning by fetal brain transplants in gustatory neocortex. *Behavioral and Neural Biology, 55,* 179–193.

Gage, F. H. (1990). NGF-dependent sprouting and regeneration in the hippocampus. *Progress in Brain Research, 83,* 357–370.

Gage, F. H., & Björklund, A. (1986). Enhanced graft survival in the hippocampus following selective denervation. *Neurosciences, 17,* 89–98.

Gallo, M., & Bures, J. (1991). Acquisition of conditioned taste aversion in rats is mediated by ipsilateral interaction of cortical and mesencephalic mechanisms. *Neuroscience Letters, 133,* 187–190.

Garcia, J., Lasiter, P. S., Bermúdez-Rattoni, F., & Deems, D. A. (1985). General theory of aversion learning. *Annals of the New York Academy of Sciences, 443,* 8–20.

Garcia, J., Rusiniak, K., Kiefer, S. W., & Bermúdez-Rattoni, F. (1982). The neural integration of feeding and drinking habits. In C. Woody (Ed.), *Conditioning* (pp. 567–579). New York: Plenum Press.

Hagg, T., Vahlsing, H. L., Manthorpe, M., & Varon, S. (1990). Nerve growth factor infusion into denervated adult rat hippocampal formation promotes its cholinergic reinnervation. *Journal of Neurosciences, 10,* 3087–3092.

Hatfield, T., Phillips, W. G., & Gallagher, M. (1992). Taste-potentiated odor aversion learning:

Role of the amygdaloid basolateral complex and central nucleus. *Behavioral Neuroscience*, *106*, 286–293.

Kesner, R. P. (1991). Neurobiological views of memory. In J. L. Martinez, Jr., & R. P. Kesner (Eds.), *Learning and memory: A biological view* (pp. 499–547). San Diego, CA: Academic Press.

Kesslak, J. P., Brown, L., Steichen, C., & Cotman, C. W. (1986). Adult and embryonic frontal cortex transplants after frontal cortex ablation enhance recovery on a reinforced alternation task. *Experimental Neurology*, *94*, 615–626.

Kiefer, S. W. (1985). Neural mediation of conditioned food aversions. *Annals of the New York Academy of Sciences*, *443*, 100–109.

Krushel, L. A., & van der Kooy, D. (1988). Visceral cortex: Integration of the mucosal senses with limbic information in the rat agranular insular cortex. *Journal of Comparative Neurology*, *270*, 34–541.

Lasiter, P. S., & Glanzman, D. I. (1985). Cortical substrates of taste aversion learning: Involvement of the dorsalateral amygdaloid nuclei and temporal neocortex in taste aversion learning. *Behavioral Neuroscience*, *99*, 257–276.

Lapchak, P. A., Jenden, D. J., & Hefti, F. (1991). Compensatory elevation of acetylcholine synthesis *in vivo* by cholinergic neurons surviving partial lesions of the septohippocampal pathway. *Neuroscience*, *11*, 2821–2828.

López-García, J. C., Bermúdez-Rattoni, F., & Tapia, R. (1990). Release of acetylcholine, G-aminobutirate, dopamine and glutamate, and activity of some related enzymes, in rat gustatory neocortex. *Brain Research*, *523*, 100–104.

López García, J. C., Fernández-Ruíz, J., Bermúdez-Rattoni, F., & Tapia, R. (1990). Correlation between acetylcholine release and recovery of conditioned taste aversion induced by fetal neocortex grafts. *Brain Research*, *523*, 105–110.

McGaugh, J. L., Introini-Collison, I. B., & Nagahara, A. H. (1988). Memory enhancement with intra-amygdala posttraining naloxone is blocked by concurrent administration of propanolol. *Brain Research*, *466*, 37–49.

McGaugh, J. L., Introini-Collison, I.B., Nagahara, A. H., Cahill, L., Brioni, J.D., & Castellano, C. (1990). Involvement of the amygdaloid complex in neuromodulatory influences on memory storage. *Neuroscience and Behavioral Review*, *14*, 425–431.

Nieto-Sampedro, M., & Cotman, C. W. (1986). Growth factor induction and other events in CNS repair. In C. W. Cotman (Ed.), *Synaptic plasticity and remodeling* (pp. 407–456). New York: Gilford Press.

Norgren, R., & Wolf, G. (1975). Projections of thalamic gustatory and lingual areas in the rat. *Brain Research*, *92*, 123–129.

Ormsby, C. E., Piña, A. L., & Bermúdez-Rattoni, F. (1991). Long-term retrograde amnesia of inhibitory avoidance and conditioned taste aversion learning tasks by insular cortex lesions. *Society for Neuroscience Abstracts*, *17*, 1045.

Pascoe, J. P., & Kapp, B. S. (1987). Responses of amygdaloid central nucleus neurons to stimulation of the insular cortex in awake rabbits. *Neuroscience*, *21*, 471–485.

Robertson, R. T., Hanes, M. A., & Yu, J. (1988). Investigations of the origins of transient acetylcholinesterase activity in developing rat visual cortex. *Developmental Brain Research*, *41*, 1–23.

Robertson, R. T., Mostamand, F., Kageyama, G. H., Gallardo, K. A., & Yu, J. (1991). Primary auditory cortex in the rat: Transient expression of acetylcholinesterase activity in developing geniculocortical projections. *Developmental Brain Research*, *58*, 81–95.

Russell, R. W., Escobar, M. L., Booth, R. A., & Bermúdez-Rattoni, F. (1994). Accelerating behavioral recovery after cortical lesions II: In vivo evidence for cholinergic involvement. *Behavioral and Neural Biology*, *61*, 81–92.

Sharp, F. R., & González, M. F. (1986). Fetal cortical transplants ameliorate thalamic atrophy ipsilateral to neonatal frontal cortex lesions. *Neuroscience Letters*, *71*, 247–251.

Vahlsing, H. L., Hagg, T., Spencer, M., Conner, J. M., Manthorpe, M., & Varon, S. (1991). Dose-dependent responses to nerve growth factor by adult rat cholinergic medial septum and neostriatal neurons. *Brain Research*, *522*, 320–329.

Varon, S., Hagg, T., Vahlsing, H. L., & Manthorpe, M. (1989). Nerve growth factor in vivo actions on cholinergic neurons in the adult rat CNS. In L. E. Cañedo, L. E. Todd, L. Packer, & J. Jaz (Eds.), *Cell function and disease* (pp. 235–248). New York: Plenum Press.

6

Somatic Gene Transfer to the Brain: A Tool to Study the Necessary and Sufficient Structure/Function Requirements for Learning and Memory

Fred H. Gage
University of California, San Diego

Michael Kawaja
Queen's University

Kaaren Eagle
Gordon Chalmers
Jasodhara Ray
Lisa J. Fisher
University of California, San Diego

A standard approach to understanding structure and function in the brain is to remove part of the brain and ask whether the organism can still perform specified functions. The more selective the lesion and the more discrete the functional analysis, the more useful the information. What we learn from this approach is the extent to which the missing component is necessary for the evaluated function. To further reveal the role of that part of the lesioned brain in normal functioning, one can reintroduce components back in to the brain until some specific function is restored. In this way, we learn not only what is necessary for function, but also what is sufficient for function. For the behavioral neurobiolo gist the lesion paradigm has been useful since the late 19th century as a tool for asking what the necessary role of a structure in learning and memory may be. With better and more discrete lesion techniques, that eliminate only specific chemically defined neurons, our dissection of unique systems within the brain that are necessary for different forms of memory has escalated. More recently, the transplantation of fetal neurons into the brain has emerged as a tool for replacing some of the neurons eliminated by the discrete lesions and for asking which of the lesioned neurons are sufficient, or necessary, for the elaboration of a particular behavior (Gage & Fisher, 1991; Fisher & Gage, 1993). Although still in an early stage as a biological tool, the transplantation technique has proven useful, and is improving as better dissection techniques and transplantation techniques are developed. One of the difficulties with this method is that it requires embryonic cells for successful engraftment, and our knowledge of neuronal precursor biology is primitive, at best. In particular, the tissue that is transplanted is composed of a heterogeneous mixture of precursor cells that are at different stages of development and are expressing distinctly different phenotypes. Thus, we need to know more about the stages and conditions of neuronal development to better exploit neuronal transplantation as a tool for understanding structure–function relationships. Recently, we have introduced a modification to intracerebral grafting that does not require the transplantation of the developing tissue, and yet allows us to implant a predefined homogeneous population of cells synthesizing a predetermined relevant gene product. We refer to this approach as ex vivo somatic gene transfer (Gage, Kawaja, Fisher, 1991; Gage et al., 1987).

SOMATIC GENE TRANSFER

Our understanding of the central nervous system, immune system, and hematopoietic system has progressed greatly since the 1970's, due to the development of molecular genetic techniques. These methods have allowed for the isolation, characterization, and cloning of genes relevant to certain disease states. Over the same period, developments in the delivery of foreign genes into target cells have advanced, such that a number of techniques are now available for efficiently introducing new DNA sequences into cultured eukaryotic cells. Many studies to date have employed gene transfer with subsequent grafting as a means of augmenting a deficient enzyme or protein in animal models of human disease types. That is, cells maintained in culture are genetically modified using delivery vectors that contain a functional foreign gene (or transgene) and are then grafted onto damaged or diseased organs to provide a focal supplement of a gene product. Thus, the combination of gene transfer and grafting is a reasonable approach to alleviating biochemical deficits and ultimately, to restoring function (Mulligan, 1993; Verma, 1990).

GENE TRANSDUCTION

At present, a number of methods are available for introducing exogenous DNA into target cells for gene transfer. A portion of the exogenous DNA can be integrated stably into the chromosomal DNA of the host cell. The entry of DNA into these cells, however, is a very inefficient process. This is due to a number of physical and enzymatic barriers of cells, and to the nature of the exogenous DNA. A number of methods have been developed to overcome these problems. These techniques fall into three categories: chemical methods (e.g., calcium phosphate and liposome-mediated gene transfer), physical methods (e.g., electroporation and microinjection), and viral methods (e.g., retrovirus and DNA virus). The advantages and disadvantages of each technique for successful transduction have been recently reviewed elsewhere (Kawaja, Fisher, et al., 1992).

CELL BIOLOGY OF TRANSPLANTATION

One way to achieve focal delivery of a transgene product into the adult brain is through the genetic modification of a homogeneous population of cells in culture, followed by implantation in the brain (Gage, Wolff, et al., 1987). Using such genetically modified cells offers a clear advantage because cultured cells that have not been genetically engineered are the perfect control material, permitting effects seen with grafts of genetically modified cells to be attributable to the expression of the transgene. To date, several different cell types have been used to deliver a transgene product via genetic modification, including immortalized cell lines, primary fibroblasts, myoblasts, myotubes, and astrocytes. These cells must exhibit certain characteristics that make them amenable to gene transfer *in vitro*, as well as additional *in vivo* features following intracerebral implantation:

1. Accessibility of donor cells is an important feature when choosing a population for genetic modification. For instance, primary adult fibroblasts and keratinocytes are both readily obtainable from skin biopsies.
2. Donor cells must also exhibit robust cell division and DNA synthesis in culture; this ensures successful incorporation of the transgene by either retroviral infection or transfection (using calcium phosphate or lipofection).
3. The cells must survive within the brain for extended periods of time. To enhance long-term graft survival, histocompatibility between the donor cells and the recipient organ is of paramount importance.
4. Intracerebral grafts of genetically modified cells must not exhibit continued growth that results in the formation of tumors.
5. It would be advantageous if the grafted cells became integrated (structurally or functionally) within the host brain.
6. Finally, and most importantly, the cells must continue to synthesize and release the transgene into the surrounding host parenchyma.

Although many types of cells may be used for gene transfer and subsequent intracerebral implantation, data from our laboratory suggest that primary skin fibroblasts are a very useful cellular population for genetic modification and grafting (Kawaja, Fagan, Firestein, & Gage, 1991; Kawaja & Gage, 1992). Primary fibroblasts are readily obtainable from skin biopsies, and can be maintained and grown under standard culture conditions. Once primary cells reach confluency, however, the rate of cell division is greatly retarded or even ceases.

Immortalized cells, on the other hand, continue to grow beyond confluence. As mentioned previously, donor cells must also exhibit gene expression following implantation, as well as stable long-term survival, without having detrimental effects on the host brain. A variety of immortalized cell types (Cunningham, Short, Vielkind, Breakefield, & Bohn, 1991; Ernfors et al., 1989; Rosenberg et al., 1988) and primary skin fibroblasts (Kawaja & Gage, 1992) are able to synthesize and release significant levels of nerve growth factor (NGF) following retroviral-mediated gene transfer *in vitro*. Likewise, these genetically modified cells continue to produce NGF after implantation into the rat brain, as revealed by the percentage of NGF-dependent septal neurons rescued from cell death following axotomy (see further on). However, grafts of immortalized cells often exhibit growth patterns that are not conducive to long-term experimentation. For instance, NIH 3T3 cells give rise to intracerebral tumors three to eight weeks after grafting (Horellou, Brundin, Kalen, Mallet, & Bjorklund,1990), whereas grafts of 208F cells often atrophy after four weeks, possibly as a result of histoincompatability between the host and donor (personal observations). Using primary skin fibroblasts is one way to circumvent problems of tumor formation and immune rejection. Following implantation in the rat brain (in these scenarios, the donor and recipient are either the same animal or from the same inbred strain), grafts of primary fibroblasts maintain a constant size for three and eight weeks, and the size of these grafts does not appear to change for up to six months (Kawaja, Fagan et al., 1991; Kawaja & Gage, 1992). In fact, we have not yet observed any spontaneous tumors arising from implants of primary skin fibroblasts. Morphologically, the fibroblasts appear viable for up to six months *in vivo* and possess typical characteristics of normal skin fibroblasts: a spindle shape, an elongated nucleus with condensed chromatin, and an extensive rough endoplasmic reticulum. Finally, fibroblast grafts become structurally incorporated within the host brain via the infiltration of astrocytic processes and capillaries; the extensive vascular plexus found in these grafts resembles host-derived vessels both morphologically (e.g., a continuous-type endothelium with a surrounding basal lamina) and functionally (e.g., an intact barrier to blood-borne macromolecules by eight weeks, Kawaja & Gage, 1992). From these observations, we suggest that the genetic modification of homogeneous populations of cells to produce a functional gene product is a viable approach to the delivery of cells and molecules into the adult CNS. Furthermore, of the many types of cells that can undergo successful gene transfer and subsequent intracerebral grafting, primary skin fibroblasts offer the best characteristics, both *in vitro* and *in vivo*.

DELIVERY OF FUNCTIONAL GENE PRODUCTS TO THE BRAIN

The feasibility of using fibroblasts to deliver molecules into the CNS has been demonstrated in several animal models. For example, L-DOPA-producing fibroblasts have been implanted into the striatum of 6-hydroxy-dopamine lesioned rats (Fisher, Jinnah, Kale, Higgins, & Gage, 1991); fibroblasts expressing the *LacZ* gene (bGal) were implanted in other rats to serve as controls. Analysis of drug-induced rotational behavior showed that rats that received implants of L-DOPA-expressing fibroblasts executed fewer rotations (Fisher et al., 1991; Fig. 2), whereas bGal-expressing fibroblasts had no effect on drug-induced rotational behavior. Studies using fibroblast-derived cell lines have produced similar results (Horellou, Brundin, et al., 1990; Horellou, Marlier, Privat, & Mallet, 1990). Genetically modified fibroblasts can also be used to deliver neurotransmitters directly. In particular, Rat-1 fibroblasts transduced to express *Drosophila* choline acetyltransferase (dChAT) readily release acetylcholine (ACh) *in vitro* (Schinstine & Rosenberg et al., 1991). More recently, substantial levels of ACh were measured in the hippocampus of fimbria-fornix lesioned rats one week after dChAT-producing dermal fibroblasts were implanted into the denervated hippocampus (Fisher et al., 1993).

INTRACEREBRAL GRAFTS OF NGF-PRODUCING CELLS: NEUROTROPHIC AND TROPIC EFFECTS

Since about 1990, immortalized and primary fibroblasts genetically modified to produce NGF fibroblasts have been used to address questions concerning neuronal survival and axon regeneration following perturbation. Using the model of lesion-induced neuronal degeneration in the septohippocampal system, we grafted genetically modified primary fibroblasts to determine whether these cells would be effective in their production and secretion of NGF *in vivo* (Kawaja, Rosenberg, Yoshida, & Gage,1992).

Two different approaches have been taken to grafting NGF-producing primary fibroblasts into rat brains following unilateral fimbria-fornix ablations. First, cells were implanted directly into the septal parenchyma ipsilateral to the lesion. Second, fibroblasts were suspended in rat tail collagen *in vitro,* and pieces of this matrix material were subsequently implanted inside the lesion cavity.

Four weeks after unilateral fimbria-fornix ablation and septal implantation of the primary fibroblasts, about 75% of NGF-receptor-positive septal neurons were sustained with NGF-producing fibroblasts, whereas only 45% of septal immunoreactive neurons survived axotomy with grafts of noninfected control cells. When grafts of collagen and NGF-producing fibroblasts were implanted in the lesion cavity, some 65% of septal cholinergic NGF-receptor-positive neurons was sustained at four and eight weeks after axotomy. In comparison to the proportion of neurons sustained with NGF-producing rat 208F and mouse NIH-3T3 cells (i.e., >90%; Rosenberg et al., 1988; Strömberg et al., 1990), the cell survival achieved with primary skin fibroblasts is smaller but significant (65%-75%). The rates of NGF release appear to be comparable for both immortalized 208F cells and primary skin fibroblasts. From these data, we propose that the proportion of lesioned septal neurons saved is dependent on the available dose of NGF, such that high levels of NGF released from either mini-osmotic pumps or grafts of immortalized cells sustain a larger number of axotomized cholinergic cells than the lower levels of NGF likely to be released from grafts of primary skin fibroblasts.

Not only do grafts of NGF-producing primary fibroblasts prevent a significant proportion of septal neurons from retrograde degeneration, but they also induce axon sprouting. To more closely assess the trophic effects of such grafts on cholinergic neurons of the rat basal forebrain, we grafted suspensions of NGF-producing primary fibroblasts into the adult striatum (Kawaja & Gage, 1992). Between one and three weeks following implantation, NGF receptor-positive axons arising from the adjacent nucleus basalis grew towards and surrounded grafts of NGF-producing fibroblasts.

Grafts of control noninfected cells did not elicit the same response. By eight weeks, the NGF-producing grafts were filled with NGF-receptor-immunoreactive profiles; the control grafts lacked this pattern of immunostaining. At the electron microscope level, in grafts of NGF-producing fibroblasts, numerous unmyelinated axons were enveloped within glial processes, especially those of reactive astrocytes. Furthermore, these axons were exclusively associated with glial elements and were not found in the extracellular matrix of the grafts. Although control grafts possessed reactive astrocytic processes, axons were not observed anywhere within these grafts. From these data, we conclude that (a) reactive astrocytes can act as conducive substrates for growing axons, and (b) only in the presence of elevated levels of NGF will permissive substrates (e.g., astrocytes) support axon growth by NGF-sensitive neurons.

Our observations that intracerebral grafts of NGF-producing skin fibroblasts can induce axonal sprouting led us to ask whether these grafts could also promote axon regeneration among NGF-sensitive neuronal populations following axotomy. Also, if regenerating axons could grow through NGF-producing grafts, would they be able to reinnervate target sites in the adult brain?

To address these questions, we again focused our attention on the septohippocampal model (Kawaja, Rosenberg, et al., 1992). Following unilateral fimbria-fornix ablations, collagen-fibroblast matrices were grafted into the lesion cavity to assess the importance of NGF on the regenerative capacities of rat septal neurons after axotomy.

We found first that NGF can promote the regeneration of septal axons, because NGF-producing grafts possessed large numbers of acetylcholinesterase (AChE)-positive axons as early as four weeks after grafting. Grafts of control cells, however, usually lacked cholinergic axons. At the electron microscope level, unmyelinated axons observed in NGF-producing grafts used many different substrates for growth, including astrocytes and components of the extracellular matrix, including the basal laminae of capillaries and collagen. Grafts of control fibroblasts possessed the same cellular and matrix substrates, but contained only a very small population of axons, probably of peripheral sympathetic origin. Finally, AChE-positive axons growing through NGF-producing grafts provided a topographically organized input to the deafferented hippocampal dentate gyrus. Regenerating septal axons terminate predominantly on the dendritic processes of granular neurons of the dentate gyrus but the dentate gyrus ipsilateral to grafts of control noninfected fibroblasts remained devoid of AChE-positive fibers. From these results, we conclude that the availability of NGF is necessary for promoting axon regeneration and cholinergic reinnervation of granular neurons by lesioned septal neurons. The presence of many permissive substrates (e.g., astrocytes, basal lamina and collagen) alone, however, is not sufficient to induce axon regrowth from adult septal neurons.

INTRACEREBRAL GRAFTS OF NGF-PRODUCING CELLS: SOME PRELIMINARY BEHAVIORAL CONSEQUENCES OF SOMATIC GENE TRANSFER

We have recently begun to examine the behavioral effects of these grafts in models that allow for evaluation of recovery from long-term nonspontaneously recoverable deficits. We utilized a unilateral fimbria-fornix lesion and grafting design, in which rats were cognitively tested until sacrifice and histochemical assessment at 7 months. Only rats with NGF-producing fibroblasts in the bridging graft demonstrated AChE staining and NGFr immunoreactivity in the graft and in the adjacent hippocampus (Eagle, Chalmers, Clary, & Gage, in press), with cholinergic fibers growing an average of 1.50 mm into the hippocampus from the graft surface.

Behavioral deficits were measured in the unilaterally lesioned rats using both the Morris water maze (to assess spatial learning and memory) and the habituation task. The performance of rats with NGF-producing grafts improved on habituation, so that they were significantly different from controls. In addition, those rats with lesion only or with β-gal fibroblast-containing grafts did not habituate significantly. There were no differences in water maze performance between any pairs of experimental groups, all of which were significantly impaired relative to the nonlesioned control group. Thus, the limited cholinergic ingrowth into the hippocampus that was promoted by the NGF-producing grafts appeared to mediate only simple forms of cognitive behaviors.

CONCLUSIONS

Primary autologous cells can be used successfully for gene transfer and subsequent intracerebral implantation to achieve *in vivo* delivery of neuroactive chemicals. Following grafting into the lesioned rat brain, these cells can produce enough NGF to sustain a significant proportion of axotomized septal neurons, which, without such trophic support, would undergo retrograde degeneration. Also, NGF production induces the regrowth of damaged axons arising from cholinergic basal forebrain neurons. These regenerating axons can use a number of different cellular and extracellular matrix components as conducive substrates for growth, but only in the presence of NGF will axon regrowth be induced and promoted. Although these regenerating axons are also able to reinnervate hippocampal granule neurons, it remains to be shown what role NGF plays in the guidance of axons to appropriate target sites and in the re-formation of synaptic contacts.

We can clearly state that an intact fimbria fornix is necessary for spatial learning and memory, and that cholinergic innervation of the dorsal hippocampus may be sufficient for simple forms of spatial memory. As we more completely replace the appropriate neuro-transmitter systems in the denervated hippocampus and assess the behavioral consequences, we can more completely define the essential requirements of spatial learning and memory in the rat.

ACKNOWLEDGMENTS

We acknowledge the support of NIH grants AG10435 and NS28121, and the Hollfelder Foundation.

REFERENCES

Cunningham, L. A., Short, M. P., Vielkind, U., Breakefield, X. O. & Bohn, M. D. (1991). Survival and differentiation within the adult mouse striatum of grafted rat pheochromocytoma (PC12) genetically modified to express recombinant β-NGF. *Experimental Neurology, 112,* 174–182.

Eagle, K. L, Chalmers, G. R., Clary, D. O. & Gage, F. H. (in press). *Axonal regeneration and limited functional recovery following hippocampal deafferent-ation. Journal of Comparative Neurology.*

Ernfors, P., Ebendal, T., Olson, L., Mouton, P., Strömberg, I., & Persson, A. (1989). A cell line producing recombinant nerve growth factor evokes growth responses in intrinsic and grafted central cholinergic neurons. *Proceedings of the National Academy of Sciences,* (USA), *86,* 4756–4760.

Fisher, L. J., & Gage, F. H. (1993). Grafting in the mammalian central nervous system. *Physiological Reviews, 78*(3) 583–616.

Fisher, L. J., Jinnah, H. A., Kale, L. C., Higgins, G. A., & Gage, F. H. (1991). Survival and function of intrastriatally·grafted primary fibroblasts genetically modified to produce L-dopa. *Neuron, 6,* 371–380.

Fisher, L. J., Schinstine, M., Salvaterra, P., Dekker, A. J., Thal, L., & Gage, F. H. (1993). In vivo production and release of acetylcholine from primary fibroblasts genetically modified to express choline acetyltransferase. *Journal of Neurochemistry, 61*(4), 1323–1332.

Gage, F. H., & Fisher, L. J. (1991). Intracerebral grafting: A tool for the neurobiologist. *Neuron, 6,* 1–12.

Gage, F. H., Kawaja, M. D., & Fisher, L. J. (1991). Genetically modified cells: Applications for intracerebral grafting. *Trends in Neuroscience, 14,* 328–333.

Gage, F. H., Wolff, J. A., Rosenberg, M. B., Xu, L., Yee, J. L., Shults, C., & Friedmann, T. (1987). Grafting genetically modified cells to the brain: possibilities for the future. *Neuroscience*, 23, 795–807.

Horellou, P., Brundin, P., Kalén, P., Mallet, J., & Bjorklund, A. (1990). In vivo release of DOPA and dopamine from genetically engineered cells grafted to the denervated rat striatum. *Neuron*, 5, 393–402.

Horellou, P., Marlier, L., Privat, A., & Mallet, J. (1990). Behavioral effect of engineered cells that synthesize L-dopa or dopamine after grafting into the rat neostriatum. *European Journal of Neuroscience*, 2, 116–119.

Kawaja, M. D., Fagan, A. M., Firestein, B. L., & Gage, F. H. (1991). Intracerebral grafting of cultured autologous skin fibroblasts into the rat striatum: An assessment of graft size and ultrastructure. *Journal of Comparative Neurology*, 307, 695–706.

Kawaja, M. D., & Gage, F. H. (1991a). Nerve growth factor receptor immunoreactivity in the rat septo-hippocampal pathway: A light and electron microscope investigation. *Journal of Comparative Neurology*, 307, 517–529.

Kawaja, M. D., & Gage, F. H. (1991b). Reactive astrocytes are substrates for the growth of adult CNS axons in the presence of elevated levels of nerve growth factor. *Neuron*, 7, 1019–1030.

Kawaja, M. D., Fisher, L. J., Schinstine, M., Hyder, J, Ray, J., Chan, L. S., & Gage, F. H. (1992). Grafting genetically modified cells within the rat central nervous system: Methodological considerations. In S. Dunnett & A. Bjorklund (Eds.), *Neural transplantation: A practical approach* (pp. 21–55). Oxford: Oxford University Press.

Kawaja, M. D., & Gage, F. H. (1992). Morphological and neurochemical features of cultured primary Skin fibroblasts of Fischer 344 rats following striatal implantation. *Journal of Comparative Neurology*, 317, 102–116.

Kawaja, M. D., Rosenberg, M. B., Yoshida, K., & Gage, F. H. (1992). Somatic gene transfer of nerve growth factor promotes the survival of axotomized septal neurons and the regeneration of their axons in adult rats. *Journal of Neuroscience*, 12, 2849–2864.

Mulligan, R. C. (1993). The basic science of gene therapy. *Science*, 260, 926–932.

Rosenberg, M. B., Friedmann, T., Robertson, R. C., Tuszynski, M., Wolff, J. A., Breakefield, X. O., & Gage, F. H. (1988). Grafting genetically modified cells to the damaged brain: restorative effects of NGF expression. *Science*, 242, 1575–1578.

Schinstine, M., Rosenberg, M. B., Routledge-Ward, C., Friedmann, T., & Gage, F. H. (1992). Effects of choline and quiescence on Drosophila choline acetyltransferase expression and acetylcholine production by transduced rat fibroblasts. *Journal of Neurochemistry*, 58, 2019–2029.

Strömberg, I., Wetmore, C. J., Ebendal, T., Ernfors, P., Persson, H., & Olson, L. (1990). Rescue of basal forebrain cholinergic neurons after implantation of genetically modified cells producing recombinant NGF. *Journal of Neuroscience Research*, 25, 405–411.

Verma, I. M. (1990). Gene therapy. *Scientific American*, 263, 68–85.

Wolff, J. A., Fisher, L. J., Xu, L., Jinnah, H. A., Langlais, P. J., Iuvone, P. M., O'Malley, K. L., Rosenberg, M. B., Shimohama, S., Friedmann, T., & Gage, F. H. (1989). Grafting fibroblasts genetically modified to produce L-dopa in a rat model of Parkinson disease. *Proceedings of the National Academy of Sciences* (USA), 86, 9011–9014.

7 Reversible Lesions Reveal Hidden Stages of Learning

Jan Bures
Academy of Sciences, Prague

According to textbook definitions (Squire, 1987), *learning* is a process leading to formation of memory traces mediating subsequent retrieval of the acquired experience. Although learning is usually identified with the acquisition of new engrams, success in learning can only be demonstrated by *retrieval*, a different process, which implements the readout of the respective memories. The uncertain delimitation of acquisition and retrieval complicates the analysis of the underlying neural mechanisms in animal experiments. The following facts must be considered:

1. Not all engrams formed during learning can be retrieved by standard testing procedures. Some latent memory traces can be activated by changing the level of arousal or motivation, but some are probably irretrievable because the set of plastic changes induced by learning must necessarily be considerably larger than the set of retrievable memories.
2. Engrams formed during learning may become irretrievable when the readout mechanism is impaired. This presents a particularly difficult problem because the failure of retrieval may be erroneously interpreted as a failure of acquisition.
3. Acquisition may proceed in several stages that cannot be separately accessed by the retrieval process and whose existence may, therefore, remain undetected.

The bulk of our knowledge of the functional anatomy of learning and memory is based on lesion studies (Thompson, 1983), which usually follow one of two basic paradigms:

Paradigm 1: The progress of training is compared in naive intact and naive lesioned animals.

Paradigm 2: Retrieval is tested in pretrained animals before and after lesion.

A lesion effective in both paradigms can interfere with acquisition, with retrieval, or with both. A lesion effective in Paradigm 1 that leaves retrieval intact in Paradigm 2 impairs acquisition. A lesion impairing retrieval in Paradigm 2, but compatible with successful, albeit somewhat slower, training in Paradigm 1 indicates the availability of other learning and retrieval mechanisms activated by the brain damage. These possibilities are summarized in Table 7.1.

Most lesion studies are based on the unverified assumption that acquisition and retrieval share the same neural mechanism. In this case, failure of training in lesioned animals is automatically interpreted as due to an acquisition failure, although impaired retrieval of normally formed memories is equally probable. The latter possibility is widely considered so unlikely that Paradigm 2 is not used in most cases in which Paradigm 1 has revealed an impairment.

Although different outcomes of Paradigms 1 and 2 suggest differential participation of the lesioned part of the brain in the acquisition and retrieval mechanisms, this possibility is not excluded in cases where both paradigms show disruption. The irreversibility of the lesion precludes a more precise answer: Once a center or pathway has been destroyed, the change affects all subsequent stages of the learning process. The impairment observed indicates that the lesioned structure is important for the process, but does not allow one to decide which particular phase of the process has been affected. To answer not only the "where" but also the "when" questions necessary for disclosing the spatial and temporal dynamics of the plastic changes underlying learning and memory, it is necessary to use functional ablation procedures whose reversibility allows the brain region eliminated during an early stage of the process to be intact again during the later stages.

Reversible lesions can be implemented using a number of procedures, includ-

TABLE 7.1
Effect of Pretraining and Posttraining Lesions on Learning and Retrieval

No lesion	Pretraining Lesion	Posttraining Lesion	Interpretation
	Paradigm 1	Paradigm 2	
+	−	−	Acquisition and/or retrieval failure
+	−	+	Acquisition failure, independent retrieval mechanism
+	+	−	Retrieval failure compensated for by parallel acquisition/retrieval mechanisms

ing local injection of drugs (Hodge, Gibbs, & Ng, 1981), local cooling (Brooks, 1983), spreading depression (Bures, Buresova, & Krivanek, 1974), and focal seizure activity (Panakhova, Buresova, & Bures, 1985). Applications of the functional ablation techniques in learning and memory research were reviewed recently (Bures & Buresova, 1990). This chapter updates that review, using new evidence taken from conditioned taste aversion (CTA), reversal learning, and interhemispheric transfer studies.

CTA

The hidden stages of learning can be conveniently demonstrated in the case of CTA, a robust, vitally important adaptive behavior that protects animals against repeated ingestion of toxic foods (for reviews, see Barker, Best, & Domjan, 1977; Braveman & Bronstein, 1985). A food whose intake has been followed by bodily discomfort becomes aversive and is subsequently avoided by the animal. Lesion studies show that CTA is disrupted by ablation of the gustatory cortex (Braun, 1990), by amygdalectomy (Simbay, Boakes, & Burton, 1986; Yamamoto, Azuma & Kawamura, 1981), and by lesions of the parabrachial nuclei (Spector, Norgren, & Grill, 1992; Yamamoto, 1993) performed before or after CTA training. These studies failed, however, to disclose the fact that CTA acquisition includes a stage highly resistant to disruption.

Under natural conditions, CTA is due to the association between the taste of a food (conditioned stimulus; CS) and the noxious visceral conséquences of its ingestion (unconditioned stimulus; US). Because the US onset is necessarily delayed by the slow passage of the ingested food through the gut, the association is not formed between the CS and the US directly, but between a CS trace and the US. Thus, formation of a short-term gustatory trace, outlasting for several hours the taste stimulus, is a prerequisite of CTA learning, which proceeds in three subsequent stages: (a) processing of the gustatory signals and formation of the gustatory short-term memory (GSTM), (b) persistence of the GSTM trace, and (c) association of the GSTM with visceral signals of poisoning and formation of the gustatory long-term memory (GLTM). The first reports showing the differential sensitivity of various CTA stages to disruption appeared in the early 1970s. Berger (1970) demonstrated that rats anesthetized with pentobarbital shortly after drinking saccharin and poisoned with LiCl under deep anesthesia acquire strong CTA to saccharin. Similar results obtained with different general anesthetics and different CSs and USs (see Bures, Buresova, & Krivanek, 1988, for a review) indicate that anesthesia does not disrupt the GSTM, does not impair processing of the poison-induced visceral signals, and prevents neither the association of the GSTM with the visceral US nor the consolidation of the resulting GLTM.

On the other hand, the same anesthesia prevents formation of the GSTM (Bures & Buresova, 1989) when administered before systemic application of the taste stimulus (ip injection of 2% saccharin, 1% body weight). Also, other systemically acting disruptive procedures (e.g., hypothermia to 20°C) prevent CTA formation when applied before, but not after, presentation of the gustatory stimulus (Ionescu & Buresova, 1977).

The fact that no systemic intervention prevents the GSTM–poisoning association, suggested that the activity remaining in critical brain regions was sufficient to implement the plastic change. This prompted attempts to examine the role of different brain regions in CTA learning by functional ablation experiments, during which a particular structure was blocked either before or immediately after presentation of the gustatory CS, but before application of the visceral US.

Functional decortication by repeated waves of cortical spreading depression (Buresova & Bures, 1973) prevents CTA acquisition when elicited before, but not after, saccharin CS presentation. A local blockade of gustatory cortex by microinjection of tetrododoxin (TTX; 10 ng) has the same effect (Gallo, Roldan, & Bures, 1992).

A similar investigation of the role of the amygdala showed that TTX blockade of this structure before saccharin drinking does not disrupt CTA learning, but that postdrinking blockade of the amygdala may interfere with the processing of the visceral US and prevent its association with the GSTM (Gallo et al., 1992).

These experiments suggest that the gustatory cortex is necessary for the analysis of the taste signal, but not for the further stages of CTA acquisition, whereas the amygdala is not required for the taste signal processing, but plays an important role in the GSTM–US association, perhaps because it mediates US processing. Neither structure participates in the consolidation of the GLTM, however, because CTA is unaffected by their posttrial blockade.

The next candidate for the locus of CTA storage is the PBN, a mesencephalic relay center of the gustatory and visceral pathways, damage to which disrupts CTA retrieval and prevents CTA acquisition (DiLorenzo, 1988; Flynn, Grill, Schulkin, & Norgren, 1991; Spector et al., 1992; Yamamoto, 1993). Because PBN lesions interrupt both the CS and the US pathways, it is impossible to decide whether the effects observed are due to disruption of input/output circuits or to interference with storage. The various possible mechanisms were recently discussed by Spector et al. (1992): (a) blockade of the conditioned response (i.e., of the aversive reaction, consisting in the cessation of licking and attempts to remove the aversive fluid from the oral cavity), (b) impairment of gustatory signal processing, (c) impairment of visceral signal processing, and (d) failure in the integration of taste and visceral signals and in the formation of the corresponding CTA trace.

Some of these explanations can be directly rejected when using TTX blockade of PBN, instead of irreversible damage. Ivanova and Bures (1990a, 1990b) have shown that a PBN blockade induced after saccharin drinking, overlapping with the duration of LiCl poisoning, prevents formation of CTA, manifested by the absence of CTA during preference testing 2 days later. During the retention test, these animals have fully recovered from the TTX block, so the CTA absence could not be due to an impairment of aversive responding or to reduced taste sensitivity. Neither of these explanations can explain the CTA acquisition failure, because the gustatory stimulus was applied to intact animals. PBN blockade could have prevented processing of the visceral signals of poisoning and, thus, disrupted the GSTM association with poisoning, but CTA was also disrupted by TTX application performed 24 hours after LiCl injection (Ivanova & Bures, 1990b). This leaves the memory explanation as the only alternative.

It seems that PBN or some adjacent centers are indispensable for the integration of the gustatory CS with the visceral US and for the subsequent storage of the CTA engram. The prolonged retrograde amnesia elicited by the TTX blockade of the PBN suggests that the block affects the storage site.

The convergence of visceral and gustatory inputs in the PBN region (Hermann & Rogers, 1985) is not a sufficient condition for CTA learning. The gustatory cortex seems to be necessary during the initial presentation of the taste stimulus, and the amygdala is required during the action of the visceral stimulus. It is conceivable that during simultaneous activation of the PBN and the gustatory cortex, corticofugal feedback may cause priming of the corresponding PBN input representing the GSTM. The primed PBN neurons are prepared to be associated

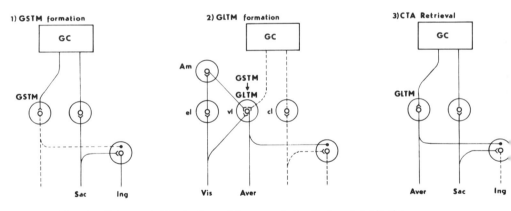

FIG. 7.1.   Schematic illustration of the neural circuits involved in the two stages of CTA acquisition and CTA retrieval. GC, gustatory cortex; Am, amygdala; cl, el, and vl, central, external, and ventral parts of the lateral subnucleus of PBN. Inputs: Sac (saccharin; CS) and Vis (visceral symptoms of poisoning; US). Ing (ingestion) and Aver (aversion): motor outputs mediating response to food. Saccharin taste activates directly the oromotor reactions mediating ingestion, but projects also through cl to GC, which primes the GSTM neurons in vl (1). If visceral US input activates vl (directly or through an el–Am–vl circuit) during the several-hours-long sensitive interval, GSTM changes into GLTM (2). As a result, ingestive oromotor reactions are inhibited and replaced by aversive ones during CTA retrieval (3).

with the visceral signals of poisoning for several hours; their effectiveness may also be enhanced by centrifugal feedback from the amygdala. The feasibility of such priming is supported by experiments showing that a novocaine blockade of the gustatory cortex modulates PBN responses to taste stimuli (DiLorenzo, 1990) and that taste-responsive PBN neurons are activated by electrical stimulation of the gustatory cortex (DiLorenzo & Monroe, 1992).

Evidence supporting the foregoing explanation was recently obtained by Yamamoto (1993), who used c-fos immunoreactivity for plotting PBN regions active during CTA retrieval. Saccharin drinking activated the central lateral subnucleus in naive rats and the ventral lateral subnucleus in rats trained to avoid saccharin. The latter subnucleus was activated in naive rats by quinine drinking. It appears that CTA acquisition is manifested by the shift of saccharin projection from one PBN subnucleus to another. Some of the putative circuits are shown in Fig. 7.1.

REVERSAL LEARNING

Another example of the use of reversible lesions for dissociation of overlapping learning processes is offered by reversal training, which changes a well-established habit into an opposite (or different) one. Two things happen during this change: (a) A new habit is formed, and (b) the old habit is inhibited. The two processes usually overlap in time and space, but the spatial overlap can be avoided when the original and reversed habits are implemented by different brain centers (e.g., by different hemispheres). In the latter case, learning of the new habit proceeds in one part of the brain, and inhibition of the old habit occurs in another, which can be independently influenced by the functional ablation procedures.

The first studies of this type (Bures et al., 1974), used functional decortication by repeated waves of spreading depression to confine conditioned reactions (e.g., a left–right discrimination in a T-maze) to one hemisphere. The reaction was then reversed, either when the animal used the same (trained) or the other (untrained) hemisphere. In the first case, reversal learning was more difficult than the original acquisition, because the animal not only had to learn the new response, but it also had to suppress the already- acquired one. Learning with the naive hemisphere was comparable with the acquisition of the original discrimination. After the trained hemisphere recovered, however, the original habit reappeared and competed with the new one. The outcome of interhemispheric conflict depended on the relative strength of the two habits at the time of testing, which was determined by the number of trials used during acquisition of the respective memories and by the decay of the memories due to forgetting (Goldowitz, Buresova, & Bures, 1972, 1973).

This paradigm was recently used to examine reversal of a more focal lateralized reaction—reaching with a preferred forepaw into a narrow tubular feeder—with the functional ablation limited to the relevant areas of the cortex and caudate (Miklyaeva & Bures, 1991). Rats displaying a strong preference (more than 80%) for one forepaw were trained to perform the same task with the nonpreferred limb while the use of the preferred extremity was prevented either peripherally (by fitting a metal bracelet larger than the feeder entrance around the wrist of the preferred paw) or centrally (by eliciting a transient paresis of the preferred forepaw by TTX inactivation of the contralateral motor cortex and caudate nucleus). The animals were forced to make 50 reaches with the non-preferred forepaw, and 3 days later their forepaw preference was tested. Each animal was allowed to make 10 reaches with an intact brain and without the bracelet. Reversal was considered accomplished when the animal made 80% or more reaches with the nonpreferred forepaw. If the preference did not change, reversal training with the nonpreferred forepaw continued in blocks of 100 reaches until the 80% criterion had been met. Reversal training proceeded significantly slower with central than with peripheral blockade: Three days after the first 50 forced reaches, reversal was found in 28% of the rats in the TTX group and in 78% of rats in the bracelet group. Cumulative results are shown in Fig. 7.2. The mean number of forced reaches required to induce reversal in the two groups was 21 ± 28 (TTX) and 91 ± 19 (bracelet).

The lower efficiency of reversal training under central blockade suggests that the behavioral change requires plastic modification, not only in the hemisphere controlling the nonpreferred forepaw, but also in the hitherto dominant hemi-

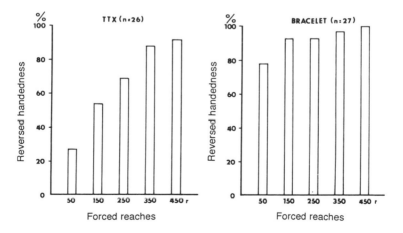

FIG. 7.2. The effectiveness of forced reversal of spontaneous fore-paw preference under conditions of central (TTX) or peripheral (brace-let) blockade of the preferred limb. Cumulative incidence of rats in which reversed preference was observed (ordinate) after 50 to 450 forced reaches (abscissa) with the nonpreferred forepaw.

sphere. During bracelet training, buildup of the new motor program overlaps with inhibition of the old program or may even include components preventing its activation. This is not the case during reversal training under TTX: In this case, there is no conflict between the original skill and the new one, because the inactivation of the cortical and striatal representation of the preferred paw leaves acquisition of the reversed preference unopposed. Reversal training can be acutely facilitated under these conditions, but as soon as the TTX block wears off, the uninhibited original preference reappears.

Essentially similar results were obtained by Martin and Webster (1974), who used cortical spreading depression to block the hemisphere contralateral to the preferred forepaw during reversal training. The somewhat smaller difference between peripheral and central blockades in their report may be due to the fact that cortical spreading depression leaves the caudate nucleus intact.

INTERHEMISPHERIC SYNTHESIS.

New information is always acquired by the intact brain in a definite context: Even when the earlier experience is not reversed, it is at least updated by the new knowledge. The novel solution to a task reduces the probability of the earlier response, even when both are simultaneously available. Although the two responses are not mutually exclusive, the isolation and sequential acquisition of the corresponding memories associates one response with the inhibition of the other response. This putative hidden stage of learning may become maladaptive when an efficient solution to the task requires the synthesis of the two component tasks. A different situation arises when the two tasks are acquired independently, that is, when the brain regions implementing Task 1 are blocked and inaccessible while memories for Task 2 are being formed.

The first attempts to approach this problem experimentally employed functional hemidecortication by spreading depression to confine different engrams to the two hemispheres (Buresova, Votava, & Bures, 1966). In a typical experiment of this type, rats were trained, with the left hemisphere, to escape electric footshock by running from start to goal in a U-shaped runway. The next day, the same rats learned, with the right hemisphere, to go from start to goal by passing through a curtain-covered opening in the wall separating two compartments in the shuttle box. In the synthesis stage, the rats were again placed in the U-shaped runway, but this time a shortcut reducing the start–goal distance by about 75% was provided by a curtain-covered opening in the partition wall. Intact-brain animals used this shortcut significantly more frequently under conditions of interhemispheric synthesis than did intact-brain animals who learned the two tests sequentially. Animals trained in the latter way paid less attention to the shortcut and persisted in using the long route.

The opportunity to examine the synthesis of two nonconflicting lateralized memories has been greatly enhanced by the finding that spatial navigation in the Morris (1981) water maze task can be confined to one intact hippocampus when the rat is trained during unilateral blockade of the other hippocampus by TTX (Fenton & Bures, 1993) or by lidocaine (Fenton & Bures, 1994). The trace remains lateralized until its transfer to the untrained hippocampus is induced by several trials performed with both hemispheres intact. These findings suggested the feasibility of storing a different task in each hippocampus and then testing the interhippocampal synthesis of the lateralized pieces of information. A controlled-cue environment developed for this purpose consisted of a set of backlit shapes serving as dimly visible extramaze landmarks hovering in the darkness (Fenton, Arolfo, Nerad, & Bures, 1994). Two such shapes were necessary and sufficient to acquire and maintain place navigation under these conditions. These preliminary findings were then combined so that we could examine the possibility that place navigation to the same target learned by one hippocampus for remote landmarks A and B and by the other hippocampus for the landmarks C and D could be directly synthesized by the intact brain when only cues A and C are presented (Fenton, Arolfo, Nerad, & Bures, 1995).

A group of 21 rats with implanted cannulae aimed at the dorsal hippocampus were trained during 4 days in two daily 8-trial sessions to swim to the underwater platform in the northwest quadrant of the pool. In one session, the rats were trained, with the blockade of one hippocampus, to use cues A and B. In the following session, with the blockade of the other hippocampus, they were trained to use cues C and D. After 4 days, the rats reached asymptotic performance on both tasks, each learned by a different hippocampus (Fig. 7.3). During the retrieval test, performed with an intact brain, the animals were presented with

FIG. 7.3. A: Place navigation with two cues (AB or CD) under unilateral hippocampal blockade at the end of the Acquisition (ACQ) phase. B: Retrieval (RET) performance with intact brain is asymptotic with a pair of cues used in acquisition (e.g., AB), as well as with a pair of cues composed of one cue from each acquisition training sets (e.g., AC). Performance with one cue used in acquisition training and a novel cue (e.g., AE) is disturbed ($p < .05$). C: Moving the platform to the opposite quadrant (PROBE) disrupted all animals ($p < .02$), indicating the use of a target-directed navigation strategy on the previous blocks.

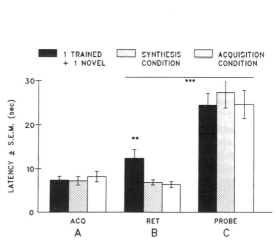

one cue from each learned pair (e.g., A and C, the synthesis condition). Control groups were trained with one of the pairs used during acquisition (e.g., A and B) or with one training cue and one novel cue. Only the latter group was disturbed (Fig. 7.3), but the disturbance was less in this condition than when the platform was moved to a different position. The synthesis was immediate and the rats' performance was indistinguishable from the performance achieved with the trained pair of cues.

The implied interhippocampal synthesis is a complex process. Its demonstration is based on a number of assumptions, only some of which have been experimentally verified. The intrahippocampal synthesis was demonstrated by Fenton et al. (1994), in experiments using four visible remote landmarks for place navigation to a particular target. The task learned with such a redundant set of landmarks was not disrupted by removal of any two of these cues. The same level of cue redundancy can be achieved by training the rats with cues A and B in odd sessions and cues C and D in even sessions. Pilot experiments showed, however, that under such daily alternation of the tasks, acquisition is slowed, and there are signs of interference, which are absent in the lateralized learning situation. More efficient intrahemispheric synthesis is achieved by mastering one task before being trained on the other one.

Although the two engrams were stored in different hemispheres before the synthesis test, it is still possible that some interhemispheric transfer may have occurred during the first or subsequent synthesis trials. A single trial with an intact brain can induce significant interhemispheric transfer, manifested by improved relearning of the task with the naive eye and hemisphere when the trained hippocampus was inactivated by lidocaine (Fenton & Bures, 1994). On the other hand, excellent navigation demonstrated even in the first synthesis trial suggests that the neural computation generating the correct start–target trajectory was based on interhippocampal comparisons mediated by commissural connections. The role of interhippocampal transfer in the synthesis experiment is limited by the fact that only one element of each of the learned pairs is available during the synthesis. Further experiments are required to test whether lateralized learning with pairs AB and CD, followed by synthesis training with pair AC, changes the engram representation in the two hemispheres to ABC and ACD, or whether the engrams for the not-explicitly-presented cues B and D were transferred, too, transforming the engram representation in each hemisphere to ABCD.

Interhemispheric synthesis of relevant engrams offers new possibilities for assessing the importance of estimating target–cue distance and target–cue azimuth (related to a general spatial gradient) for place navigation. A rat learning under minimum cue conditions to navigate with each hippocampus to a different target will direct the interhemispheric synthesis based on two unilaterally represented cues to a location corresponding to the intersection of the memorized target–cue distances or to a definite angle between the two memorized target–cue azimuths. With a suitable choice of landmarks, the target locations construed by synthesis may be quite different for the distance and azimuth predictions. Results of probe trials made in the absence of an escape platform will show the animal's preference.

The interhippocampal synthesis of place navigation behavior is an example of the parallel synthesis of lateralized input data needed for the correct the solution of an overtrained task. No new response is produced, but the behavior is generated under conditions requiring simultaneous use of the information contained in separate hemispheres that can interact through commissural pathways or by influencing the shared circuits controlling locomotion. In the latter case, each hemisphere will produce one locomotion vector; when they are summed, the animal finds its way to the target just as a boat might be successfully steered by two sailors, one knowing the latitude of the destination harbor and the other knowing its longitude.

CONCLUSION

The examples discussed in this review show that many plastic changes induced by learning cannot be revealed by standard methods of investigation. Some of these hidden events can be detected when irreversible lesions are replaced with functional blockades, which eliminate a particular structure during a definite phase of learning but leave it intact during later stages, particularly during retrieval. This is the method of choice when the same center or circuit may participate in both acquisition and retrieval and when reversible lesions allow dissociation of the respective component processes. Another class of hidden events is represented by putative processes accompanying overt reversal learning. Functional ablation makes it possible to dissociate these otherwise inseparable component processes. At a more subtle level, functional ablation makes it possible to break the usual connections formed whenever a new engram is added to the already-available experience. Engrams acquired independently from other engrams present in the blocked part of brain are devoid of such connections and are, therefore, particularly well suited for synthesis unbiased by the routine of sequential learning.

REFERENCES

Barker, L. M., Best, M. R., & Domjan, M. (Eds.). (1977). *Learning mechanisms in food selection.* Waco, TX: Baylor University Press.

Berger, B. D. (1970). Learning in anesthetized rat. *Federation Proceedings, 29,* 749.

Braun, J. J. (1990). Gustatory cortex: Definition and function. In B. Kolb & B. C. Tees (Eds.), *The cerebral cortex of the rat* (pp. 407–430). Cambridge, MA: MIT Press.

Braveman, N. S., & Bronstein, P. (Eds.). (1985). *Experimental assessment and clinical applications of conditioned food aversions.* (*Annals of the New York Academy of Sciences*, Vol. 443).

Brooks, V. B. (1983). Study of brain function by local, reversible cooling. *Reviews of Physiology, Biochemistry and Pharmacology, 95*, 1–109.

Bures, J., & Buresova, O. (1989). Conditioned taste aversion to injected flavor: Differential effects of anesthesia on the formation of the gustatory trace and on its association with poisoning in rats. *Neuroscience Letters, 98*, 305–309.

Bures, J., & Buresova, O. (1990). Reversible lesions allow reinterpretation of system level studies of brain mechanisms of behavior. *Concepts in Neuroscience, 1*, 69–89.

Bures, J., Buresova, O., & Krivanek, J. (1974). *The mechanism and applications of Leao's spreading depression of electroencephalographic activity.* San Diego: Academic Press.

Bures, J., Buresova, O., & Krivanek, J. (1988). *Brain and behavior: Paradigms for research in neural mechanisms.* Chichester: Wiley.

Buresova, O., & Bures, J. (1973). Cortical and subcortical components of the conditioned saccharin aversion. *Physiology and Behavior, 11*, 435–439.

Buresova, O., Votava, J., & Bures, J. (1966). Interhemispheric synthesis of competing and complementing experiences. *Physiology and Behavior, 1*, 59–63.

DiLorenzo, P. M. (1988). Long-delay learning in rats with parabrachial pontine lesions. *Chemical Senses, 13*, 219–229.

DiLorenzo, P. M. (1990). Corticofugal influence on taste responses in the parabrachial pons of the rat. *Brain Research, 530*, 73–84.

DiLorenzo, P. M., & Monroe, S. (1992). Corticofugal input to taste-responsive units in the parabrachial pons. *Brain Research Bulletin, 29*, 925–930.

Fenton, A. A., Arolfo, M. P., Nerad, L., & Bures, J. (1995). Interhippocampus synthesis of lateralized place navigation engrams. *Hippocampus, 5*, 16–24.

Fenton, A. A., Arolfo, M. P., Nerad, L., & Bures, J. (1994). Place navigation in the Morris water maze under minimum and redundant extra-maze cue conditions. *Behavioral and Neural Biology, 62*, 178–189.

Fenton, A. A., & Bures, J. (1993). Place navigation in rats with unilateral tetrodotoxin inactivation of the dorsal hippocampus: Place but not procedural learning can be lateralized to one hippocampus. *Behavioral Neuroscience, 107*, 552–564.

Fenton, A. A., & Bures, J. (1994). Interhippocampal transfer of place navigation monocularly acquired by rats during unilateral functional ablation of the dorsal hipocampus and visual cortex with lidocaine. *Neuroscience, 58*, 481–491.

Flynn, F. W., Grill, H. J., Schulkin, J., & Norgren, R. (1991). Central gustatory lesions: II. Effects on salt appetite, taste aversion learning and feeding behaviors. *Behavioral Neuroscience, 105*, 944–955.

Gallo, M., Roldan, G., & Bures, J. (1993). Differential involvement of gustatory insular cortex and amygdala in the acquisition and retrieval of conditioned taste aversion in rats. *Behavioural Brain Research, 52*, 91–97.

Goldowitz, D., Buresova, O., & Bures, J. (1972). Time labelling of independently acquired lateralized engrams in rats. *Physiology and Behavior, 9*, 699–704.

Goldowitz, D., Buresova, O. & Bures, J. (1973). Forgetting of lateralized engrams studied by interhemispheric conflict in rats. *Behavioral Biology, 8*, 183–192.

Hermann, G. E., & Rogers, R. C. (1985). Convergence of vagal and gustatory afferent input within the parabrachial nucleus of the rat. *Journal of the Autonomous Nervous System, 13*, 1–17.

Hodge, R. J., Gibbs, M. E., & Ng, K. T. (1981). Engram duplication in the day-old chick. *Behavioral and Neural Biology, 31*, 283–298.

Ionescu, E., & Buresova, O. (1977). Effects of hypothermia on the acquisition of conditioned taste aversion in rats. *Journal of Comparative and Physiological Psychology, 91*, 1297–1307.

Ivanova, S. F., & Bures, J. (1990a). Acquisition of conditioned taste aversion in rats is prevented by tetrodotoxin blockade of a small midbrain region centered around the parabrachial nuclei. *Physiology and Behavior, 48*, 543–549.

Ivanova, S. F., & Bures, J. (1990b). Conditioned taste aversion is disrupted by prolonged retrograde effects of intracerebral injection of tetrodotoxin in rats. *Behavioral Neuroscience, 104*, 948–954.

Martin, D., & Webster, W. G. (1974). Paw preference shifts in the rat following forced practice. *Physiology and Behavior, 13*, 745–748.

Miklyaeva, E. I., & Bures, J. (1991). Reversal of handedness in rats is achieved more effectively by training under peripheral than under central blockade of the preferred forepaw. *Neuroscience Letters, 125*, 89–92.

Morris, R. G. M. (1981). Spatial localization does not require the presence of local cues. *Learning and Motivation, 12*, 239–260.

Panakhova, E., Buresova, O., & Bures, J. (1985). Functional hemidecortication by spreading depression or by focal epileptic discharge disrupts spatial memory in rats. *Behavioural Processes, 10*, 387–398.

Simbay, L. C., Boakes, R. A., & Burton, M. J. (1986). Effects of basolateral amygdala lesions on taste aversions produced by lactose and lithium chloride in the rat. *Behavioral Neuroscience, 100*, 455–456.

Spector, A. S., Norgren, R., & Grill, H. J. (1992). Parabrachial gustatory lesions impair taste aversion learning in rats. *Behavioral Neuroscience, 106*, 147–161.

Squire, L. R. (1987). *Memory and brain.* London: Oxford University Press.

Thompson, R. (1983). Brain systems and long-term memory. *Behavioral and Neural Biology, 37*, 1–45.

Yamamoto, T. (1993). Neural mechanisms of conditioned taste aversion. *Neuroscience Research, 16*, 181–185.

Yamamoto, T., Azuma, S., & Kawamura, Y. (1981). Significance of cortical-amygdalar-hypothalamic connections in retention of conditioned taste aversion in rats. *Experimental Neurology, 74*, 758–768.

8 Cerebellar Localization of a Memory Trace

Richard F. Thompson
Jo Anne Tracy
University of Southern California

Different forms or aspects of memory critically involve different neural systems and structures in the brain (Dudai, 1989; McGaugh, 1989; Squire, 1992; R. F. Thompson, 1986; Wagner & Brandon, 1989). The specific focus of this chapter is on identification of the essential memory trace circuit and on localization of the memory trace for a basic form of long-term associative memory: delay classical conditioning of discrete behavioral responses. Even in this simple paradigm of associative learning and memory, higher brain structures become essential when the task is made more complex. Thus, hippocampal lesions prevent discrimination reversal learning in eye-blink conditioning (Berger & Orr, 1983) and prevent trace eye-blink conditioning, where an interval with no stimulation intervenes between the conditioned stimulus (CS) offset and the unconditioned stimulus (US) onset (Moyer, Deyo, & Disterhoft, 1990; Solomon, Vander Schaaf, R. F. Thompson, & Weisz, 1986). These paradigms would seem to involve relational aspects of stimuli, including information about context (see Eichenbaum, Young, & Bunsey, this volume, chapter 9; Lynch, 1986).

Eye-blink conditioning (the basic delay paradigm, in which the CS and US overlap) is the most widely used procedure for the classical conditioning of discrete responses, but other responses, particularly limb flexion, provide additional evidence. Perhaps the simplest descriptor of these aspects of basic associative learning is sensorimotor memory. I argue here that the evidence now strongly favors the following hypotheses: that the essential memory trace circuit for basic delayed conditioning includes the cerebellum and its associated brain stem circuitry, and that the memory traces are formed and stored in the cerebellum. For reasons that are not entirely clear, this has been an extremely contentious field. Several workers appear to have an unshakable a priori belief that associative memory traces cannot possibly be formed and stored in the cerebellum (Bloedel, 1992; Welsh & Harvey, 1989).

The cerebellum has long been a favored structure for modeling a neuronal learning system, dating from the classic papers of Brindley (1964), Marr (1969), and Albus (1971). Recent empirical studies, reviewed furtheron, have been guided by these models and by the related views of Eccles, Ito, and Szentagothai (1967), Eccles (1977), and Ito (1972, 1984). The results of these studies constitute a remarkable verification of the spirit of these theories. The highly simplified schematic block diagram in Fig.8.1 summarizes the results to date and may be considered a qualitative model of the role of the cerebellum in the classical conditioning of discrete behavioral responses (see also reviews by Lavond, Kim, & R. F. Thompson, 1993; J. E. Steinmetz, Lavond, Ivkovich, Logan, & R. F. Thompson, 1992; Thach, Goodkin, & Keating, 1992; R. F. Thompson, 1986, 1990). The earlier Russian literature had indicated that removal of the cerebellum impaired or abolished classical conditioning of the leg-flexion response (e.g., Karamian, Fanaralijian, & Kosareva, 1969; see also discussion in R. F. Thompson, Berger, & Madden, 1983), but these observations were not subsequently pursued.

THE INTERPOSITUS NUCLEUS AND THE CONDITIONED RESPONSE PATHWAY

In single-unit studies (Foy, J. E. Steinmetz, & R. F. Thompson, 1984; Tracy, Weiss, & R. F. Thompson, 1991), we described several populations of units in the anterior interpositus: One population responded to a tone conditioned stimulus (CS) onset, another population to corneal air-puff unconditioned stimulus (US) onset (tactile, rather than auditory, component), others responded to both CS and US onsets, and yet another population responded in relation to the behavioral response (it is difficult to distinguish between somatosensory-evoked and motor-related responses in untrained animals). In trained animals, a significant population of units responded in close association with, and substantially precede and predict, the form of the behavioral conditioned response (CR; see also Berthier & Moore, 1990; McCormick & R. F. Thompson, 1984a, 1984b; McCormick, G. A. Clark, Lavond, & R. F. Thompson, 1982; McCormick et al., 1981). Perhaps most relevant is the recent study by Yang and Weisz (1992). They recorded activity of single neurons in the anterior dentate and interpositus nuclei (identified as principal excitatory neurons by antidromic activation and collision from stimulation of the red nucleus) to the CS and US at the very beginning of training. The great majority of these neurons showed increased discharge frequency to the US (substantial) and the CS (small, but significant). Paired CS–US presentations resulted in marked enhancement of the response to the US in cells in the interpositus and a depression of response to the US in cells in the dentate nucleus. Small lesions in the region of recording in the interpositus completely prevented acquisition of the eye-blink CR, but lesions of the dentate recording region had no effect at all on learning (see further on). It would seem clear that complex information processing may occur in the interpositus.

McCormick et al. (1981), using a tone CS and a corneal air-puff US in the basic delay paradigm (CS, 350 msec; US, 100 msec; coterminating), initially reported that lesions of the cerebellum ipsilateral to the trained eye (large aspirations and electrolytic lesions of the interpositus nucleus) abolished the eye-blink CR completely and selectively, that is, the CR was completely abolished, but the lesion had no effect on the unconditioned response (UR; see also, McCormick, Clark, et al., 1982). The lesions did not prevent learning in the contralateral eye. If the lesion was made before training, animals were completely unable to learn any CRs at all with the eye ipsilateral to the lesion (Lincoln, McCormick, & R. F. Thompson, 1982). In other studies, the same results obtained with lesions of the superior cerebellar peduncle, the efferent pathway from the interpositus to the red nucleus (Lavond, McCormick, G. A. Clark, Holmes, & R. F. Thompson, 1981; McCormick, Guyer, & R. F. Thompson, 1982; Rosenfeld, Dovydaitis, & Moore, 1985).

Electrolytic lesions of the interpositus nucleus ipsilateral to the trained eye demonstrated, again, that if the lesions completely destroyed the critical region of the interpositus nucleus the CR was abolished, with no effect on the UR (G. A. Clark, McCormick, Lavond, & R. F. Thompson, 1984). It is important to note that if the lesions were incomplete, there was a marked decrease in the amplitude and frequency of occurrence of the CR and a marked increase in CR onset latency, which did not recover with postoperative training (see also Welsh & Harvey, 1989). Because electrolytic lesions of the interpositus cause retrograde degeneration in the inferior olive, kainic acid lesions of the critical region of the interpositus were made, with identical results: (complete and selective abolition of the CR (Lavond, Hambree, & R. F. Thompson, 1985). Yeo, Hardiman, and Glickstein (1985a) replicated the interpositus lesion result, using light and white noise CSs and a periorbital shock US, thus extending the generality of the findings. A number of subsequent studies have shown identical effects of interpositus lesions: (complete and selective abolition of the ipsilateral eye-blink CR, with no effect on the UR (e.g., Lavond, Lincoln, McCormick, & R. F. Thompson, 1984; Lavond, McCormick, & R. F. Thompson, 1984; Lavond, J. E. Steinmetz, Yokaitis, & R. F. Thomspon, 1987; McCormick & Thompson, 1984a; Polenchar, Patterson, Lavond, & R. F. Thompson, 1985; Sears & J. E. Steinmetz, 1990; J. E. Steinmetz et al., 1992; Weisz & LoTurco, 1988; Woodruff-Pak, Lavond, & R. F. Thompson, 1985). This effect was extremely localized. Electrolytic interpositus-lesioned animals were periodically trained for periods up to 8 months; no CRs ever developed on the side of the lesion (Lavond, McCormick, et al., 1984).

Reversible inactivation by microinfusion of nanomolar amounts of neurotransmitter antagonists in the critical region of the interpositus completely and reversibly abolished the CR, with no effect at all on the UR, in a dose-dependent fashion (Mamounas, R. F. Thompson, & Madden, 1987).

Recently, the interpositus-lesion abolition of the CR was studied in great detail (J. E. Steinmetz et al., 1992). Appropriate interpositus lesions were found to completely and permanently prevent acquisition and completely and permanently abolish retention of the eye-blink CR, regardless of the amount of pre-operative or postoperative training, over all conditions of training and measurement that have been used, and have no persistent effects on performance of the UR (see also J. E. Steinmetz & G. S. Steinmetz, 1991). Finally, there are now several human studies showing that appropriate cerebellar damage completely prevents learning of the eye-blink CR (Daum et al., 1993; Lye, Boyle, Ramsden, & Schady, 1988; Solomon, Stowe, & Pendibeury, 1989).

Electrical microstimulation of the critical region of the anterior interpositus nucleus evokes an eye-blink response in naive animals, and lesion of the superior cerebellar peduncle abolishes this response; thus, the eye-blink circuit is hard-wired from the interpositus nucleus to behavior (Chapman, J. E. Steinmetz, & R. F. Thompson, 1988; McCormick & Thompson, 1984a). The region of the contralateral magnocellular red nucleus that receives projections from the region of the anterior interpositus critical for eye-blink conditioning also exhibits a learning-induced pattern of increased unit activity in eye-blink conditioning very similar to that shown by interpositus neurons (Chapman, J. E. Steinmetz, Sears, & R. F. Thompson, 1990). Microstimulation of this region of the red nucleus in naive animals also elicits eye-blink responses. If the red nucleus is reversibly inactivated in trained animals, the eye-blink CR is reversibly abolished, but the learning-induced neuronal model of the CR in the interpositus nucleus is un-affected. In contrast, when the anterior interpositus nucleus is reversibly inacti-vated, both the behavioral CR and the learning-induced neuronal model of the CR in the magnocellular red nucleus are completely abolished (Chapman et al., 1990; R. E. Clark, & Lavond, 1992; R. E. Clark, Zhang, & Lavond, 1992). These data argue strongly that neural activity flows from the interpositus to the red nucleus in performance of the CR.

A small lesion of the appropriate region of the magnocellular red nucleus contralateral to the trained eye causes complete abolition of the CR, with no effect on the UR (Chapman et al., 1988; Haley, Lavond, & R. F. Thompson, 1983; Rosenfeld et al., 1985; Rosenfeld & Moore, 1983). This same lesion also abolishes the eye-blink response elicited in untrained animals by stimulation of the interpositus nucleus. Microinfusions of nanomolar amounts of neurotransmit-ter antagonists in a very localized region of the magnocellular red nucleus revers-ibly abolishes the conditioned eye-blink response, with no effect on the UR (Haley, R. F. Thompson, & Madden, 1988). Identical results were obtained for the conditioned limb-flexion response: Appropriate interpositus lesions abolished the conditioned hindlimb-flexion response, with no effect on reflex flexion in the rabbit (Donegan, Lowry, & R. F. Thompson, 1983). Lesions of the red nucleus or descending rubral pathway abolished the conditioned limb-flexion response in the cat, with no effect on the reflex limb-flexion response and no effect on normal behavioral movement control of the limb (Smith, 1970; Tsukahara, Odar, & Notsu, 1981; Voneida, 1990).

THE ISSUE OF PERFORMANCE

One of the advantages of classical conditioning for neurobiological analysis is that performance of the behavioral response per se (the UR) can be measured independently of the performance of the learned response (the CR). A consistent finding of the many studies showing interpositus lesion abolition of the CR is that the lesion has no effect on the UR (as already discussed). Welsh and Harvey (1989) claimed that interpositus lesions did effect the UR, but they did not actually measure the effects of interpositus lesions on reflex responses in the same animals. Rather, they compared only some of their postlesion animals separated post hoc into different groups. Importantly, they did not find any effect of interpositus lesions on the amplitude of the UR at any US intensity, and they reported only very small lesion effects on UR topography at low US intensities. Many factors can influence the UR, and there are extreme individual animal differences in properties of the UR. In order to demonstrate the effects of lesions on the UR, it is essential to compare URs in the same animals before and after lesion. Given the fact that the evidence necessary to demonstrate interpositus lesion effects on performance of the UR does not exist, it is somewhat surprising that the performance argument could have been taken seriously. In any event, possible effects of interpositus lesions (that abolished the CR) on the UR to US-alone stimuli have been examined in detail over a wide range of US intensities, comparing prelesion versus postlesion URs in the same animals. No persistent effects of the lesions were found on any property of the UR (J. E. Steinmetz et al., 1992).

Welsh and Harvey (1989) asserted that, "when one attempts to equate the CS and the UCS [US] as response-eliciting stimuli, the deficits in the CR and the UCR [UR] become more alike" (p. 309). The only way to evaluate this statement is to equate the CS and the US in terms of response elicitation prior to lesion and then determine the effect of the lesion on the two responses that were psychophysically equivalent prior to lesion.

Welsh and Harvey did not make this comparison and did not provide any information on the properties of the URs prior to lesion in their animals. When this is done—that is, when the intensity of the US is reduced so that the UR (US-alone trials) is matched in amplitude and percent response to the CR before lesion—the interpositus lesion abolishes the CR and has no effect at all on the prelesion equivalent UR (Steinmetz et al., 1992). All of these studies used a standard US intensity for training (e.g., ≥3 psi), which typically yields a UR (US-alone trials) larger in amplitude than the CR. Recently, animals were trained with a low-intensity US, just suprathreshold, to establish learning (Ivkovich, Lockard, & R. F. Thompson, 1993). Under these conditions, the CR (CS-alone trials) and the UR (US-alone trials) are equivalent in amplitude: The CR is numerically, but not statistically, larger than the UR. Interpositus lesions completely abolished the CR and had no effect at all on the UR.

There is, in fact, a double dissociation, in terms of various brain-lesion effects, on the CR and the UR in eye-blink conditioning. Appropriate partial lesions of the motor nuclei involved in generating the CR and the UR cause immediate abolition of both the CR and the UR. With postoperative training, the CR recovers almost to the preoperative level, but the UR shows little recovery (Disterhoft, Quinn, Weiss, & Shipley, 1985; J. E. Steinmetz et al., 1992). Large lesions of appropriate regions of cerebellar cortex that markedly impair or abolish performance of the CR (see furtheron) result in an *increase* in the amplitude of the UR (Logan, 1991; Yeo, 1991).

Finally, the performance argument requires that the interpositus nucleus play a role in generating the behavioral reflex response, that is, in performance. The onset latency of the reflex response to a 3 psi corneal air-puff US, measured as an extension of the nictitating membrane (NM), ranges from 25 to 40 msec; it is somewhat shorter with a periorbital shock US. As already noted, electrical stimulation of the critical region of the anterior interpositus evokes an eye-blink response in untrained animals. The minimum onset latency of this response (measured as a NM extension) is approximately 50 msec (see further on). The minimum time for activation of the cerebellum by peripheral somatosensory stimulation is about 20 msec. Therefore, the earliest time that the interpositus nucleus could play any role at all in performance following US onset is about 70 msec; consequently, it plays no role in performance of the reflex response.

Collectively, this evidence decisively rules out the performance argument, that interpositus lesion abolition of the CR is somehow due to lesion effects on the UR.

THE ESSENTIAL CIRCUIT

The anterior interpositus nucleus is, thus, completely necessary for both learning and memory of the classically conditioned eye-blink and other discrete responses, and the necessary CR pathway appears to be entirely limited to the interpositus nucleus, the magnocellular red nucleus, and the premotor and motor nuclei. These data do not prove, however, that the memory trace is in the interpositus nucleus. To localize the memory trace, we must first identify the circuitry essential for the classical conditioning of discrete behavioral responses, which we have done. This literature has been reviewed in several sources (e.g.,

Lavond et al., 1993; Thompson, 1986, 1990), so I summarize it very briefly here (see Fig. 8.1).

The CS pathway consists of sensory projections via mossy fiber projections, in significant part via the pontine nuclei to the cerebellum. Large lesions of the pontine nuclei or middle cerebellar peduncle (conveying mossy fibers to the cerebellum) completely abolish the eye-blink CR to all modalities of stimulation. More localized lesions in the pontine nuclei can selectively abolish the CR to a tone, but not a light, CS. Electrical microstimulation of the pontine nuclei serves as a "supernormal" CS, yielding more rapid learning than that achieved with peripheral CSs. Further, if animals are trained with electrical stimulation of the pontine nuclei–mossy fibers as a CS, some animals show immediate and complete (100%) transfer to a tone CS, demonstrating that the tone must activate a

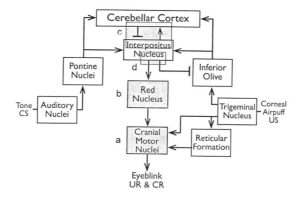

FIG. 8.1. Schematic of the cerebellar–brain stem circuitry essential for classical conditioning of discrete behavioral responses (e.g., eyeblink response). The reflex response pathways (US–UR) include direct projections from the trigeminal nucleus and indirect projections via the reticular formation to motor nuclei. The CS pathway includes projections from sensory (auditory) nuclei to the pontine nuclei and to the cerebellum via mossy fibers. The US pathway includes trigeminal projections to the inferior olive and its climbing fiber projections to the cerebellum. The CR pathway includes projections from the interpositus nucleus to the magnocellular red nucleus and from there to premotor and motor nuclei. The direct inhibitory projection from the interpositus to the inferior olive is hypothesized to function as the error-correcting system. Arrows indicate excitatory projections; bars inhibitory connections. Laterality is not indicated; the pontine nuclei, red nucleus, and inferior olive are all contralateral to the trained eye and cerebellum. a: Reversible inactivation of the motor nuclei generating the UR and CR. b: Reversible inactivation of the magnocellular red nucleus. c: Reversible inactivation of the anterior interpositus nucleus and overlying cerebellar cortex of lobule HVI. d: Reversible inactivation of the output of the anterior interpositus nucleus (see text for details and outcomes).

substantial number of neurons or axons activated by the prior electrical stimulation (J. E. Steinmetz, 1990). Finally, with a pontine stimulation CS, the threshold to evoke the CR drops to a very low level (as low as 2 μA), but the threshold to interpositus stimulation does not change, arguing that a massive increase in synaptic efficacy occurs between the pontine and interpositus electrodes. (Subsequent lesion via the interpositus electrode abolishes the CR to pontine stimulation, showing that the latter is, indeed, activating mossy fiber afferents to the cerebellum.)

The US pathway includes the trigeminal nucleus, its projection to the inferior olive, and olivary-climbing fiber projections to the cerebellum. Lesion of the appropriate region of the inferior olive (dorsal accessory olive; DAO) completely prevents learning if made before training, and results in extinction of the CR with continued paired training if made after training. Electrical microstimulation of the DAO elicits discrete behavioral responses (eye-blink, head-turn, etc., depending on electrode locus). When paired with a tone CS, the exact response elicited by DAO stimulation is learned as a CR to the CS. Further, responses evoked by stimulation of cerebellar white matter can also be conditioned to a neutral stimulus. Finally, stimulation of pontine nuclei or mossy fibers as a CS and DAO-climbing fibers as a US results in normal behavioral learning of the response elicited by DAO stimulation. To our knowledge, this is the only system in the brain (other than reflex afferents) where the exact response elicited by electrical stimulation can be learned for any neutral stimulus.

CEREBELLAR CORTEX

Many Purkinje neurons, particularly in lobule HVI, are responsive to the tone CS and the corneal air-puff US in naive animals (extracellular single-unit recording). Before training, the majority of Purkinje neurons that are responsive to the tone show variable increases in simple spike discharge frequency in the CS period (Foy & Thompson, 1986). After training, the majority show learning-induced decreases in simple spike frequency in the CS period that correlate closely in onset latency with the behavioral CR; however, a significant number show the opposite effect (Berthier & Moore, 1986; Donegan, Foy, & R. F. Thompson, 1985; Foy, Krupa, Tracy, & R. F. Thompson, 1992). These results are consistent with the possibility that a process of long-term depression may be a mechanism of synaptic plasticity in the cerebellar cortex during eye-blink conditioning (Chen & R. F. Thompson, 1992; Ito, 1989; Schreurs & Alkon, 1992).

Before training, Purkinje neurons that are influenced by the corneal air-puff consistently show an evoked complex spike to US onset. In trained animals, this US-evoked complex spike is virtually absent on paired CS–US trials when the animal gives a CR, but it is present and normal on US-alone test trials (Foy & R. F. Thompson, 1986; Krupa, Weiss, R. F. Thompson, 1991). This learning-induced reduction in US-evoked complex spikes is consistent with a similar decrease with training in US-evoked activity of units in the inferior olive (Sears & J. E. Steinmetz, 1991). These results led to the hypothesis that the DAO-climbing fiber system, a necessary part of the US pathway, could function as the error-correcting algorithm in classical conditioning (Rescorla & Wagner, 1972) by way of the direct γ-amino-butiric-acid-related (GABAergic) descending pathway from the interpositus to the inferior olive (Nelson & Mugnoini, 1987, see Fig. 1; see also Donegan, Gluck, & R. F. Thompson, 1989; Gluck, Reifsnider, & R. F. Thompson, 1990; R. F. Thompson, 1990). Current evidence supports this view: When animals are trained in the "blocking" paradigm, infusion of the GABA antagonist, picrotoxin, into the DAO during the compound stimulus training phase completely prevents blocking, as revealed in subsequent training to the novel stimulus component of the compound stimulus (Kim, Krupa, & R. F. Thompson, 1992).

In the initial studies, there appeared to be some disagreement about the effects of cerebellar cortical lesions on eye-blink conditioning (McCormick & Thompson, 1984a; Yeo, Hardiman, & Glickstein, 1985b). However, there now appears to be a growing consensus. In trained animals, lesions limited largely to HVI cause variable degrees of impairment in the CR, but with substantial or complete recovery (Lavond et al., 1987; Yeo & Hardiman, 1992). Larger lesions can cause greater impairments, and very large lesions (HVI, Crus I, Crus II, and paramedian and anterior lobes) can cause substantial and, in some animals, persistent impairments (Lavond et al., 1987; Perrett, Ruiz, & Mauk, 1993; Yeo, 1991; Yeo & Hardiman, 1992). If they are made before training, lesions limited to HVI slowed acquisition somewhat; somewhat larger lesions (HVI, Crus I, Crus II, and paramedian lobule, and in one study, the flocculus and paraflocculus, as well) markedly impaired acquisition (Lavond & J. E. Steinmetz, 1989; Logan, 1991); and very large lesions that included some anterior lobe markedly impaired and, in a few cases, prevented acquisition (Logan, 1991). Animals with these very large lesions that neither learn nor retain CRs exhibit disruption of adaptive timing of the CR (Logan, 1991; Perrett et al., 1993). Such lesions also prevent acquisition of conditioned inhibition (Logan, 1991). Experimentally, it is extremely difficult to remove a very large portion of the cerebellar cortex without damaging the cerebellar nuclei, but it seems clear that the cerebellar cortex plays a critically important role in normal learning of the eye-blink CR; whether it is essential remains unresolved.

Latency measures are consistent with the cerebellar hypothesis. Under standard training conditions (85 dB tone CS, 3 psi corneal air-puff, 250 msec CS–US onset interval), the mean minimum onset latency of the NM extension CR is about 90–100 msec. The onset of the learning-induced increase in unit activity in the interpositus nucleus varies somewhat from animal to animal; it can precede onset of the learned NM response by as much as 60–70 msec, and a typical value is about 50 msec. Learning-induced decreases in Purkinje neuron simple spikes can precede the onset of the learned NM response by as much as 60–80 msec (Foy & R. F. Thompson, 1986). The latency of activation of the cerebellum by peripheral somatosensory stimuli is about 20 msec (Ekerot, Gustavsson, Oscarsson, & Schouenborg, 1987). Finally, as already noted, onset of the NM extension response to electrical stimulation of the interpositus nucleus is about 50 msec (McCormick & R. F. Thompson, 1984a). These time delays account for the otherwise puzzling facts (a) that the minimum onset latency of the conditioned NM response is about 90–100 msec, substantially longer than the minimum onset latency of the reflex NM response to a corneal air-puff (25 msec); and (b) that no learning occurs if the CS–US onset interval (the interstimulus interval used in training) is shorter than about 80 msec (e.g., Gormezano, Kehoe, & Marshall-Goodell, 1983; J. E. Steinmetz, 1990).

REVERSIBLE INACTIVATION

The diagram in Fig. 8.1 shows, in highly simplified, schematic form, the essential memory trace circuit for the classical conditioning of discrete responses, based on the lesion, recording, and stimulation evidence I have described. Interneuron circuits are not shown, only net excitatory or inhibitory actions of projection pathways. Other pathways, known and unknown, may also, of course, be involved. Many uncertainties still exist, concerning, for example, details of sensory-specific patterns of projection to pontine nuclei and cerebellum (CS pathways), details of red nucleus projections to premotor and motor nuclei (CR pathways), the relative roles of the cerebellar cortex and interpositus nucleus, and the possible roles of recurrent circuits.

Several parts of the circuit can be reversibly inactivated for the duration of training (eye-blink conditioning) in naive animals; these are indicated by boxes labeled a, b, c, and d. The motor nuclei essential for generating the UR and CR (primary 7th and accessory 6th) were inactivated by infusion of muscimol (6 days) or cooling (5 days) during standard tone–air-puff training (a in Fig. 8.1; J. K. Thompson, Krupa, Weng, & R. F. Thompson, 1993; Zhang & Lavond, 1991). The animals showed no CRs and no URs during this inactivation training; indeed, they showed no behavior at all: Performance was completely abolished. The animals did, however exhibit asymptotic CR performance and normal URs immediately after inactivation. Thus, performance of the CR and UR are completely unnecessary for normal learning, and the motor nuclei make no contribution to formation of the memory trace; they are efferent from the trace.

Inactivation of the magnocellular red nucleus is indicated by b in Fig. 8.1. Inactivation by low doses of muscimol for 6 days of training had no effect on the UR, but completely prevented expression of the CR (Krupa, J. K. Thompson, & R. F. Thompson, 1993). Nevertheless, animals showed asymptotic learned performance of the CR from the beginning of postinactivation training (see Fig.

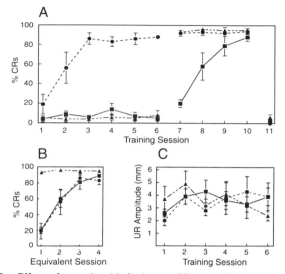

FIG. 8.2.   Effect of muscimol infusion on CRs and URs. A: All animals received an infusion before training on Sessions 1 to 6. The cerebellar group (■; n = 6) received muscimol infusions into the ipsilateral lateral cerebellum, the red nucleus group (▲; n = 6) received muscimol in the contralateral red nucleus, and the saline group (●; n = 6) received 1 μl of saline vehicle into the ipsilateral lateral cerebellum. No infusions were administered on Days 7 to 10. All animals received muscimol infusions before Session 11. Data are expressed as percent CRs averaged over all animals in each group for each training session. B: Percent CRs for Sessions 1 to 4 of the saline group and sessions 7 to 10 of the cerebellar and red nucleus groups. C: UR amplitudes on air-puff–only test trials during the six sessions in which infusions were administered. There were no significant differences between groups on these days. All data points are $M \pm$ SEM; symbols are the same for all figures (from Krupa et al., 1993).

8.2). Training during cooling of the magnocellular red nucleus gave identical results: Animals learned during cooling, as evidenced in postinactivation training, but did not express CRs at all during inactivation training (R. E. Clark & Lavond, 1993). However, cooling did impair performance of the UR (although the animals learned normally), yet another line of evidence against the performance argument. Consequently, the red nucleus must be efferent from the memory trace.

Inactivation of the dorsal anterior interpositus and overlying cortex (c in Fig. 8.1) by low doses of muscimol (6 days), by lidocaine (3 days and 6 days), and by cooling (5 days) resulted in no expression of CRs during inactivation training and no evidence of any learning at all having occurred during inactivation training (R. E. Clark et al., 1992; Krupa et al., 1993; Nordholm, J. K. Thompson, Dersarkissian, & R. F. Thompson, 1993). In subsequent postinactivation

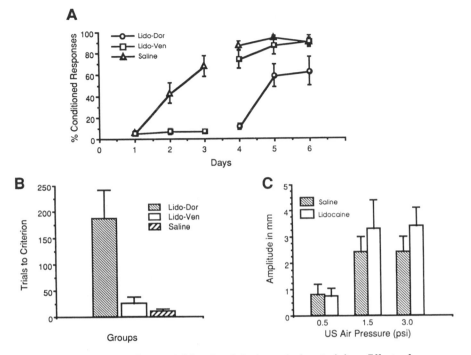

FIG. 8.3.   A: Effects of lidocaine infusions during training. Effect of lidocaine (dorsal and ventral) vs. saline. Lidocaine animals show no CRs during infusion (dorsal and ventral group data combined). In post-infusion training, animals with ventral cannula placements show virtually asymptotic learning, whereas those with dorsal placements learn as if naive. B: Mean postinfusion trials to criterion for the two lidocaine-infusion groups and the saline control group (Days 4–6 for all groups). The number of trials to criterion for the dorsal group is significantly greater than the number of trials for the saline or ventral groups, which do not differ from each other. C: Performance on US-alone trials at 0.5, 1.5, and 3.0 psi, with dorsal infusion of saline and effective infusions of lidocaine. There were no differences between UR amplitudes during saline or lidocaine infusion. (from Nordholm et al., 1993).

training, animals learned normally as though completely naive: They showed no savings at all relative to noninactivated control animals (see Figs. 8.2 and 8.3). None of the methods of inactivation had any effect at all on performance of the UR in US-alone trials. In one study (Nordholm et al., 1993), cerebellar lidocaine infusions effective in abolishing the CR and preventing learning were subsequently tested on US-alone trials over a wide range of US intensities and had no effect on performance of the UR; indeed, URs were numerically larger with lidocaine inactivation of CRs than with saline control infusions that had no effect on CRs (see Fig. 8.3c). The distribution of [3H]-muscimol completely effective in preventing learning included the anterior dorsal interpositus and overlying cortex of lobule HVI, a volume approximately 2% of the total volume of the cerebellum (Krupa et al., 1993; (see Fig. 8.4). The region of the cerebellum essential for learning this task is extremely localized.

Welsh and Harvey (1991) gave rabbits extensive training to a light CS, then gave them transfer training to a tone CS with interspersed light CSs (one session) with lidocaine infusion in the anterior interpositus, and then trained them to the tone without infusion. Control animals were treated identically, except that they

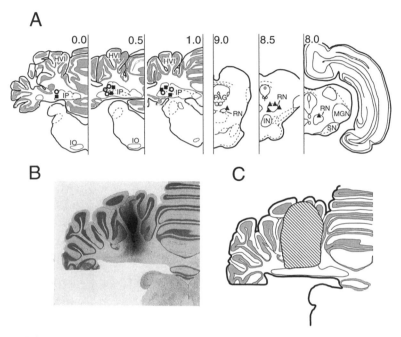

FIG. 8.4. Localization of muscimol-inactivated regions in Fig.8.2. A: Locations of all cannulae tips. Filled squares, cerebellar muscimol cannulae; open circles, saline controls; filled triangles, red nucleus cannulae. The numbers above the first three sections are the distances (in mm) rostral to lambda; above the last three are distances caudal from the bregma skull sutures. HVI, hemispheric lobule VI; IN, interpeduncular nucleus; IP, interpositus nucleus; IO, inferior olive; MGN, medial geniculate nucleus; PAG, periaqueductal grey; RN, red nucleus; SN, substantia nigra. B: Digitized image of an autoradiograph showing the greatest extent of [3H]-muscimol diffusion in the lateral cerebellum. Labeling encompasses dorsal aspects of the anterior interpositus and the overlying cortex, including lobule HVI. In no instance was any labeling found outside the cerebellum. The autoradiograph is shown superimposed on the Nissl-stained section from which it was exposed. C: Outline drawing of micrograph in B. Hatched area delineates maximal extent of [3H]-muscimol diffusion (from Krupa et al., 1993).

were given saline infusions during the transfer training session. The authors reported that CRs to the light CS were prevented during lidocaine infusion, but that the animals exhibited virtually asymptotic performance to the tone CS in postinfusion training. As noted earlier, if naive animals are given tone CS training during lidocaine infusion (3 days or 6 days), they do not learn at all at the time, and learn subsequently with no savings. The simplest explanation of Welsh and Harvey's results is that substantial transfer of training occurred; indeed, their control animals showed very substantial transfer compared to naive animals (see also Schreuers & Kehoe, 1987). Cannula location may also be a contributing factor: When lidocaine was infused in the white matter ventral to the interpositus to inactivate the efferent projections from the interpositus (see *d* in Fig. 8.1, and Fig. 8.3), normal learning occurred, although no CRs were expressed during infusion training (Nordholm et al., 1993), a result analogous to that reported by Welsh and Harvey. In any event, all studies where naive animals were trained during inactivation of the anterior interpositus and overlying cortex (by cooling, muscimol, or lidocaine) are consistent in showing that no learning occurs during inactivation training.

The white matter ventral to the interpositus nucleus includes the efferent projections conveying information from this portion of the cerebellum to other brain structures. Nordholm et al. (1993) trained animals for 3 days during lidocaine inactivation of this fiber region (*d* in Fig. 8.1). The animals showed no evidence of CRs during inactivation training, but exhibited asymptotic CR performance from the beginning of postinactivation training (see Figs. 8.3 and 8.5). These ventral infusions had no effect on performance of the UR. This result argues that interpositus projections to other brain regions play no essential role in *this* act of learning and memory, but this is not to say that such circuits play no role in learning. Indeed, as noted earlier, the GABAergic projection from the interpositus to the DAO appears to play a critical role as the error-correcting system in classical conditioning. A recent connectionist-level computational model of this circuit (Gluck, Goren, Myers, & R. F. Thompson, in press) suggests that feedback to the cerebellum from the output of the interpositus, possibly via other structures, may play a key role in the adaptive timing of the CR: the fact that, over a wide CS–US onset interval range, the peak of the CR occurs at about the time as the onset of the US.

Collectively, these data strongly support the hypothesis that the memory trace is formed and stored in a localized region of the cerebellum (anterior interpositus and overlying cortex). Inactivation of region *c* during training completely prevents learning, but inactivation of the output pathway from region *d* and its necessary (for the CR) efferent target, the red nucleus, *b*, does not prevent learning at all. In no case do the drug inactivations have any effect at all on performance of the reflex response on US-alone trials. If even a part of the essential memory trace were formed prior to the cerebellum in the essential circuit, then, following cerebellar inactivation training, the animals would have

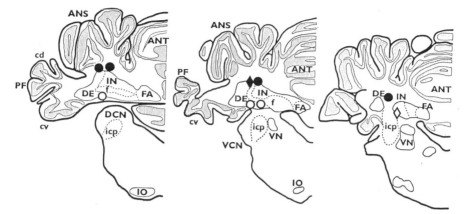

FIG. 8.5.   Cannula placements for the lidocaine animals described in
Fig. 8.3. Diamonds represent lowest concentration for the dorsal (solid
diamond and circles) and ventral (open diamond and circles) placements. Circles represent all other concentrations. ANS, ansiform
lobule; ANT, anterior lobe; DE, dentate nucleus; DCN, dorsal cochlear
nucleus; FA, fastigial nucleus; IN, interpositus nucleus; IO, inferior
olive; PF, paraflocculus; VN, vestibular nuclei; VCN, ventral cochlear
nucleus; cd, dorsal crus; cv, ventral crus; f, fibers; iop, inferior cerebellar peduncle (from Nordholm et al., 1993).

to show savings, and they show none. Similarly, if a part of the essential memory
trace were formed in the red nucleus or in other efferent targets of the interpositus, then, following red nucleus (*b*) or interpositus efferent (*d*) inactivation
training, animals could not show asymptotic CR performance, but they do.

These results would seem to rule out conclusively the possibility that the
essential memory trace is formed and stored in the brain-stem reflex pathways, as
hypothesized by Bloedel (1992) and Welsh and Harvey (1989, 1991). The brain-
stem hypothesis has not been elaborated much beyond the assertion that the
memory trace occurs in the brain-stem, and there is, at present, no evidence to
support it. There are, perhaps, two alternative possibilities: (a) the trace is
established in the brain stem largely independently of the cerebellum, but the
excitatory drive from the cerebellum is necessary for its behavioral expression; or
(b) the trace is established in the brain-stem at least in part as a result of the
actions of the cerebellum on the brain-stem circuitry. Insofar as expression of the
CR is concerned, lesions of the interpositus nucleus, of its efferent projection to
the red nucleus via the superior cerebellar peduncle, of the target region of the
magnocellular red nucleus, and of the descending rubral pathway projecting to
the brainstem and motor nuclei completely prevent and abolish expression of the
CR, with no effect on the UR (as discussed). Consequently, the cerebellum must
exert its actions on the brain-stem and motor nuclei for the eye-blink CR via its
efferent projection to the red nucleus and rubral projections to the brain-stem. So,
if the cerebellum–red nucleus circuit simply facilitates expression of the brain-

stem CR, then inactivation of the critical region of the cerebellum during training could not possibly prevent learning, yet it does. On the other hand, if the cerebellum–red nucleus circuit actually establishes the brain-stem CR, reversible inactivation of either structure, each of which completely prevents expression of the CR, would have the same effect on learning the CR in naive animals. However, as noted, inactivation of the critical cerebellar region completely prevents learning, but inactivation of the red nucleus region does not prevent learning at all, even though, in both cases, the necessary cerebellar actions on the brain-stem are completely prevented.

The evidence summarized here would seem to demonstrate that the memory traces for classical conditioning of discrete responses are formed and stored in the cerebellum. To date, all of our reversible inactivations that prevent learning include the dorsal anterior interpositus and at least the ventral overlying cortex of lobule HVI. There are substantial direct projections from the interpositus to the cerebellar cortex; hence, interpositus inactivation would also inactivate these nucleocortical projections. The permanent cortical lesion data would seem to indicate that a very large volume of cerebellar cortex must be removed to substantially impair or, in a few cases, to prevent, learning of the eye-blink response. Consequently, the most conservative hypothesis remains that the memory trace is formed and stored in multiple sites in the cerebellar cortex and in the anterior interpositus nucleus (R. F. Thompson, 1986). If so, then the memory trace is, indeed, localized to particular regions of one brain structure, although it is distributed over many thousands of neurons, possibly in multiple sites.

As noted earlier, our Purkinje neuron recording data support the view that long-term depression (LTD) may be a mechanism underlying the learning of discrete responses. Decreases in simple spike discharges in the CS period will disinhibit the appropriate interpositus neurons, hence increasing the excitatory drive via the red nucleus to generate the behavioral CR. If this is the case, the rapidly growing understanding of the mechanisms of LTD (see Ito, 1993), should ultimately lead to the molecular mechanisms of memory storage in the cerebellum.

An understanding of the molecular biology of memory trace formation will lead to an understanding of the mechanisms of memory storage, but this information can never inform us of the content of a memory store. The memory itself, be it an appropriately timed eye-blink, the correct turn in a maze, or a particular experience, is a property of the neural network that encodes the memory. It seems very likely that the mechanisms of storage are embedded within this network; indeed, it is difficult to think otherwise. In the case of the cerebellum and the memories for learned discrete movements, much of the essential circuitry has been identified; Recordings from single interpositus neurons or Purkinje neurons can predict rather accurately the content of the memory and the actual nature and temporal course of the learned response. Granted, this is a simple form of associative memory, but here, at least, we are rapidly gaining an understanding of the neuronal networks that encode the memories.

ACKNOWLEDGMENTS

I thank all the people in my laboratory for the work reported here, which was supported by National Institute on Aging grant AF05142, Office of Naval Research contract NOOO14–91-J-0112, NSF (BNS-8117115), and Sankyo.

REFERENCES

Albus, J. S. (1971). A theory of cerebellar function. *Mathematical Bioscience, 10*, 25–61.

Berger, T. W., & Orr, W. B. (1983). Hippocampectomy selectively disrupts discrimination reversal conditioning of the rabbit nictitating membrane response. *Behaviroal Brain Research, 210*, 411–417.

Berthier, N. E., & Moore, J. W. (1986). Cerebellar Purkinje cell activity related to the classical conditioned nictitating membrane response. *Experimental Brain Research, 63*, 341–350.

Berthier, N. W., & Moore, J. W. (1990). Activity of deep cerebellar nuclear cells during classical conditioning of nictitating membrane extension in rabbits. *Experimental Brain Research, 83*, 44–54.

Bloedel, J. R. (1992). Functional heterogeneity with structural homogeneity: How does the cerebellum operate? *Behavioral Brain Science, 15*, 666–678.

Brindley, C. S. (1964). The use made by the cerebellum of the information that it receives from sense organs. *International Brain Research Organization Bulletin, 3*, 80.

Chapman, P. F., Steinmetz, J. E., Sears, L. L., & Thompson, R. F. (1990). Effects of lidocaine injection in the interpositus nucleus and red nucleus on conditioned behavioral and neuronal responses. *Brain Research, 537*, 149–156.

Chapman, P. F., Steinmetz, J. E., & Thompson, R.F. (1988). Classical conditioning does not occur when direct stimulation of the red nucleus or cerebellar nuclei is the unconditioned stimulus. *Brain Research, 442*, 97–104.

Chen, C., & Thompson, R. F. (1992). Associative long-term depression revealed by field potential recording in rat cerebellar slice. *Society for Neuroscience Abstracts, 18*, 1215.

Clark, G. A., McCormick, D. A., Lavond, D. G., & Thompson, R. F. (1984). Effects of lesions of cerebellar nuclei on conditioned behavioral and hippocampal neuronal response. *Brain Research, 291*, 125–136.

Clark, R. E., & Lavond, D. G.(1993). Reversible lesions of the red nucleus during acquisition and retention of a classically conditioned behavior in rabbit. *Behavioral Neuroscience, 107*, 264–270.

Clark, R. E., Zhang, A. A., & Lavond, D. G. (1992). Reversible lesions of the cerebellar interpositus nucleus during acquisition and retention of a classically conditioned behavior. *Behavioral Neuroscience, 106*, 879–888.

Daum, I., Schugens, M. M., Ackermann, H., Lutzenberger, W., Dichgans, J., & Birbaumer, N. (1993). Classical conditioning after cerebellar lesions in humans *Behavioral Neuroscience, 107*, 748–756.

Disterhoft, J. F., Quinn, K. J., Weiss, C., & Shipley, M. T. (1985). Accessory abducens nucleus and conditioned eye retraction/nictitating membrane extensions in rabbit. *Journal of Neuroscience, 5*, 941–950.

Donegan, N. H., Foy, M. R., & Thompson, R. F. (1985). Neuronal responses of the rabbit cerebellar cortex during performance of the classically conditioned eyelid response. *Society for Neuroscience Abstracts, 11*, 835.

Donegan, N. H., Gluck, M. A., & Thompson, R. F. (1989). Integrating behavioral and biological models of classical conditioning. In R. D. Hawkins & G. H. Bower (Eds.), *Psychology of Learning and Motivation* (pp. 109–156). New York: Academic Press.

123

Donegan, N. H., Lowry, R. W., & Thompson, R. F. (1983). Effects of lesioning cerebellar nuclei on conditioned leg-flexion responses. *Society for Neuroscience Abstracts, 9,* 331.

Dudai, Y. (1989). *The neurobiology of memory: Concepts, findings, trends.* New York: Oxford University Press.

Eccles, J. C. (1977). An instruction-selection theory of learning in the cerebellar cortex. *Brain Research, 127,* 327–352.

Eccles, J. C., Ito, M., & Szentagothai, J. (1967). *The cerebellum as a neuronal machine.* Berlin: Springer.

Ekerot, C. F., Gustavsson, P., Oscarsson, O., & Schouenborg, J. (1987). Climbing fibres projecting to cat cerebellar anterior lobe activated by cutaneous A and C fibres. *Journal of Physiology, 386,* 529–538.

Foy, M. R., Krupa, D. J., Tracy, J., & Thompson, R. F. (1992). Analysis of single unit recordings from cerebellar cortex of classically conditioned rabbits. *Society for Neuroscience Abstracts, 18,* 1215.

Foy, M. R., Steinmetz, J. E., & Thompson, R. F. (1984). Single unit analysis of the cerebellum during classically conditioned eyelid responses. *Society for Neuroscience Abstracts, 10,* 122.

Foy, M. R., & Thompson, R. F. (1986). Single-unit analysis of Purkinje cell discharge in classically conditioned and untrained rabbits. *Society for Neuroscience Abstracts, 12,* 518.

Gluck, M. A., Goren, O., Myers, C., & Thompson, R. F. (in press). A higher order recurrent network model of the cerebellar substrates of response timing in motor-reflex conditioning. *Journal of Cognitive Neuroscience.*

Gluck, M. A., Reifsnider, E., & Thompson, R. F. (1990). Adaptive signal processing and the cerebellum: Models of classical conditioning and VOR adaptation. In M. A. Gluck & D. E. Rumelhart (Eds.), *Neuroscience and connectionist models* (pp. 131–185). Hillsdale, NJ: Lawrence Erlbaum Associates.

Gormezano, I., Kehoe, E. J., & Marshall-Goodell, B.S. (1983). Twenty years of classical conditioning research with the rabbit. In J. M. Sprague & A. N. Epstein, (Eds.), *Progress in physiological psychology* (pp. 197–275). New York: Academic Press.

Haley, D. A., Lavond, D. G., & Thompson, R. F. (1983). Effects of contralateral red nuclear lesions on retention of the classically conditioned nictitating membrane/eyelid response. *Society for Neuroscience Abstracts, 9,* 643.

Haley, D. A., Thompson, R. F., & Madden, J., IV. (1988). Pharmacological analysis of the magnocellular red nucleus during classical conditioning of the rabbit nictitating membrane response. *Brain Research, 454,* 131–139.

Ito, M. (1972). Neural design of the cerebellar motor control system. *Brain Research, 40,* 81–84.

Ito, M. (1984). *The cerebellum and neural control.* New York: Raven.

Ito, M. (1989). Long-term depression. *Annual Review of Neuroscience, 12,* 85–102.

Ivkovich, D., Lockard, J. M., & Thompson, R. F. (1993). Interpositus lesion abolition of the eyeblink CR is not due to effects on performance. *Behavioral Neuroscience, 107,* 530–532.

Karamian, A. I., Fanaralijian, V. V., & Kosareva, A. A. (1969). The functional and morphological evolution of the cerebellum and its role in behavior. In R. Llinas (Ed.), *Neurobiology of cerebellar evolution and development: First international symposium.* Chicago: American Medical Association.

Kim, J. J., Krupa, D. J., & Thompson, R. F. (1992). Intra-olivary infusions of picrotoxin prevent "blocking" of rabbit conditioned eyeblink response. *Society for Neuroscience Abstracts, 18,* 1562.

Krupa, D. J., Thompson, J. K., & Thompson, R. F. (1993). Localization of a memory trace in the mammalian brain. *Science, 260,* 989–991.

Krupa, D. J., Weiss, C., & Thompson, R. F. (1991). Air puff evoked Purkinje cell complex spike activity is diminished during conditioned responses in eyeblink conditioned rabbits. *Society for Neuroscience Abstracts, 17,* 322.

Lavond, D. G., Hambree, T. L., & Thompson, R. F. (1985). Effects of kainic acid lesions of the cerebellar interpositus nucleus on eyelid conditioning in the rabbit. *Brain Research, 326,* 179–182.

Lavond, D. G., Kim, J. J., & Thompson, R. F. (1993). Mammalian brain substrates of aversive classical conditioning. *Annual Review of Psychology, 44,* 317–342.

Lavond, D. G., Lincoln, J. S., McCormick, D. A., & Thompson, R. F. (1984). Effect of bilateral lesions of the dentate and interpositus cerebellar nuclei on conditioning of heart-rate and nictitating membrane/eyelid responses in the rabbit. *Brain Research, 305,* 323–330.

Lavond, D. G., McCormick, D. A., Clark, G. A., Holmes, D. T., & Thompson, R. F. (1981). Effects of ipsilateral rostral pontine reticular lesions on retention of classically conditioned nictitating membrane and eyelid response. *Physiological Psychology, 9,* 335–339.

Lavond, D. G., McCormick, D. A., & Thompson, R. F. (1984). A nonrecoverable learning deficit. *Physiological Psychology, 12,* 103–110.

Lavond, D. G., & Steinmetz, J. E. (1989). Acquisition of classical conditioning without cerebellar cortex. *Behavioral Brain Research, 33,* 113–164.

Lavond, D. G., Steinmetz, J. E., Yokaitis, M. H., & Thompson, R. F. (1987). Reacquisition of classical conditioning after removal of cerebellar cortex. *Experimental Brain Research, 67,* 569–593.

Lincoln, J. S., McCormick, D. A., & Thompson, R. F. (1982). Ipsilateral cerebellar lesions prevent learning of the classically conditioned nictitating membrane/eyelid response of the rabbit. *Brain Research, 242,* 190–193.

Logan, C. G. (1991). Cerebellar cortical involvement in excitatory and inhibitory classical conditioning. Unpublished doctoral dissertation, Stanford University, Stanford.

Lye, R. H., Boyle, D. J., Ramsden, R. T., & Schady, W. (1988). Effects of a unilateral cerebellar lesion on the acquisition of eye-blink conditioning in man. *Journal of Physiology, 403,* 58.

Lynch, G. (1986). *Synapses, circuits, and the beginnings of memory.* Cambridge, MA: MIT Press.

Mamounas, L. A., Thompson, R. F., and Madden, J., IV. (1987). Cerebellar GABAergic processes: Evidence for critical involvement in a form of simple associative learning in the rabbit. *Proceedings of the National Academy of Sciences, 84,* 2101–2105.

Marr, D. (1969). A theory of cerebellar cortex. *Journal of Physiology, 202,* 437–470.

McCormick, D. A., Clark, G. A., Lavond, D. G., & Thompson, R. F. (1982). Initial localization of the memory trace for a basic form of learning. *Proceedings of the National Academy of Sciences, 79,* 2731–2742.

McCormick, D. A., Guyer, P. E., & Thompson, R. F. (1982). Superior cerebellar peduncle lesions selectively abolish the ipsilateral classical conditioned nictitating membrane/eyelid response of the rabbit. *Brain Research, 244,* 347–350.

McCormick, D. A., Lavond, D. G., Clark, G. A., Kettner, R. E., Rising, C. E., & Thompson, R. F. (1981). The engram found? Role of the cerebellum in classical conditioning of nictitating membrane and eyelid responses. *Bulletin of the Psychonomic Society, 18,* 103–105.

McCormick, D. A., & Thompson, R. F. (1984a). Cerebellum: Essential involvement in the classically conditioned eyelid response. *Science, 223,* 296–299.

McCormick, D. A., & Thompson, R. F. (1984b). Neuronal responses of the rabbit cerebellum during acquisition and performance of a classically conditioned nictitating membrane eyelid response. *Journal of Neuroscience, 4,* 2811–2822.

McGaugh, J. (1989). Involvement of hormone and neuromodulatory systems in the regulation of memory storage. *Annual Review of Neuroscience, 12,* 255–287.

Moyer, J. R., Jr., Deyo, R. A., & Disterhoft, J. F. (1990). Hippocampectomy disrupts trace eyeblink conditioning in rabbits. *Behavioral Neuroscience, 104,* 243–252.

Nelson, B., & Mugnaini, E. (1987). GABAergic innervation of the inferior olivary complex and experimental evidence for its origin. In P. Strata, (Ed.), *The olivocerebellar system in motor control.* New York: Springer-Verlag.

Nordholm, A. F., Thompson, J. K., Dersarkissian, C., & Thompson, R. F. (1993). Lidocaine infusion in a critical region of cerebellum completely prevents learning of the conditioned eyeblink response. *Behavioral Neuroscience, 107*, 882–886.

Perrett, S. P., Ruiz, B. P., & Mauk, M. D. (1993). Cerebellar cortex lesions disrupt the timing of conditioned eyelid responses. *Journal of Neursocience, 13*, 1708–1718.

Polenchar, B. E., Patterson, M. M., Lavond, D. G., & Thompson, R. F. (1985). Cerebellar lesions abolish an avoidance response in rabbit. *Behavioral and Neural Biology, 44*, 221–227.

Rescorla, R., & Wagner, A. (1972). A theory of Pavlovian conditioning: Variations in the effectiveness of reinforcement. In A. Black, & W. Prokasy, (Eds.), *Classical conditioning: II: Current Research Theory* (pp. 64–99). New York: Appleton-Century-Crofts.

Rosenfeld, M. E., Dovydaitis, A., & Moore, J. W. (1985). Brachium conjunctivum and rubrobulbar tract: Brainstem projections of red nucleus essential for the conditioned nictitating membrane response. *Physiology and Behavior, 34*, 751–759.

Rosenfeld, M. E., & Moore, J. W. (1983). Red nucleus lesions disrupt the classically conditioned nictitating membrane response in rabbits. *Behavioral Brain Research, 10*, 393–398.

Schreurs, B. G., & Alkon, D. L. (1992). Long-term depression and classical conditioning of the rabbit nictitating membrane response: An assessment using the rabbit cerebellar slice. *Society for Neuroscience Abstracts, 18*, 337.

Schreurs, B. G., & Kehoe, E. J. (1987). Cross-model transfer as a function of initial training level in classical conditioning with the rabbit. *Animal Learning and Behavior, 15*, 47–54.

Sears, L. L., & Steinmetz, J. E. (1990). Acquisition of classical conditioned-related activity in the hippocampus is affected by lesions of the cerebellar interpositus nucleus. *Behavioral Neuroscience, 104*, 681–692.

Sears, L. L., & Steinmetz, J. E. (1991). Dorsal accessory inferior olive activity diminishes during acquisition of the rabbit classically conditioned eyelid response. *Brain Research, 545*, 114–122.

Smith, A. M. (1970). The effects of rubral lesions and stimulations on conditioned forelimb lexion responses in the cat. *Physiology and Behavior, 5*, 1121–1126.

Solomon, P. R., Stowe, G. T., & Pendibeury, W. W. (1989). Disrupted eyelid conditioning in a patient with damage to cerebellar afferents. *Behavioral Neuroscience, 103*, 898–902.

Solomon, P. R., Vander Schaaf, E. R., Thompson, R. F., & Weisz, D. J. (1986). Hippocampus and trace conditioning of the rabbit's classically conditioned nictitating membrane response. *Behavioral Neuroscience, 100*, 729–744.

Squire, L. R. (1992). Memory and the hippocampus: A synthesis from findings with rats, monkeys, and humans. *Psychological Review, 99*, 195–231.

Steinmetz, J. E. (1990). Classical nictitating membrane conditioning in rabbits with varying interstimulus intervals and direct activation of cerebellar mossy fibers as the CS. *Behavioral Brain Research, 38*, 91–108.

Steinmetz, J. E., & Steinmetz, G. S. (1991). Rabbit classically conditioned eyelid responses fail to reappear after interpositus lesions and extended postlesion training. *Society for Neuroscience Abstracts, 17*, 323.

Steinmetz, J. E., Lavond, D. G., Ivkovich, D., Logan, C. G., & Thompson, R. F. (1992). Disruption of classical eyelid conditioning after cerebellar lesions: Damage to a memory trace system or a simple performance deficit? *Journal of Neuroscience, 12*, 4403–4426.

Thach, W. T., Goodkin, H. G., & Keating, J. G. (1992). The cerebellum and the adaptive coordination of movement. *Annual Review of Neuroscience, 15*, 403–442.

Thompson, J. K., Krupa, D. J., Weng, J.,& Thompson, R. F. (1993). Inactivation of motor nuclei blocks expression but not acquisition of rabbit's classically conditioned eyeblink response. *Society for Neuroscience Abstracts, 19*, 999.

Thompson, R. F. (1986). The neurobiology of learning and memory. *Science, 233*, 941–947.

Thompson, R. F. (1990). Neural mechanisms of classical conditioning in mammals. *Philosophical Transactions of the Royal Society of London* (Series B) *329*, 161–170.

Thompson, R. F., Berger, T. W., & Madden, J., IV (1983). Cellular processes of learning and memory in the mammalian CNS. *Annual Review of Neuroscience, 6*, 447–491.

Tracy, J., Weiss, C., & Thompson, R. F. (1991). Single unit recordings of somatosensory and auditory evoked responses in the anterior interpositus nucleus in the naive rabbit. *Society of Neuroscience Abstracts, 18*, 344.

Tsukahara, N., Oda, T., & Notsu, T. (1981). Classical conditioning mediated by the red nucleus in the cat. *Journal of Neuroscience, 1*, 72–79.

Voneida, T. J. (1990). The effect of rubrospinal tractotomy on a conditioned limb response in the cat. *Society for Neuroscience Abstracts, 16*, 170.

Wagner, A. R., & Brandon, S. E. (1989). Evolution of a structured connectionist model of Pavlovian conditioning (AESOP). In S. B. Klein, & R. R. Mowrer (Eds.), *Contemporary learning theories: Pavlovian Conditioning and the status of traditional Learning Theory* (pp. 149–189). Hillsdale, NJ: Lawrence Erlbaum Associates.

Weisz, D. J., & LoTurco, J. J. (1988). Reflex facilitation of the nictitating membrane response remains after cerebellar lesions. *Behavioral Neuroscience, 102*, 203–209.

Welsh, J. P., & Harvey, J. A. (1989). Cerebellar lesions and the nictitating membrane reflex: Performance deficits of the conditioned and unconditioned response. *Journal of Neuroscience, 9*, 299–311.

Welsh, J. P., & Harvey, J. A. (1991). Pavlovian conditioning in the rabbit during inactivation of the interpositus nucleus. *Journal of Physiology, 444*, 459–480.

Woodruff-Pak, D. S., Lavond, D. G., & Thompson, R. F. (1985). Trace conditioning: Abolished by cerebellar nuclear lesions but not lateral cerebellar cortex aspirations. *Brain Research, 348*, 249–260.

Yang, B.-Y., & Weisz, D. J. (1992). An auditory conditioned stimulus modulates unconditioned stimulus-elicited neuronal activity in the cerebellar anterior interpositus and dentate nuclei during nictitating membrane response conditioning in rabbits. *Behavioral Neuroscience, 106*, 889–899.

Yeo, C. H. (1991). Cerebellum and classical conditioning of motor responses. *Annals of the New York Acadademy of Sciences, 627*, 292–304.

Yeo, C. H., & Hardiman, M. J. (1992). Cerebellar cortex and eyeblink conditioning. *Experimental Brain Research, 88*, 623–638.

Yeo, C. H., Hardiman, M. J., & Glickstein, M. (1985a). Classical conditioning of the nictitating membrane response of the rabbit: I. Lesions of the cerebellar nuclei. *Experimental Brain Research, 60*, 87–98.

Yeo, C. H., Hardiman, M. J., & Glickstein, M. (1985b). Classical conditioning of the nictitating membrane response of the rabbit: II. Lesions of the cerebellar cortex. *Experimental Brain Research, 60*, 99–113.

Zhang, A. A., & Lavond, D. G. (1991) Effects of reversible lesions of reticular or facial neurons during eyeblink conditioning. *Society for Neuroscience Abstracts, 17*, 869.

9 Persistent Questions About Hippocampal Function in Memory

Howard Eichenbaum
Brian Young
Michael Bunsey
State University of New York at Stony Brook

Although the hippocampal region has been the focus of intense investigation since the 1960s, we do not yet fully understand the role this part of the brain plays in memory, or how it fulfills that role. In this chapter, we consider some of the persistent questions about hippocampal function and review our own efforts to address these questions. The focus of our work is a cognitive and neural-systems analysis of hippocampal function, rather than the synaptic or molecular mechanisms of plasticity, although we hope that our findings will shed light on, or even guide, investigations at the cellular level.

Our overall goals are to discover the fundamental role the hippocampus plays in memory processing, and to reveal the coding schemes and functional circuitry that underlie it. We outline our efforts toward these goals by addressing three central questions whose answers reflect different strategies through which progress has been made:

1. What kind of memory relies on hippocampal function?
2. How are experiences encoded by the hippocampus?
3. Can information processing by the hippocampal system be subdivided into component functions?

We can provide only preliminary and somewhat speculative answers to these questions. Nevertheless, taken together, the findings from these three lines of investigation suggest a coherent framework for understanding the role of the hippocampus in mnemonic processing. In the following sections we consider each of these questions separately, and then attempt to synthesize some answers.

WHAT KIND OF MEMORY IS DEPENDENT
ON HIPPOCAMPAL FUNCTION?

Since the earliest studies on amnesia following damage in the hippocampal region in humans, it has been known that the hippocampus plays a selective role in memory (Scoville & Milner, 1957). The early findings focused its time-limited role the hippocampal region plays in memory, and indicated that the hippocampus and its associated cortical structures are not required for immediate or short-term memory, nor for the retrieval of permanent memories, but are critical to mediating the long-term storage of information. More recently, it has become clear that the role of the hippocampal system is limited to the permanent storage of a particular kind of memory, and that other forms of learning proceed normally in the absence of normal hippocampal function. Considerable progress has been made in distinguishing domains of impaired versus spared learning capacity in human amnesics and in animals with experimental damage to the hippocampal region. However, separate investigations on different species have led to different, and seemingly unrelated, formulations about the nature of the distinction between hippocampal-dependent and hippocampal- *in*dependent memory.

In studies on humans, substantial consensus has been reached in characterizing the amnesia due to hippocampal system damage as a selective impairment in *declarative* or *explicit memory.* This kind of memory is exemplified by our recall of everyday facts and events. Such memories can be brought to conscious recollection, are typically subject to verbal reflection or other explicit forms of recall, and can be used flexibly in a variety of situations outside the learning experience (Cohen & Squire, 1980; Squire, 1987). Nearly all conventional assessments of human recall and recognition require or emphasize that the explicit expression of memories, and performance across a wide range of tasks is severely impaired in amnesia associated with hippocampal system dysfunction. By contrast, the domain of preserved learning in amnesia has been described as *procedural memory*, a collection of learning capacities that can be revealed in the absence of conscious recollection or verbal reflection and that are expressed implicitly through enhanced or altered performance during repetition of the learning experience (Cohen & Squire, 1980; Schacter, 1987). Most of the behavioral paradigms in which procedural memory has been studied involve the acquisition of various perceptual, motor, or cognitive skills, and several forms of adaptation and bias in performance (reviewed in Cohen, 1984; Cohen & Eichenbaum, 1993; Corkin, 1984; Squire, 1992). Perhaps the most popular of these paradigms involves the priming phenomenon in which normal subjects are more likely to complete or recognize pictorial or verbal items from familiar partial information or are able to read recently experienced text more quickly than "new" material. Human amnesics often perform normally on such tasks, although they are unable to recollect their experiences consciously during testing. Notably, such enhanced performance in both normal subjects and amnesics is inflexible, in that it succeeds only when the physical form of the test item closely matches that of the previously experienced item (Schacter, 1985).

In contrast to the high level of consensus on the phenomenology characterizing human amnesia, there are currently several distinct proposals regarding the selective role of the hippocampus in learning and memory in animals. The most widely held view, and therefore the one considered in detail here, posits that the hippocampus is critical to the acquisition of a cognitive map of the environment and is not involved in nonspatial memory (O'Keefe & Nadel, 1978). This account is based on a large quantity of data indicating selective or disproportionate deficits in spatial versus nonspatial learning in animals following hippocampal lesions and on the finding that many hippocampal neurons fire in association with an animal's location in its environment. Although these data are compelling, the conclusion that hippocampal function is fundamentally dedicated to spatial information processing is clearly at odds with the findings from studies on humans. Human amnesics are, in fact, severely impaired in spatial learning, but to a degree no greater than that associated with various forms of nonspatial learning and memory (Cave & Squire, 1991).

How can the conclusions from the study of human amnesia and those from studies on animal models be reconciled? Our view is that declarative memory, as described in human subjects, and cognitive mapping, as described in animals, share a common fundamental basis in something we call *relational representation*. This view, which we have elaborated in detail elsewhere (Cohen & Eichenbaum, 1993; Eichenbaum, Cohen, Otto, & Wible, 1992; Eichenbaum, Otto, & Cohen, 1992), posits that the hippocampus mediates the storage of memories in a multidimensional network, in which items are organized according to the relevant relationships among them. Relational representation is distinguished from the individual representation of separate items by two properties of that define its operation: First, relational representations are created through and, once acquired, support the comparing and contrasting of items. By contrast, individual representations do not require comparisons among items, but involve the acquisition of biases, preferences, or mere familiarity for describing perceptually distinct items and habitual performance routines. Second, relational representations support the ability to make inferences and generalizations across items that are only indirectly related in the memory network. This ability permits the flexible expression of memories in new situations. Individual representations, in contrast, are characterized by the inflexibility of their expression; they are revealed only through repetition of the procedures that characterized their acquisition.

Characterizations of declarative memory in humans place heavy demands on relational representations, emphasizing both the capacity for making comparisons among memories and the ability to express memories flexibly, that is, in various and even novel ways (Cohen, 1984). How are these two properties related to characteristics of cognitive mapping in animals? Even more importantly, how can they be employed to understand the patterns of performance in nonspatial learning and memory in animals? Some of our studies have focused directly on these questions.

Our initial investigations exploited the excellent learning and memory capacities rats demonstrate in odor discrimination learning (Eichenbaum, Fagan, Mathews, & Cohen, 1988; Eichenbaum, Mathews, & Cohen, 1989). The learning ability of intact rats versus rats with fornix transection was evaluated in variations of the odor discrimination learning paradigm, which assesses the capacity for relational representation by manipulating the demands for comparison and for the representation of relations among identical odor cues (Eichenbaum et al., 1988). In a simultaneous discrimination task, two odor cues were presented at the same time and in close spatial juxtaposition; the discriminative response required a selection between equivalent left and right choices. Under these training conditions, rats with fornix lesions were severely and persistently impaired on a series of different odor discrimination problems (Fig. 9.1A). In a successive discrimination task, odors were presented separately, hindering comparison among items, and the response required only completing or discontinuing the stimulus sampling behavior, thus eliminating the response choice. In contrast to the results on simultaneous discrimination, under these training conditions, rats with fornix lesions were superior to normal rats in acquiring the same series of discriminations that they had failed to learn in the simultaneous condition (Fig. 9.1B; see also Eichenbaum, Fagan, & Cohen, 1986; Otto, Schottler, Staubli, Eichenbaum, & Lynch, 1991; Staubli, Ivy, & Lynch, 1984). Our interpretation of these findings is that, with identical stimulus materials, hippocampal damage can cause severe impairment, transient impairment, or even facilitation, depending on the demands of the task. More specifically, the differences in performance caused by hippocampal system damage can be related to the demand for stimulus and response comparison.

To assess the capacity for representational flexibility in normal rats and in rats with hippocampal system damage, we pursued a follow-up experiment using the simultaneous discrimination task (Eichenbaum et al., 1989). Our investigation exploited a surprising finding in Eichenbaum et al. (1988): Although rats with fornix lesions were generally impaired at simultaneous discriminations, they succeeded in learning some of the discrimination problems at least as rapidly as normal animals. To understand why they occasionally succeeded and to explore the nature of memory representation when they did succeed, we trained yoked pairs of normal and fornix-lesioned rats on a series of simultaneous odor discrimination problems until the fornix-lesioned rat in each pair had acquired two such "instruction" problems within the normal range of scores. We then assessed the flexibility of their representations by challenging them with probe trials composed of familiar odors that were "mispaired", that is, were presented in combinations not previously experienced. According to our notion of relational representation, normal animals encode all the odor stimuli presented, both within and across trials, using an organized scheme that would support comparisons even

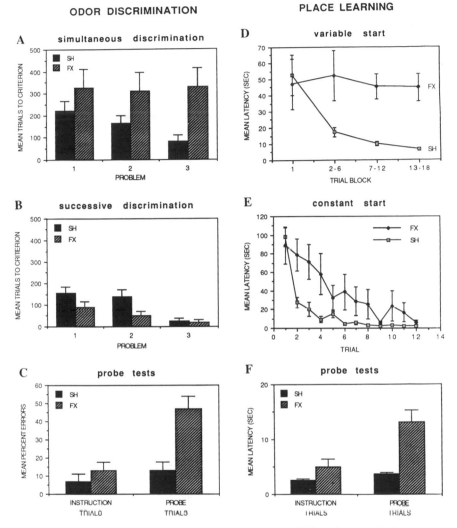

FIG. 9.1. Performance of sham operated rats (SH) and rats with lesions of the fornix (FX) on different versions of odor discrimination and place learning tasks and their probe trials (from Eichenbaum & Cohen, 1992).

among odors not previously experienced together. Conversely, we postulated that the representation of rats with hippocampal system damage would not support the recognition of the separate elements within each combination. To test these predictions, we intermixed within a series of trials on two different instruction problems occasional probe trials composed of the rewarded odor from one problem and the nonrewarded odor from another. Both normal rats and rats with fornix lesions continued to perform well on the trials composed of the odor pairings used on the instruction trials. The normal rats also performed accurately on the probe trials (Fig. 9.1C), but the rats with fornix lesions performed at chance levels on these trials, as if they had been presented with novel stimuli.

A further analysis focusing on the response latencies of animals performing the simultaneous discrimination provided additional evidence that the nature of learned odor representation was abnormal in rats with hippocampal system damage. This analysis also provided insight into how these animals succeeded in learning some of the simultaneous discrimination problems. We determined that rats with fornix lesions had shorter average response latencies than normal rats, even though all rats performed at consistently high accuracy levels and showed the speed-inaccuracy tradeoff typical of RT measures. Furthermore, rats' normal latencies were distributed bimodally: Each of the two modes was associated with one of the positions where the rewarded odor was presented and the response was executed. This pattern of response latencies suggests that normal rats sample both odor ports in an orderly fashion. In contrast, rats with fornix lesions had a unimodal distribution of response latencies, and the pattern of their response latencies was the same, regardless of odor and response positions. Our interpretation of these results was that rats with hippocampal system damage sample the entire stimulus compound at once, requiring less time to complete the trial. On those problems in which the left-right combinations of odors were distinguishable, they succeeded in learning an individual association for each odor compound and thus learned the appropriate response. Indeed, this account of representational strategies suggests that their performance was inflexible on our probe tests because novel mispairings of odors were perceived as unfamiliar odor compounds.

Our investigations have also included experiments on place learning, which have been performed to more directly extend our notions of relational representation and representational flexibility to spatial learning *per se*. Perhaps the clearest demonstration of the critical role the hippocampus plays in place learning comes from experiments using the Morris water maze (Morris, Garrud, Rawlins, & O'Keefe, 1982). A large circular swimming pool is filled with an opaque water solution; the pool contains an escape platform slightly submerged at a fixed location relative to salient extramaze visual cues. On each training trial the rat is placed in the water at the edge of the pool and must find its way to the escape platform. In the standard version of this task, rats are released into the water at different starting points on successive trials, a manipulation that strongly encourages them to compare the views of extramaze stimuli and their own positions across trials, and to form a representation of the spatial relations among the cues that consistently predicts the locus of the platform. To assess the importance of the demand for relational representation in place learning, we compared the performance of intact rats and rats with fornix lesions on the standard, variable-start version of this task with a version of the task that eliminates the need to compare views across different starting positions by using the same starting position on all trials (Eichenbaum, Stewart, & Morris, 1990). In the variable-start condition, intact animals rapidly learned the place of the platform, demonstrating their memory in progressively shorter escape latencies (Fig. 9.1D). By contrast, rats with fornix lesions failed to learn the escape locus, as expected. In the constant-start version of the task, however, rats with fornix lesions learned to escape nearly as rapidly as normal animals (Fig. 9.1E). To confirm that both sets of rats were using the same extramaze cues to guide performance, we applied the standard "transfer" test developed by Morris (1984), in which the escape platform is removed and the swimming pattern of the rats is observed for a fixed period. Both normal rats and rats with fornix lesions swam near the former location of the platform, indicating that they could identify the place of escape by the same set of available extramaze cues, rather than solely by the approach trajectory.

To assess the flexibility of the memory representations supporting accurate performance on the constant-start version of the task, we presented rats with different types of probe trials, each involving an alteration of the cues or starting points, intermixed within a series of repetitions of the instruction trial. One of our probe tests demonstrated a particularly striking dissociation between the subject groups. In this test, the platform was left in its normal place, but the start position was moved to various novel locations. When the start position was the same as that used during the instruction trials, both normal and fornix-lesioned rats had short escape latencies (Fig. 9.1F). On probe trials, normal rats swam directly to the platform, regardless of the starting position, but lesioned rats swam in various directions and, consequently, had abnormally long average escape latencies, sometimes never locating the platform.

These findings support our view that the hippocampal system is involved in learning all types of materials, that this system participates in the creation and updating of an organization of memories based on critical relations among items in memory, and that this form of representation supports the flexible use of memories in novel situations. Viewing hippocampal system function in terms of relational representation and representational flexibility serves to bridge the gap between the phenomenologies of animal and human amnesia, suggesting a common set of fundamental characteristics distinguishing the representational demands of hippocampal-dependent and hippocampal-independent memory processing. This view can account for the pattern of behavioral impairments and spared performance across a wide variety of behavioral paradigms used in the assessment of memory in humans and animals. The qualities of declarative memory representation are emphasized in nearly all conventional recall and recognition tasks used with human subjects, and in most place-learning, contextual, conditional, and working-memory tasks used with rats. Consistent with our interpretation, human amnesics and animals with hippocampal system damage are severely impaired on these tasks. By contrast, the absence of a demand for declarative processing characterizes most priming and skill-learning tasks used on human subjects and most simple conditioning and discrimination tasks used in animal experiments, and, indeed, human amnesics and animals with hippocampal system damage acquire these tasks normally (see Cohen & Eichenbaum, 1993; Eichenbaum, 1994 for a review of these data).

WHAT ASPECTS OF EXPERIENCE ARE ENCODED BY HIPPOCAMPAL NEURONS?

If we are to understand the mechanisms by which a relational representation is mediated by the hippocampus, we must discover the coding schemes employed by the hippocampus in processing relational information. Earlier findings from recordings of hippocampal neuronal activity in behaving rats indicated that hippocampal neurons could be characterized as *place cells*, neurons whose activity reflect the position of an animal in its environment (O'Keefe, 1976). These data were interpreted as strongly supporting the cognitive mapping view of hippocampal function, but are also consistent with our theory of relational representation. Thus, the place of an animal in its environment is defined by the spatial relations among environmental cues and between them and the animal. However, to support our view that hippocampal representation extends to relations among all types of cues, we must demonstrate that place cells are just one example of relational coding.

In our own studies, we have monitored the activity of isolated hippocampal neurons in animals performing nonspatial and spatial learning and memory tasks that employ representational demands similar to those of the neuropsychological studies discussed earlier. In this work, we have observed that hippocampal cellular activity encodes both spatial and nonspatial relations among cues, as well as actions made with regard to those cues. Thus, for example, we found that the activity of hippocampal neurons was associated with an animal's position in an open field as it performed a spatial working-memory task based on Olton's (see Olton, Becker, & Handleman, 1979) radial maze paradigm. However, the activity of these cells is also related to aspects of spatial movement, such as the animal's speed, direction, and turning angle, indicating that multiple spatial variables associated with intentional actions may be encoded along with spatial position (Eichenbaum & Cohen, 1988; Eichenbaum & Otto, 1993; Wiener, Paul, & Eichenbaum, 1989).

More recently, we have been able to provide evidence that the predominance of spatial correlates of hippocampal neuronal activity is at least partly due to the exaggeration of the salience and significance of distal spatial cues, as opposed to nonspatial cues, in the experimental environment. For example, O'Keefe and Speakman (1987) reported that distal spatial cues predominated in governing hippocampal cell activity as rats searched for food on an elevated-plus maze.

However, in this task, local cues that might have distinguished the maze arms were minimized and made irrelevant to the task solution. Conversely, prominent distal cues were present, and their spatial configuration consistently predicted the reward. In a recent experiment, we reversed this disparity, minimizing and making irrelevant the distal spatial cues surrounding an elevated-plus maze, and providing local visual-tactile cues that identified each maze arm (Young, Fox, & Eichenbaum, 1994). Following the paradigm for nonspatial working memory established by Olton and Feustle (1981), rats were required to visit each arm, as defined by its local cues, only once within a session. The topological arrange-

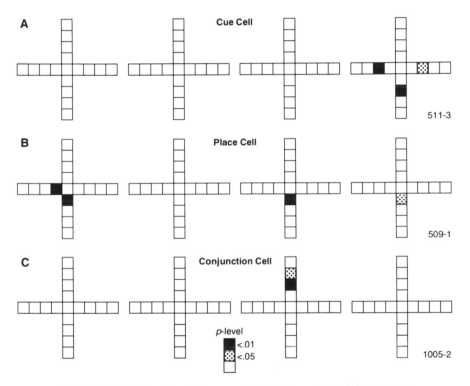

FIG. 9.2. Significant local increases in the firing rate of (A) a cue cell, (B) a place cell, and (C) a conjunction cell. Each of the three panels shows four schematic diagrams of the radial maze viewed from overhead. The individual diagrams represent a particular cue in each of the north, south, east, and west locations. The relative position of an animal on an arm was also considered in the analysis by subdividing each arm into four regions. Means were calculated for each of the four relative positions associated with each Cue and Location combination. A single-ended confidence interval was then constructed around the overall mean, with firing rates greater than 1.65 SD above the mean (p < .05) regarded as significant.

ment of the arms was varied pseudorandomly after each arm entry within a session, so that spatial location did not predict the loci of rewards. It is important to note that these procedures did not preclude the rat's ability to establish a spatial framework for the environment; uncontrolled and consistently located auditory stimuli, as well as the entry point into the apparatus, likely provided sufficient spatial cues. Our procedures simply reduced the usual overemphasis on distal spatial cues while providing salient nonspatial cues.

Many hippocampal cells increased their activity associated with both the spatial and nonspatial cues during performance of this task. The activity of some cells was associated with a local visual-tactile cue; these neurons were classified as *cue cells* in that they fired when the rat was on the same arm as defined by its local cues, independent of its spatial location (Fig. 9.2A). A similar proportion of cells were classified as *place cells*, in that they fired when the rat was in a particular location in the maze, irrespective of the local cue assignments (Fig. 9.2B). Thus, under maze performance conditions where distal spatial cues were not emphasized, there were about as many cue cells as place cells. However, the activity of every cell was governed (in some measure) by both spatial and nonspatial cues. Even the most selective place cells did not display significant increases in firing in the appropriate location if one particular cue was present. Similarly, the firing of the most well-defined cue cells did not increase significantly in response to the appropriate cue in some location. In some cases, the cell activity was associated only with very particular location-and-cue combinations (Fig. 9.2C), or with multiple combinations of locations, cues, and direction of motion.

Further evidence showing that hippocampal function extends beyond the representation of spatial relations comes from recordings we have made of hippocampal cells in rats performing in the same odor discrimination tasks employed in our lesion experiments (Eichenbaum, Kuperstein, Fagan, & Nagode, 1986; Otto & Eichenbaum, 1992; Wiener et al., 1989). In each task, we found cells that fired in a time-locked way to nearly every significant behavioral event. For example, some cells fired as the animal approached the area where the odor stimuli were sampled, others fired selectively during odor sampling or response generation, and still others fired during the retrieval of rewards. In each task, we focused our analyses on a subset of cells that fired selectively when the rat sampled the odors and prepared to make the behavioral response. Some of these cells were activated throughout the stimulus sampling period on all types of trials, beginning to fire with the onset of the cues and ceasing to fire abruptly on response. Other cells were much more selective: The increases in their firing depended on the conjunction or combination of multiple odors presented in either different spatial configurations or different temporal sequences. During simultaneous discriminations, these cells fired maximally only while the rat sampled a specific left–right configuration of a particular pair of odors. During successive odor discriminations, these cells fired maximally only when the rat sampled the rewarded odor immediately after having sampled the nonrewarded odor on the previous trial; that is, the firing of these cells was dependent on the sequence of odor presentations.

Combing the data across experimental paradigms, hippocampal neuronal activity reflects conjunctions of, or relations between, spatial and nonspatial information, as well as temporal relations among cues without any spatial component. More recent data indicate that, at least for some hippocampal cells, the particular cues involved in a relationship may not be critical. We have developed a recognition memory task in which subjects are presented with a sequence of odor stimuli, much as in successive discrimination learning, but are required to re-

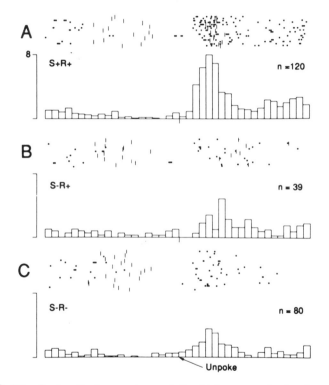

FIG. 9.3.   Raster displays and cumulative histograms of spikes from a single hippocampal neuron active during stimulus sampling during performance of the odor-guided delayed nonmatch to sample task. This cell fired sharply at the time when the discriminative response was initiated on correct nonmatch trials (A), and fired much less when the same behavioral response occurred erroneously (B) and when no response was made on correct match trials (C). Vertical tic marks to the left of the synch point indicate the time of trial initiation; tic marks to the right of the synch point indicate the occurrence of a water port response (from Otto & Eichenbaum, 1992).

spond differentially, depending on whether the present cue is the same as the preceding odor (matches), or is different from its predecessor (nonmatches) (Otto & Eichenbaum, 1992b). A subset of hippocampal cells fire selectively either for all match or for all nonmatch combinations, regardless of the particular cues involved in any specific comparison (Fig. 9.3). Thus, the activity of these cells reflects the *abstract* relationship between the odors, very strongly supporting our view that the hippocampus represents relations among items.

IS THE HIPPOCAMPAL FORMATION A UNITARY ORGAN OR A MEMORY SYSTEM WITH FUNCTIONALLY DISTINCT COMPONENTS?

The hippocampal region involves a number of anatomically distinct structures that are systematically interconnected to provide a flow of information between the hippocampus and cortical and subcortical structures. One possible conceptualization is that the hippocampus is a "unitary" organ whose fundamental function can be disrupted at any stage of processing. Many studies from the literature on animals, as well as some on humans, have supported this notion, indicating that substantial bilateral damage to any component of the system produces equivalent effects on a variety of learning and memory tasks (see Eichenbaum, Otto, & Cohen, 1994; Squire, 1992). However, some recent studies on nonhuman primates and rats suggest that, in fact, some aspects of hippocampal function may be dissociable along anatomical boundaries. In monkeys, removal of the entire hippocampal region produces a severe deficit in recognition memory for single objects (Mishkin, 1978). The deficit is much less severe after selective removal of the hippocampus or transection of the fornix (which disconnects the hippocampus from subcortical areas), but the full-blown deficit is observed following damage to the cortical areas surrounding the hippocampus (Gaffan & Murray, 1992; Zola-Morgan, Squire, Amaral, & Suzuki, 1989). These data indicate that a capacity to hold the representation of an isolated item for an extended period may be accomplished by parahippocampal cortical areas, without requiring hippocampal involvement. More generally, these data support the notion that different components of the hippocampal formation support related but distinct types of processing, rather than acting as a unitary organ. Combined with the results discussed earlier, our work suggests a sequence of stages of memory processing by the hippocampal system. In the first stage, very-short-term storage of individual items might occur outside the hippocampal system, presumably in the cortical areas responsible for specific perceptual and other representations. In the second stage, the parahippocampal cortical areas receive convergent representations from these areas, and they are capable of storing these elaborated individual representations for extended periods. This function may be sufficient to support simple recognition memory. In the third stage, the hippocampus itself might integrate these stored items, processing the relations among them and updating and modifying the relational network (Eichenbaum, Otto, & Cohen, 1994).

Data from our recent experiments are consistent with this account. In tests assessing retention for single odors, we employed our recently developed continuous delayed nonmatch to sample task (Fig. 9.4; Otto & Eichenbaum, 1992a). In this task, a series of odors, selected from a collection of 16, are presented at differing memory delays (intertrial intervals). On each trial, the rat must compare the current stimulus to the immediately preceding one and respond differentially, depending on whether the current odor is a match or a nonmatch with the previous one. Normal rats acquire this task very rapidly and demonstrate over 90% retention at short delays, with a gradual decline in performance at longer delays. Comparing the performance of normal rats with that of rats with fornix and parahippocampal lesions (Fig. 9.4), we found that short-term retention was completely independent of the hippocampal region, and that longer term retention for individual items was dependent on the parahippocampal region, but independent of the hippocampus proper. Fornix lesions or selective hippocampal lesions had no effect at any delay (Wilner, Otto, Gallagher, & Eichenbaum, 1993). These findings support our notion that parahippocampal areas are capable of storing individual odor representations even in the absence of intact hippocampal function.

Other recent studies involving the development of a paradigm for paired associate learning in rats demonstrated an even more striking dissociation between parahippocampal and hippocampal functions (Bunsey & Eichenbaum, 1993a, 1993b). In the paired associate task, as typically used for humans, the subject studies a list of arbitrarily paired words; this is followed by testing in which the subject is cued with the first item of each pair and must recall the second item. For rats, we designed an analogous task using odor stimuli and a recognition format that required them to distinguish appropriate odor pairings from a large number of foils. Animals were trained to sample a stimulus sequence comprised of two odors separated by a period when airflow was reversed to prevent the stimuli from blending (Fig. 9.5A). When the stimulus sequence was one of four arbitrarily assigned paired associates, approaching a water port was rewarded; no reward was given for water port responses to either of two types of foils (Fig. 9.5B). One type of foil involved odors taken from different paired associates and recombined to form 48 different mispairs. Distinguishing mispairs from paired associates thus required learning the arbitrarily assigned relations among items. The other type of foil involved 64 different nonrelational pairs that included one of four odors that was never associated with reward. Distinguishing nonrelational pairs from paired associates did not require relational processing, because these sequences could be identified by single never-rewarded items.

Both sham-operated rats and rats with parahippocampal area lesions rapidly learned to distinguish nonrelational pairs from paired associates (Fig. 9.5C). In

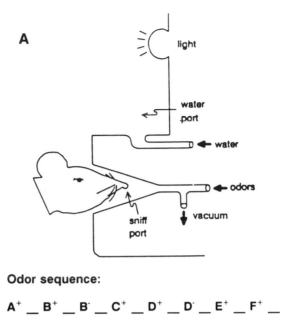

Odor sequence:

$$A^+ \_ B^+ \_ B^- \_ C^+ \_ D^+ \_ D^- \_ E^+ \_ F^+ \_$$

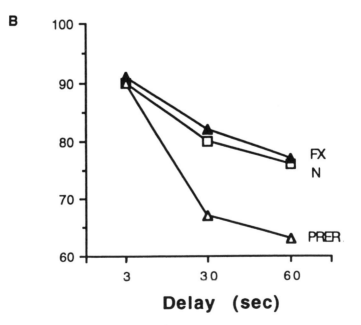

FIGURE 9.4.

addition, normal rats gradually learned to distinguish paired associates from odor mispairs. By contrast, rats with parahippocampal lesions could not learn to distinguish paired associates from mispairs, even when given nearly twice as many training trials as normal rats. Examination of the learning curves also indicated qualitative differences in the pattern of performance on the two types of foils. Both groups rapidly acquired appropriate responses to the nonrelational pairs, and normal rats incrementally learned to distinguish mispairs from paired associates. Rats with parahippocampal lesions, in contrast, remained near-chance levels of performance with respect to mispairs throughout testing. Taken together, these observations indicate a specific deficit in learning appropriate stimulus relationships following parahippocampal lesions.

In a subsequent study, we evaluated the role of the hippocampus itself in paired associate learning using the same task (Fig. 9.5D). In this study, selective neurotoxic lesions of the hippocampus significantly affected paired associate learning. However, in contrast to the severe impairment seen after parahippocampal region lesions, hippocampal lesions resulted in a *facilitation* of paired associate learning. This combination of findings indicates that the parahippocampal region and the hippocampus play important, but different and likely interactive, roles in paired associate learning. One possible explanation is that stimuli involved in a paired associate could be represented in two fundamentally different ways, one subserved by the hippocampus and another mediated by the parahippocampal region. First, the two stimuli could be represented as a "unitized structures" (Schacter, 1985) or "configural cues" (Sutherland & Rudy, 1989). This kind of representation is often made when stimuli are presented simultaneously, such as when elements of a scene are combined to form a single compound cue. Unitized structures can also be formed even when stimuli are presented successively, as in the case of verbal idioms (e.g., *sour grapes*, *small potatoes*; Schacter, 1985). Recent evidence from both human amnesics and studies of animals with hippocampal damage (reviewed in Eichenbaum et al., 1991) indicate that such learning may be accomplished, in some circumstances, even after damage to the hippocampus but that this learning is rigid or *hyperspecific*, in that memories for the elements of such unitized structures cannot be expressed in amnesic humans or in animals with hippocampal damage. We propose that the representation of unitized structures may be mediated by the parahippocampal

---

FIG. 9.4. The continuous delayed nonmatch to sample task. A: Schematic diagram of the apparatus and testing procedure, where letters (A, B, etc.) represent different odors indicating the assignment of rewarding (plus) nonmatch and nonrewarding (minus) match trials; the underscore indicates the memory delay (intertrial interval). B: Performance of normal rats (N) and rats with lesions of the fornix (FX) or parahippocampal region (PRER) at different memory delays (from Otto & Eichenbaum, 1992).

A

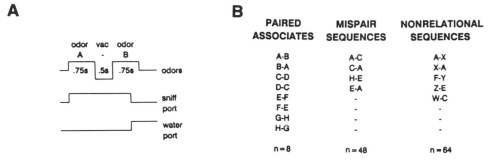

B

PAIRED ASSOCIATES	MISPAIR SEQUENCES	NONRELATIONAL SEQUENCES
A-B	A-C	A-X
B-A	C-A	X-A
C-D	H-E	F-Y
D-C	E-A	Z-E
E-F	-	W-C
F-E	-	-
G-H	-	-
H-G	-	-
n = 8	n = 48	n = 64

C   **D**

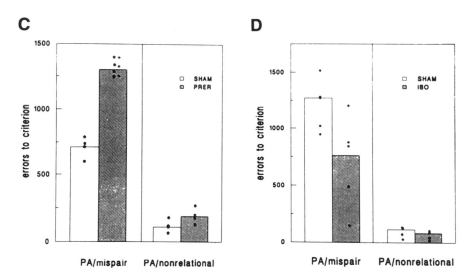

FIG. 9.5. Odor-guided paired associate learning experiments. a: Sequence of odor presentations and timing of behavioral responses on a typical trial. Odor A, period of first item presentation; VAC, period when vacuum flow away from the rat prevents odor sampling; Odor B, period of second item presentation. b: Types of odor sequences; letters (A, B, etc.) designate different odors. The four paired associates were methyl-salicylate and geovertal, dimyrcetol and anethole, o-tertiary butylphenol and Siberian pine needle, D-carvone and Mevantraal. The four odors used only in nonrelational sequences were phenyl ethyl buterate, C-16 Alkene, Eugenol, Cis-3-hexen-1–01. c, d: Mean errors to criterion in the two experiments for sham-operated rats (SHAM), rats with lesions of the perirhinal and entorhinal cortices (PRER), and rats with ibotenic-acid-induced lesions of the hippocampus (IBO) on discriminating paired associates from mispairs and from nonrelational sequences.

region and, in the present case, can mediate the representation of odor pairs as unitized or configural cues. The second form of representation that could support paired associate learning involves an encoding of stimulus elements as perceptually distinct items, in terms of assigned pair-wise relations. Such a representation differs from learning unitized structures, in that relational representation would support the expression of memories for the odor elements and novel applications of knowledge about the relationships between them. The acquisition of such relational representations is proposed to be dependent on the hippocampus.

In normal paired associate learning, we suggest that the hippocampus "wins" a competition between the representational strategies mediated by the hippocampus and the parahippocampal regions, and consequently, the odors are stored separately, according to their pairing relationships. In rats with hippocampal damage, processing by the parahippocampal region is unimpeded and its connections with cortical areas remains intact, supporting performance based on the storage of unitized odor-pair representations. Indeed, our data indicate this form of representation is associated with abnormally rapid acquisition of this particular variant of the task. By contrast, after damage to the parahippocampal region, neither the unitized nor the relational form of representation is intact. The ability of the parahippocampal region to make unitized representations is directly eliminated, and this lesion disconnects the hippocampus from cortical inputs carrying the odor information, also effectively preventing the hippocampus from mediating a relational representation of odor pairings. Ongoing research is aimed at distinguishing these forms of representation through tests for flexible expression of paired associate memories, akin to our approach with discrimination learning described earlier.

CONCLUSIONS

Our study of the selective role of hippocampal function in memory representation, the coding properties of hippocampal neurons, and the distinct roles of different components of the hippocampal system has generated a working hypothesis about what happens during memory processing in this system. These findings indicate that the parahippocampal region may play a special role in the temporary storage of convergent representations for single, specific items of information for extended periods, and may mediate the configuring of multiple stimulus elements under some circumstances. During this time, the hippocampus itself may detect the relevant relations among perceptually distinct items and integrate these bits of new information within the existing relational network of memories. This processing and ultimate storage of relational representations support a capacity for the inferential expression of memories, the hallmark of declarative memory in both humans and animals.

ACKNOWLEDGMENTS

Preparation of this manuscript was supported, in part, by NIA grant AG09973 and ONR grant N0014–91-J-1881.

REFERENCES

Bunsey, M., & Eichenbaum, H. (1993a). Paired associate learning in rats: Critical involvement of the parahippocampal region. *Behavioral Neuroscience*, *107*(5), 1–8.

Bunsey, M., & Eichenbaum, H. (1993b). Selective hippocampal lesions facilitate performance in a paired associate task in rats. *Society for Neuroscience Abstracts*, *19*, 358.

Cave, C. B., & Squire, L. R. (1991). Equivalent impairment of spatial and nonspatial memory following damage to the human hippocampus. *Hippocampus*, *1*, 329–340.

Cohen, N. J. (1984). Preserved learning capacity in amnesia: Evidence for multiple memory systems. In N. Butters & L. R. Squire (Eds.), *The neuropsychology of memory* (pp. 83–103). New York: Guilford.

Cohen, N. J., & Eichenbaum, H. (1993). *Memory, amnesia, and the hippocampal system*. Cambridge, MA: MIT Press.

Cohen, N. J., & Squire, L. R. (1980). Preserved learning and retention of a pattern-analyzing skill in amnesia: Dissociation of knowing how and knowing that. *Science*, *210*, 207–210.

Corkin, S. (1984). Lasting consequences of bilateral medial temporal lobectomy: Clinical course and experimental findings in H.M. *Seminars in Neurology*, *4*, 249–259.

Eichenbaum, H. (1994). The hippocampal system and declarative memory in humans and animals: Experimental analysis and historical origins. In D. L. Schacter & E. Tulving (Eds.), *Memory Systems* (pp. 147–201). Cambridge, MA: MIT Press.

Eichenbaum, H., & Cohen, N. J. (1988). Representation in the hippocampus: What do the neurons code? *Trends in Neuroscience*, *11*, 244–248.

Eichenbaum, H., Cohen, N. G., Otto, T., & Wible, C. (1991). A snapshot without the album. *Brain Research Reviews*, *16*, 209–215.

Eichenbaum, H., Cohen, N. J., Otto, T., & Wible, C. (1992). Memory representation in the hippocampus: Functional domain and functional organization. In L. R. Squire, G. Lynch, N. M. Weinberger, & J. L. McGaugh (Eds.), *Memory: Organization and locus of change* (pp. 163–204). New York: Oxford University Press.

Eichenbaum, H., Fagan, A., & Cohen, N. J. (1986). Normal olfactory discrimination learning set and facilitation of reversal learning after combined and separate lesions of the fornix and amygdala in rats: Implications for preserved learning in amnesia. *Journal of Neuroscience*, *6*, 1876–1884.

Eichenbaum, H., Fagan, A., Mathews, P., & Cohen, N. J. (1988). Hippocampal system dysfunction and odor discrimination learning in rats: Impairment or facilitation depending on representational demands. *Behavioral Neuroscience*, *102*, 331–339.

Eichenbaum, H., Kuperstein, M., Fagan, A., & Nagode, J. (1986). Cue-sampling and goal-approach correlates of hippocampal unit activity in rats performing an odor discrimination task. *Journal of Neuroscience*, *7*, 716–732.

Eichenbaum, H., Mathews, P., & Cohen, N. J. (1989). Further studies of hippocampal representation during odor discrimination learning. *Behavioral Neuroscience*, *103*, 1207–1216

Eichenbaum, H., & Otto, T. (1993). Where perception meets memory: Functional coding in the hippocampus. In T. Ono, L. R. Squire, R. E. Raicle, D. Perrett, & M. Fukuda (Eds.), *Brain mechanisms of perception and memory: From neuron to behavior* (pp. 301–329). New York: Oxford University Press.

Eichenbaum, H., Otto, T., & Cohen, N. J. (1992). The hippocampus—What does it do? *Behavioral and Neural Biology, 57*, 2–36.

Eichenbaum, H., Otto, T., & Cohen, N. J. (1994). Two functional components of the hippocampal memory system. *Behavioral and Brain Sciences, 17*, 449–518.

Eichenbaum, H., Stewart, C., & Morris, R. G. M. (1990). Hippocampal representation in spatial learning. *Journal of Neuroscience, 10*, 331–339.

Gaffan, D., & Murray, E. A. (1992). Monkeys (*Macaca fascicularis*) with rhinal cortex ablations succeed in object discrimination learning despite 24-hr intertrial intervals and fail at matching to sample despite double sample presentations. *Behavioral Neuroscience, 106*, 30–38.

Mishkin, M. (1978). Memory in monkeys severely impaired by combined but not separate removal of the amygdala and hippocampus. *Nature, 273*, 297–298.

Morris, R. G. M. (1984). Developments of a water-maze procedure for studying spatial learning in the rat. *Journal of Neuroscience Methods, 11*, 47–60.

Morris, R. G. M., Garrud, P., Rawlins, J. N. P., & O'Keefe, J. (1982). Place navigation impaired in rats with hippocampal lesions. *Nature, 297*, 681–683.

O'Keefe, J. A. (1976). Place units in the hippocampus of the freely moving rat. *Experimental Neurology, 51*, 78–109.

O'Keefe, J., & Nadel, L. (1978). *The hippocampus as a cognitive map.* Oxford: Oxford University Press.

O'Keefe, J., & Speakman, A. (1987). Single unit activity in the rat hippocampus during a spatial memory task. *Experimental Brain Research, 68*, 1–27.

Olton, D. S., Becker, J. T., & Handleman, G. E. (1979). Hippocampus, space, and memory. *Brain and Behavioral Sciences, 2*, 313 365.

Olton, D. S., & Feustle, W. A. (1981). Hippocampal function required for nonspatial working memory. *Experimental Brain Research, 41*, 380–389.

Otto, T., & Eichenbaum, H. (1992a). Complementary roles of orbital prefrontal cortex and the perirhinal-entorhinal cortices in an odor-guided delayed non-matching to sample task. *Behavioral Neuroscience, 106*, 763–776.

Otto, T., & Eichenbaum, H. (1992b). Neuronal activity in the hippocampus during delayed non-match to sample performance in rats: Evidence for hippocampal processing in recognition memory. *Hippocampus, 2*, 323–334.

Otto, T., Schottler, F., Staubli, U., Eichenbaum, H., & Lynch, G. (1991). Hippocampus and olfactory discrimination learning: Effects of entorhinal cortex lesions on olfactory learning and memory in a successive-cue, go/no-go task. *Behavioral Neuroscience, 105*, 111–119.

Scoville, W. B., & Milner, B. (1957). Loss of recent memory after bilateral hippocampal lesions. *Journal of Neurology, Neurosurgery, & Psychiatry, 20*, 11–21.

Schacter, D. L. (1985). Multiple forms of memory in humans and animals. In N. M. Weinberger, J. L. McGaugh, & G. Lynch (Eds.), *Memory systems of the brain* (pp. 351–380). New York: Guilford Press.

Schacter, D. L. (1987). Implicit memory: History and current status. *Journal of Experimental Psychology: Learning, Memory, & Cognition, 13*, 510–518.

Squire, L. R. (1987). *Memory and brain.* New York: Oxford University Press.

Squire, L. R. (1992). Memory and the hippocampus: A synthesis of findings with rats, monkeys, and humans. *Psychological Reviews, 99*, 195–231.

Staubli, U., Ivy, G., & Lynch, G. (1984). Hippocampal denervation causes rapid forgetting of olfactory information in rats. *Proceedings of the National Academy of Sciences (USA), 81*, 5885–5887.

Sutherland R. J., & Rudy J. W. (1989). Configural association theory: The role of the hippocampal formation in learning, memory, and amnesia. *Psychobiology, 17*, 129–144.

Wiener, S. I., Paul, C. A., & Eichenbaum, H. (1989). Spatial and behavioral correlates of hippocampal neuronal activity. *Journal of Neuroscience, 9*, 2737–2763.

Wilner, J., Otto, T., Gallagher, M., & Eichenbaum, H. (1993). Hippocampal lesions that impair place learning facilitate delayed non-matching performance in rats. *Society for Neuroscience Abstracts*, *19*, 358.

Young, B. J., Fox, G. D., & Eichenbaum, H. (1994). Correlates of hippocampal complex-spike cell activity in rats performing a nonspatial radial maze task. *Journal of Neuroscience*, *14*, 6553–6563.

Zola-Morgan, S., Squire, L. R., Amaral, D. G., & Suzuki, W. A. (1989). Lesions of perirhinal and parahippocampal cortex that spare the amygdala and hippocampal formation produce severe memory impairment. *Journal of Neuroscience*, *9*, 4355–4370.

10 Frontal Cortex and the Cognitive Support of Behavior

Joaquin M. Fuster
University of California, Los Angeles

An important recent development is the reemergence of the notion of the cortex of the frontal lobe as a cerebral structure devoted, in its totality, to the representation and organization of action, in the broadest sense, including skeletal movement, ocular movement, spoken language, and even certain forms of internal action, such as logical reasoning. Thus, the frontal cortex may be called the *motor* cortex, in the widest sense of the word.

In this chapter, I argue that the reason the frontal lobe is so important for organizing behavior is that it is indispensable for what Lashley (1951) called the *syntax of action*, the logical and goal-directed binding of perceptual and motor acts in the temporal domain. I argue, further, that the syntax of action depends on the interplay of two basic cognitive functions of the dorsolateral frontal cortex that are essential for the bridging of cross-temporal contingencies: a temporally retrospective function, *active short-term memory* (called by some, *working memory*), and a temporally prospective function, *preparatory set*

I begin with some of the neuropsychological evidence that, in the primate, the dorsolateral prefrontal cortex is necessary for the mediation of cross-temporal contingencies. Since the pioneering work of Jacobsen (1935), it has been known that monkeys with ablations of Brodmann areas 9 and 46 (area FD of von Bonin & Bailey, 1947) are incapable of properly performing delay tasks. This category includes delayed response, delayed alternation, and delayed matching, all of which require the temporary retention of a discrete item of sensory information for the performance of an equally discrete behavioral act. All of these tasks that suffer after prefrontal ablation share the fundamental principle of *cross-temporal contingency*. Twin logical propositions define this principle: *"If now this, then later that action; if earlier that, then now this action"*. The first proposition implies the activation of motor memory and preparatory set; the second, the activation and retention of perceptual memory. Sequential behavior is like a domino of motor acts extended in the time domain, each piece touching the past and the future through successive bridges of cross-temporal contingency.

It is my contention that the prefrontal cortex supports the two temporally symmetrical functions of active perceptual memory and preparatory motor set that allow the mediation of cross-temporal contingencies. What follows, briefly described, is some empirical evidence for that contention from the monkey, as well as the human. First, I demonstrate that the deficit in prefrontal animals in delay tasks is not restricted, as it has been commonly and mistakenly assumed, to the retention of spatially defined cues, as in delayed response or delayed alteration. My colleagues and I have been able to show this by inducing reversible lesions of the dorsolateral prefrontal cortex in a variety of delay tasks, spatial and nonspatial.

The cryogenic depression of dorsolateral prefrontal cortex, for example, leads to a deficit in a nonspatial visual task, such as delayed matching to sample with colors (Bauer & Fuster, 1976; see Fig. 10.1). In the same apparatus, the frontally cooled monkey shows a deficit of about the same magnitude in performance of the classical (spatial) delayed response task. In a recent study (Sierra-Paredes & Fuster, 1993), we have been able to observe a comparable deficit in an auditory memory task. In yet another study (Shindy, Posley, & Fuster, 1994), frontal cooling impaired tactile tasks that required not only cross-temporal, but cross-modal, mediation of contingencies (Figs. 10.2, 10.3).

How much is the prefrontal cortex involved in active perceptual memory and how much is it involved in active motor memory and preparatory set? To answer these questions, we must turn to functional data from unit studies and neuroimaging. I do not dwell here on the evidence of perceptual memory cells in dorsolateral prefrontal cortex. That evidence has been available since the 1970s (Fuster, 1973), and has been confirmed and expanded in several laboratories (Funahashi, Bruce, & Goldman-Rakic, 1989; Fuster, Bauer, & Jervey, 1982; Quintana, Yajeya, & Fuster, 1988). I simply remind you that a series of concomitant studies of inferotemporal (Fuster, 1990; Fuster et al., 1982) and parietal (Koch & Fuster, 1989) cortex indicate that those prefrontal cells are part of extensive memory networks that, depending on the modality of the memorandum, encroach on one or another portion of the posterior (i.e., post-Rolandic, postcentral) cortex.

Instead, my emphasis here is on the other factor of the cross-temporal equation: the temporally prospective function of *active motor memory*. The first indications that there were motor-coupled cells alongside perceptual memory cells came in Fuster et al. (1982), as we systematically explored the prefrontal cortex with microelectrodes in monkeys performing delay tasks. Figure 10.4 shows the average frequency histograms from a series of cells during delayed matching to sample with colors. Activity during the delay, (i.e., the memoriza-

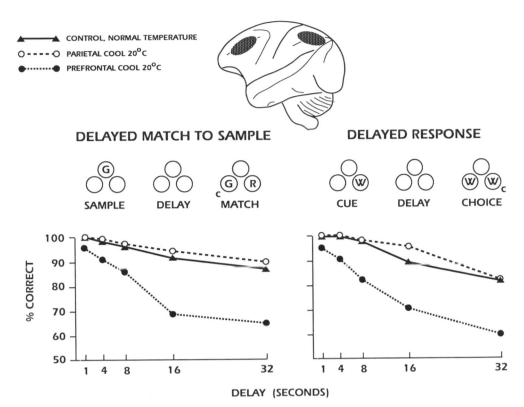

FIG. 10.1.   Effects of cooling dorsolateral and posterior parietal cortex
on performance of a nonspatial delay task (delayed matching to sample, left graphs) and a spatial delay task (delayed response, right
graphs). Both tasks, performed on a triangle of stimulus–response
buttons, require the retention of a visual cue through a period of delay
of variable length. In the first task, the cue is a color, red (R) or green
(G); in the second task, it is the position of a white (W) light. (Sample
and match colors in delayed matching change at random, as does the
cue in delayed response.) Note the drop in correct performance, especially on long delays, during prefrontal cooling.

tion period) is indicated by the black histogram. During that period, some cells
show descending discharge, whereas others show the opposite, that is, accelerating discharge as the response grows near. The former would be the temporally
backward-looking memory cells, whereas the latter would be the temporally
forward-looking motor-coupled cells. Both types can be observed along prac-
tically any given electrode tract.

   More convincing evidence of motor-coupled cells has been obtained by use of
a delay task with a double contingency between temporally separate color cues
(Quintana & Fuster, 1992). The essential feature of the task is that, because of

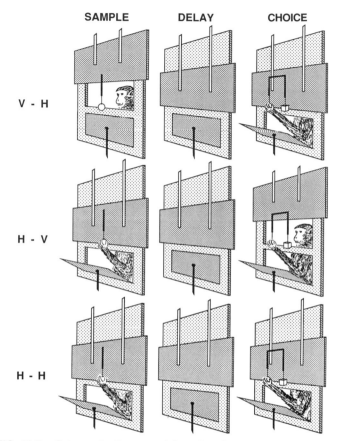

FIG. 10.2. Schematic diagram of three haptic memory tasks. Task on top requires mediation of a visual–haptic (V–H) contingency; task in the middle is haptic–visual (H–V); task on the bottom is unimodal, requiring exclusively haptic mediation (H–H).

that double contingency, the color of the cue at the start of each trial allows the animal to predict, with more or less certainty, the direction of an arm movement at the end of the trial. Yellow and blue predict with 100% certainty the direction, right or left, of that movement, whereas green or red predict it with only 75% probability. The study of prefrontal units under these conditions reveals, of course, the traditional memory cells, whose activity is coupled to the color of the cue and tends to diminish in the course of the 10–12-second delay (Fig. 10.5). In addition, however, one can find, intermingled with them, a substantial number of motor-coupled cells whose activity accelerates in anticipation of the motor response. What's more, the activity of these cells during the delay shows a different degree of acceleration, depending on how well the animal can predict the direction of the prospective response.

In conclusion, both types of cells, sensory-coupled and motorcoupled, can be found in the prefrontal cortex, and, perhaps with different temporal scales, in other parts of the frontal motor substrate (the premotor and primary motor cortices), as well. Cells of the first type reflect the cue during its memorization, and their activity generally goes down in the course of it. Cells of the second type, on the other hand, reflect the consequent and approaching motor response, and their

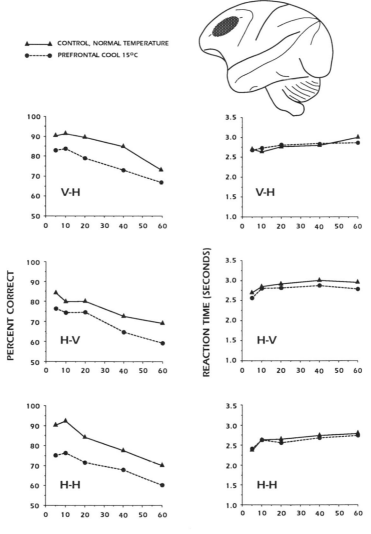

FIG. 10.3.   Effects of prefrontal cooling on the three tasks in Fig. 10.2.

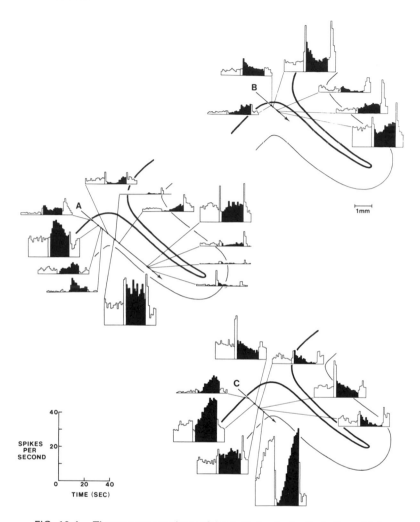

FIG. 10.4.   Three cross-sections of the sulcus principalis, in the middle of dorsolateral prefrontal cortex, showing the frequency histograms of neurons recorded along three separate electrode tracts during performance of delayed matching.

activity increases as that response grows near. It is only reasonable to suppose that these cells not only *represent* movement, but prepare the motor system for it. The networks to which they belong are not only representational, but, as needed to attain a goal, can become operational.

Quite recently, my colleagues and I (Swartz, Halgren, Fuster, Simpkins, Gee, & Mandelkern, 1995) have acquired some indirect evidence for the last assertion in the human. We trained human subjects to perform a delayed matching to sample task, much like those we used with monkeys, but this one used abstract color designs. By imaging with positron emission tomography (PET), we observed that labeled glucose uptake in prefrontal cortex (areas 9, 10, and 46) was significantly greater during performance of the memory task (delayed matching) than during performance of a control task that required the same number of matchings and motor responses, but without the memory requirement. In addition, delayed matching performance was accompanied by significantly increased metabolic activation of premotor and motor areas. It is, indeed, reasonable to conclude that, in anticipation of motor response, those areas are primed by the downflow of excitatory influences from prefrontal areas, although the underlying mechanisms are obscure.

Delay tasks can be construed as sequential behaviors with temporal gaps (i.e., cross-temporal contingencies) that need cognitive bridging. The role of dorsolateral prefrontal cortex, with its two mutually complementary cognitive func-

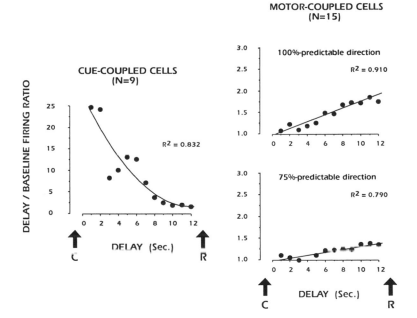

FIG. 10.5.   Activity of sensory-coupled (left) and motor-coupled (right) prefrontal cells during the delay period of a double contingency memory task. Sensory cells show descending discharge during memorization of a color, whereas motor cells accelerate their firing as the motor response approaches. Their accelerating slope of discharge is steeper when the monkey can predict with 100% certainty the side of response—right or left—than when the probability of predicting the cells' "preferred" side is only 75%.

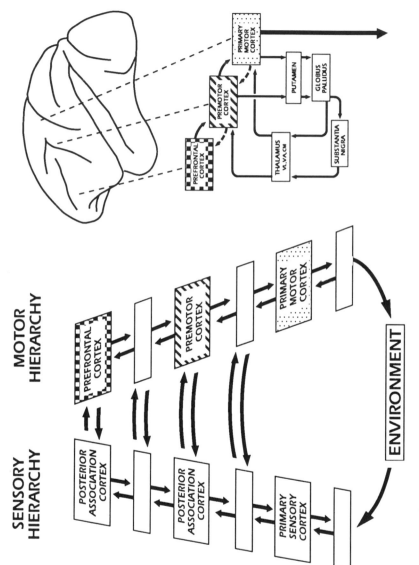

FIG. 10.6. Schematic respresentation of the connectivity through cortical regions in-volved in the perception–action cycle.

tions of perceptual and motor memory, can best be appreciated in the context of the broader role of cortical areas in those behaviors.

All behavioral sequences depend on the smooth operation of the *perception–action cycle* (Fuster, 1989), the circular flow of neural information processing between sensory and motor structures: The sensory processing areas of the postcentral cortex process sensory input from the environment; the result of that processing leads to the organization and execution of motor acts in the frontal cortex; those acts lead to environmental changes, which lead, in turn, to new sensory input; and so on.

Fig. 10.6 shows the cortical substrate of the perception–action cycle. The scheme is based on a solid body of neuroanatomical evidence of connectivity, which need not be reviewed here. All connections in the diagram are reciprocal, as indicated by bidirectional arrows. At all hierarchical levels of the perception–action cycle, extending from the spinal cord to the cortex, there are feed-forward and feed-back shunts between sensory and motor structures. These shunts subserve the automatic acts and reflexes in behavioral sequences. Information is only passed to higher cortical levels if it needs to be used for the bridging of cross-temporal contingencies. There, the prefrontal cortex, in cooperation with the posterior association cortex, mediates those contingencies by supporting both active perceptual memory and active motor memory. Motor priming influences originating by the activation of motor memory flow from the prefrontal cortex, down the frontal motor hierarchy (and through subcortical loops), to the effectors of the motor system. It is the successful bridging of cross-temporal contingencies, thus achieved by the prefrontal cortex, that leads the behavioral sequence to its goal. That bridging of cross-temporal contingencies within the perception–action cycle is the essence of the *syntax of action* and of the role of the prefrontal cortex in it.

To summarize, the neuropsychological evidence is now overwhelming that the dorsolateral prefrontal cortex of the primate plays a critical role in the mediation of cross-temporal contingencies of behavior. Our use of reversible—cryogenic—lesions demonstrates that the mediation of those contingencies, for which that cortex is essential, may require the processing of spatial, as well as nonspatial, information. That information may be in the visual, auditory, or tactile modality. Single-unit research in monkeys performing delay tasks shows that the role of the dorsolateral prefrontal cortex in cross-temporal contingencies, and thus in the temporal organization of behavior, is based on the coordination of two cognitive functions supported by that cortex: a retrospective function of active *perceptual memory* and a prospective function of active *motor memory*. A single-unit study and a PET metabolic study indicate that, in cross-temporal mediation, the latter representational function of motor memory becomes operational and prepares motor systems for the execution of behavioral action. The role of the prefrontal cortex in crosstemporal mediation is essential for the sequencing of goal-directed behavior, and can be best understood as an integral component of the *perception–action cycle*.

The position I have taken in this matter, however, may lead to misinterpretations and unjustified inferences. Therefore, having attempted to make the case for the role of the prefrontal cortex in cross-temporal integration, I must conclude with a few qualifications of my central theme and put it in the context of the work of others, Thompson and Eichenbaum in particular.

It is important to emphasize, first, that the cortex of the frontal lobe or any of its parts, such as the prefrontal cortex, is not the only cognitive support of motor behavior. It may be the highest one, but it is certainly not the only one.

Motor memory is hierarchically organized along the nerve axis in accord with certain phylogenetic and functional gradients and criteria. At the lowest level, phyletic motor memory—the motor memory "of the species"—would be represented in the spinal cord and the brain stem, the substrate for adaptive and defensive reflexes. Plasticity at these levels, from the point of view of the individual organism, is undoubtedly limited. At a somewhat higher level, in the cerebellum, motor memory is apparently more modifiable and subject to conditioning (Thompson, this volume, chapter 8). We now know, thanks to the work of Thompson and his colleagues, that certain cerebellar structures, notably the nucleus interpositus, are much more than downstream coordinators of action. They seem to provide support to elementary forms of acquired motor behavior that, in all likelihood, constitute the essential components of more elaborate behavior.

The basal ganglia also appear to be a depository of motor memory. After the programs of complex behavior, motor sequences, and automatic actions have been established with neocortical participation, they may be relegated to certain regions of the basal ganglia, where they are permanently stored. They may then be retrieved and executed with minimal participation of the frontal neocortex.

The frontal cortex—and its prefrontal region, in particular—seems necessary for the novel structures of behavior that require the kind of temporal integration that I have referred to in this chapter. Of course, it can be argued that the single trial in a delay task is hardly a "novel structure of behavior," and that the trained animal is thoroughly familiar with both the stimuli to be remembered for performing the task and the motor responses that the task demands. This argument ignores the essence of delay tasks. It ignores the fact that these tasks, with the built-in randomness of stimuli and responses from one trial to the next, do, indeed, require the formation of ever-novel structures of behavior. In the monotonous succession of trials with thoroughly familiar stimuli and responses, each trial is a unique structure of behavior. That trial is independent of all previous, as well as all succeeding, trials. *"The game is old but the play is new."* Under the circumstances, the animal must treat each stimulus and each response as *new* if it is to obtain the reward with higher than chance probability. And, inasmuch as the response and the stimulus are novel and must be made congruent with each other across time, the prefrontal cortex is necessary. That is why, no matter how well trained the monkey is, the lesion—or cooling—of the prefrontal cortex will lead the animal to make errors on the task, especially if the delay between stimulus and response is substantial. Substantial delays tax the short-term memory functions of the prefrontal cortex (active perceptual and motor memory). Without the functional integrity of this structure, these functions fail.

Eichenbaum, Young, and Bunsey (this volume, chapter 9) propose a critical role for the hippocampus in the representation of relationships within and between percepts or memories. Thus, it could be argued that the cross-temporal relationship is a special case of hippocampal representation, and, consequently, the hippocampus has a representational function identical to that of the prefrontal cortex, perhaps competing with it. This argument has some general validity, but does not fully take into consideration the fundamental difference between the representational functions of the two cortices. For all we know, the hippocampus is involved in the formation *of permanent memory* (relational or otherwise), and the prefrontal cortex is involved in the *temporary* activation *of memory* for behavioral action related to it.

The mnemonic functions of the prefrontal cortex are *ad hoc*, for the occasion, and devoted to novel material in the sense already mentioned, even if that material is part of old and well-established memory. My main point is that the prefrontal cortex exerts its temporally integrative role in behavior by supporting two mutually complementary cognitive functions—active perceptual memory and active motor set—which derive directly from motor memory. Both are part of the integrative role of the prefrontal cortex. That role depends not only on this cortex, but on the coordinated roles of other neocortical regions in the *perception–action* cycle.

In any case, prefrontal function is fundamentally geared to behavioral action. Prefrontal memory, with its perceptual and motor aspects, is memory of the action, in the action, and for the action.

REFERENCES

Bauer, R. H. & Fuster, J. M. (1976). Delayed-matching and delayed-response deficit from cooling dorsolateral prefrontal cortex in monkeys. *Journal of Comparative Physiological Psychology, 90*, 293–302.

Bonin, G. V., & Bailey, P. (1947). *The neocortex of Macaca mulatta*, Urbana: University of Illinois Press.

Funahashi, S., Bruce, C. J., & Goldman-Rakic, P. S. (1989). Mnemonic coding of visual space in the monkey's dorsolateral prefrontal cortex. *Journal of Neurophysiology, 61*, 331–349.

Fuster, J. M. (1973). Unit activity in prefrontal cortex during delayed-response performance: Neuronal correlates of transient memory. *Journal of Neurophysiology, 36*, 61–78.

Fuster, J. M. (1989). *The prefrontal cortex: Anatomy, physiology, and neuropsychology of the frontal lobe*. New York: Raven.

Fuster, J. M. (1990). Inferotemporal units in selective visual attention and short-term memory. *Journal of Neurophysiology, 64*, 681–697.

Fuster, J. M., Bauer, R. H., & Jervey, J. P. (1982). Cellular discharge in the dorsolateral prefrontal cortex of the monkey in cognitive tasks. *Experimental Neurology, 77*, 679–694.

Jacobsen, C. F. (1935). Functions of the frontal association area in primates. *Archives of Neurology and Psychiatry, 33,* 558–569.

Koch, K. W., & Fuster, J. M. (1989). Unit activity in monkey parietal cortex related to haptic perception and temporary memory. *Experimental Brain Research, 76,* 292–306.

Lashley, K. S. (1951). The problem of serial order in behavior. In L. A. Jeffress (Ed.), *Cerebral mechanisms in behavior,* (pp. 112–146). New York: Wiley.

Quintana, J., & Fuster, J. M. (1992). Mnemonic and predictive functions of cortical neurons in a memory task. *NeuroReport, 3,* 721–724.

Quintana, J., Yajeya, J., & Fuster, J. M. (1988). Prefrontal representation of stimulus attributes during delay tasks: I. Unit activity in cross-temporal integration of sensory and sensory-motor information. *Brain Research, 474,* 211–221.

Shindy, W. W., Posley, K. A., & Fuster, J. M. (1994). Reversible deficit in haptic delay tasks from cooling prefrontal cortex. *Cerebral Cortex, 4,* 443–450.

Sierra-Paredes, G., & Fuster, J. M. (1993). Auditory-visual association task impaired by cooling prefrontal cortex. *Society for Neuroscience Abstracts, 19,* 801.

Swartz, B. E., Halgren, E., Fuster, J. M., Simpkins, F., Gee, M., & Mandelkern, M. (1995). Cortical metabolic activation in humans during a visual memory task. *Cerebral Cortex, 5,* 205–214.

11 Correlates of Taste and Taste-Aversion Learning in the Rodent Brain

Yadin Dudai
Kobi Rosenblum
Noam Meiri
Ruth Miskin
Rina Schul
Weizmann Institute of Science

Intriguing data have been accumulating in recent years on the molecular and cellular mechanisms that subserve learning and memory (reviewed in Dudai, 1989; Kandel & Hawkins, 1992). A substantial fraction of these data stems from studies of relatively simple organisms (e.g., *Aplysia*; Schacher et al., 1990), or of long-term potentiation (LTP), a cellular phenomenon considered to model memory (Bliss & Collingridge, 1993). However, these experimental systems cannot substitute for direct analysis of natural types of learning and memory in the mammalian brain.

In our laboratory, we are investigating taste and odor learning in rodents and the involvement of the cortex in such learning. The advantages of the rodent brain for the molecular and cellular analysis of brain function need not be reiterated here. It is worth noting, however, that recent developments in molecular biology make it possible to add neurogenetics, though still to a rather limited extent, to the arsenal of tools available for the analysis of mouse brain and behavior. Until now, this powerful experimental tool was restricted to the analysis of *Drosophila* only (Dudai, 1989).

The choice of learning mediated by the chemical senses is guided by the fact that the rodent brain has evolved to acquire, store, and retrieve chemical information. It is probably because of that that taste and odor learning can occur very fast and leave robust memory traces. Furthermore, conditioned taste aversion (CTA) and taste-potentiated odor aversion (TPOA) can tolerate long delays between the exposure to a novel taste or odor and the association of that stimulus with poisoning (reviewed in Bures, Buresova, & Krivanek, 1988; Garcia, 1989). Paradigms of taste and odor learning, hence, provide the opportunity to analyze mechanisms of acquisition and consolidation of memory of a sensory item in well-defined time windows and in the absence of salient exogenous reinforcers. In addition, such paradigms permit analysis of the association of the memory of that sensory item with a reinforcer.

We summarize here some of our recent findings, concentrating on the analysis of taste learning and its molecular correlates in the insular cortex (IC), which contains the central cortical taste area (Braun, 1990). In brief, our data demonstrate that (a) the IC is instrumental in the formation of the memory of a novel taste; (b) modulation of protein tyrosine phosphorylation takes place in the IC following exposure to a novel taste; (c) protein synthesis in the IC is required for the formation of taste memory; and (d) overexpression of the extracellular protease urokinase-type plasminogen activator (PA) in the brain markedly diminishes CTA learning.

THE BEHAVIORAL PARADIGMS: CONDITIONED AVERSION AND INCIDENTAL LEARNING

In CTA and TPOA, individuals learn to associate taste or odor with poisoning. This leads to subsequent aversion to that taste or odor. In nature, the poisoning is due to toxins in the foodstuff; in the laboratory, ip injection of LiCl is usually used to elicit transient malaise. Effective CTA and TPOA can be obtained even if the injection is administered several hours after the novel taste or odor. But even a separation in time of several hours may not suffice to permit a clear distinction between the time window, and hence the mechanisms, of acquisition of memory of the novel taste or odor, and the association of the same taste or odor with the poisoning. This is because the temporal resolution of current transient lesion techniques may be too low. For example, in experiments in which the protein synthesis inhibitor, anisomycin, is used to block protein synthesis in a certain brain region (see further on), the effect of the drug lasts several hours, overlapping both the acquisition and the association periods of CTA.

We have, therefore, taken advantage of *latent inhibition*, the well-known behavioral observation that preexposure to a sensory stimulus attenuates the associability of that same stimulus in subsequent learning (Lubow, 1989). The idea was to briefly preexpose the rat to a novel taste or odor, and to use that same taste or odor in CTA or TPOA training a few days later. The assumption was that the conditioned aversion would be attenuated by the preexposure. This, indeed, happened. We found that a single preexposure to a taste markedly attenuated subsequent CTA to that same taste (Fig. 11.1), and that preexposure to an odor markedly attenuated aversion to that odor in subsequent TPOA training using that odor (Fig. 11.2). The aversion paradigms in these experiments served as measures of the memory of the preexposed stimulus; that is, these paradigms became detectors of the incidental learning of the preexposed stimuli. All of our subsequent molecular work was performed using either aversion paradigms (CTA and TPOA), incidental learning paradigms (latent inhibition combined with CTA and TPOA), or a combination of the paradigms.

FIG. 11.1. Latent inhibition of CTA. Rats preexposed once to 0.1% saccharin (Sacch) two days before CTA training, display much diminished CTA to that taste as compared to rats who receive water on the preexposure day. Test was conducted for 2 consecutive days. CTA can therefore be used as a detector for incidental learning of a taste. (For methods, see Rosenblum et al., 1993.)

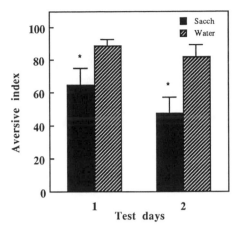

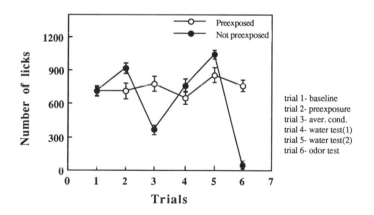

FIG. 11.2. Latent inhibition of TPOA. Water consumption of rats licking from a liquid spout was measured on Day 1 (baseline). On Day 2, the preexposed group was presented with an airstream of diluted isopropyl acetate while drinking. A small neophobic effect toward the odor was evident from the suppression of water consumption in the preexposed group during the preexposure trial. On Day 3, both groups of rats were subjected to TPOA using saccharin and isopropyl acetate. There was a significant attenuation of neophobia to the odor–taste compound in the preexposed group. On Day 6, both groups were presented with isopropyl acetate while sampling the water spout. The rats preexposed to the odor were not aversive, whereas the nonpreexposed group displayed strong aversion to the odor (from Schul, unpublished data).

MODULATION OF PROTEIN TYROSINE
PHOSPHORYLATION IN THE IC BY CTA

Protein tyrosine phosphorylation is modulated in the course of action of the signal transduction pathways that regulate cellular differentiation and growth (reviewed in Schlessinger & Ullrich, 1992). Recently it became apparent that tyrosine phosphorylation also plays a key function in neuronal activity and plasticity. For example, inhibitors of protein tyrosine kinase (PTK) block ionic channel modulation induced by neuronal contact in the leech (Catarsi & Drapeau, 1993), and LTP in hippocampal CA1 in the guinea pig (O'Dell, Kandel, & Grant, 1991). Furthermore, a knockout of the *fyn* PTK gene impairs LTP and spatial learning, as well as hippocampal morphology, in transgenic mice (Grant et al., 1992).

We set out to search for modulation by taste learning and CTA training of signal transduction systems which are expected to trigger learning-induced neuronal remodeling in the IC. Because protein tyrosine phosphorylation cascades are prime candidates for such a trigger, we have analyzed protein tyrosine phosphorylation in the rat IC following CTA training as well as following separate exposure to the conditioned stimulus (CS; the novel taste) and the unconditioned stimulus (US; (LiCl injection) used in CTA training. The methodology involved behavioral manipulation, followed by excision of the appropriate brain area and immunoblotting of the homogenate with specific antiphosphotyrosine (αPY) antibodies. We found that CTA led to a marked increase in the phosphorylation level of a selected set of PTK substrates (dubbed here pXgc) in a MW range of 97–180 kD, in the IC (Fig. 11.3), but not in other brain areas. Exposure to a novel taste increased the phsophorylation of these proteins, but to a smaller degree. The major protein of molecular mass of 180kD modulated this way is a membrane-associated glycoprotein enriched in synaptosomes. It remained modulated for at least 1 hour following training. To the best of our knowledge, this is the first demonstration of the modulation of protein tyrosine phosphorylation in

FIG. 11.3. Proteins of MW— 180, 115, and 97 kD—are modulated in CTA training. The figure depicts the level of protein tyrosine phosphorylation (PY), as quantified by antiphosphotyrosine antibodies that have reacted with a blot of IC proteins, following CTA training, administration of saccharin, or no oral input. No effect on protein tyrosine phosphorylation was detected in other cortices. (from Rosenblum et al., 1995).

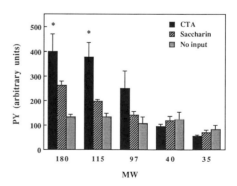

the brain of a behaving animal following sensory experience.

Because CTA training involves LiCl administration, and the latter is expected to have marked effects on metabolism and behavior, it is pertinent to inquire whether LiCl alone is capable of inducing alteration in pXgc. Our data showed that LiCl alone was incapable of bringing about the enhancing effect observed after CTA training. Furthermore, neither exposure to a novel odor nor transfer to a new cage, modulated the phosphorylation of pXgc in the IC.

The findings concerning protein tyrosine phosphorylation in the IC indicate that the activity of this cortex is specifically correlated with training in taste and CTA learning paradigms. These findings do not prove that the IC is *necessary* for taste and CTA learning. This we have established in another set of experiments, involving the transient block of protein synthesis in the IC.

PROTEIN SYNTHESIS IS REQUIRED FOR FORMATION OF TASTE MEMORY

Protein tyrosine phosphorylation, as a posttranslational modification, can persist for only seconds to possibly minutes or hours. Therefore, even when considered as a mechanism of cellular memory, protein tyrosine phosphorylation *per se* cannot instantiate long-term changes. Indeed, prevalent theories of memory consolidation propose that for memory to become immune to molecular turnover, gene modulation must be involved (see Davis & Squire, 1984; Dudai, 1989; Goelet, Castelucci, Schacher, & Kandel, 1986). We have investigated whether protein synthesis in the IC is involved in the formation of memory of taste or CTA, using anisomycin, a potent and relatively specific protein synthesis inhibitor.

We found that focal microinjection of anisomycin into the rat IC significantly impaired CTA (Fig. 11.4). Anisomycin had no effect on the consumption of saccharin in training or on total fluid consumption during the test days. Anisomycin did not alter the perception or sensation of taste, nor did it affect the retrieval of taste memory: When rats were subjected to CTA using saccharin and

FIG. 11.4. Inhibition of protein synthesis in the IC attenuates CTA. The inhibitor, anisomycin, was microinjected locally into the IC in CTA training. Memory of CTA was measured for 3 consecutive days, starting at Day 3 after training. Black bars, anisomycin-injected rats; striped bars, saline-injected rats (from Rosenblum et al., 1993).

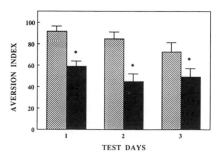

a few days later were injected with anisomycin before presentation with saccharin in the test, they displayed normal aversion, indicating that saccharin was normally perceived and its memory could be retrieved to evoke an appropriate behavioral response. No effect on CTA was seen when anisomycin was injected into an adjacent cortex.

Experiments in which anisomycin was administered at various time points before and after consumption of saccharin indicated that the protein synthesis inhibitor was most effective if injected to the gustatory cortex a few minutes before saccharin was sampled. In order to further separate in time the exposure to taste from the negative reinforcer, and thus minimize the potentially confounding effects of the negative reinforcer and better elucidate the role of protein synthesis in the memory of taste *per se*, the latent inhibition paradigm was employed. Prior exposure to a taste indeed attenuated subsequent CTA to the same taste; anisomycin injected during the preexposure period significantly impaired this effect. We can thus conclude that protein synthesis in the gustatory cortex is necessary for normal acquisition of a new taste.

OVEREXPRESSION IN THE BRAIN OF A GENE ENCODING AN EXTRACELLULAR PROTEASE ATTENUATES CTA

The observation that protein synthesis is necessary for memory consolidation is construed as indicating that modulation of gene expression is required for the formation of long-term memory (Davis & Squire, 1984; Dudai, 1989; Goelet et al., 1986). If this is so, which genes are modulated? Attractive candidates are genes involved in tissue remodeling (Qian, Gilbert, Colicos, Kandel, & Kuhl, 1993), because remodeling of neural circuits is expected to alter the internal representation of information in the circuit, and, hence, modify memory (Dudai, 1992). Plasminogen activators (PAs), serine proteases involved in controlled degradation of extracellular proteins, belong to the category of candidate circuit-remodeling genes. There are two molecular types of PA, the urokinase-type (uPA) and the tissue-type (tPA), encoded by two distinct genes (Saksela & Rifkin, 1988). In our work, we have concentrated on uPA.

The alteration of gene expression with respect to location and dosage by molecular genetics provides an immense potential for investigating the function of PAs in the brain in general, and in brain plasticity in particular. We have used transgenic mice designated αMUPA, carrying the murine uPA cDNA linked to the promoter of the αA-crystallin gene normally expressed exclusively in the ocular lens (Miskin et al., 1990). Unexpectedly, αMUPA mice also express active transgenic uPA in several ectopic sites, including the retina, the hippocampal formation, and the neocortex. We have found that αMUPA mice display defective behavior in CTA (Fig. 11.5). In contrast, αMUPA mice did not differ

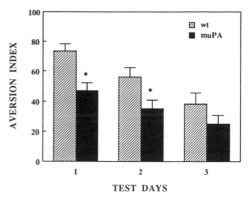

FIG. 11.5. CTA in wild-type and αMUPA transgenic mice (from Meiri et al., 1994).

significantly from normal mice in the sensory and motor capabilities that are apparently required for succeeding at this task. Transgenic mice carrying cDNA encoding the human uPA (that produces the human enzyme in the brain) did not display altered performance on the CTA task.

What is the time window of uPA action? We found that the learning disadvantage of the αMUPA mice fades with extensive training, and, if they are trained repeatedly, they come to remember the association of taste with malaise. This suggests that uPA plays a role in acquisition or consolidation, but not in long-term retention. Two explanations may be offered for the effect of overtraining on the uPA effect. The first is that the overexpression of uPA decreases the signal-to-noise ratio of the information in the learning system, and overtraining increases the signal. The second is that overtraining recruits additional or alternative pathways that are not affected by the aberration in uPA activity.

All in all, the results are in line with the assumption that uPA is involved in brain mechanisms recruited in behavioral plasticity. More specifically, the enzyme appears to play a role in mechanisms that are recruited during the initial stages of the formation of a memory trace.

THE MOLECULAR EVENTS AND THE LOCUS OF CHANGE

Our data support the following assertions:

1. The IC is involved in the learning of information about a novel taste and in the acquisition of CTA. A similar conclusion concerning the role of the IC in the acquisition of CTA has been reached by other investigators, using lesion techniques (Bermúdez-Rattoni & McGaugh, 1991; Dunn & Everitt, 1988; Gallo, Roldan, & Bures, 1992).

2. Protein tyrosine phosphorylation in the IC is correlated with taste experi-

ence and with CTA training. Although protein tyrosine phosphorylation has already been implicated in neuronal plasticity and learning (Grant et al., 1992; O'Dell et al., 1991), this is, to the best of our knowledge, the first demonstration of alteration of protein tyrosine phosphorylation in the brain *in vivo* following a behavioral experience.

3. Protein synthesis in the IC is critical for the formation of taste and CTA memory. This finding is in line with the prevailing conceptual framework that implicates gene expression in memory consolidation and corroborates the role of the cortex in memory in general (Mishkin & Appenzeller, 1987). It is still an open question, however, whether the IC is critical for long-term retention of the associative CTA trace (see Bermúdez-Rattoni, Ormsby, Escobar, & Hernandez-Echeagaray, this volume, chapter 5). Clearly, some degree of CTA can be formed in cortically lesioned or decorticated rats (Bures et al., 1988; Yamamoto & Fujimoto, 1991). It has been proposed that the IC is necessary for the memory of novel tastes, but in CTA, the association of those tastes with poisoning occurs at subcortical levels (e.g., in the brain-stem; Bures et al., 1988). Indeed, the effect that we see on the formation of CTA memory in our localized protein synthesis inhibition experiments is probably due to the interference with the formation of the normal memory of the taste rather than interference with the association of the taste with the malaise (Rosenblum, Meiri, & Dudai, 1993).

4. Enhanced activity of an extracellular protease, uPA, disrupts learning. It is plausible to suggest that extracellular proteins (e.g., cell-adhesion and basement membrane molecules) participate in the cellular mechanisms that subserve memory formation, and that their enhanced degradation by the overexpressed uPA interferes with the formation of the normal trace. Whether these mechanisms also take place in the IC is not yet established, but it is rewarding to note that uPA in αMUPA mice is overexpressed in selected brain areas that include the IC.

In sum, our data provide clues to some molecular and cellular mechanisms that take place in brain in the process of the acquisition of information about novel tastes and their hedonic valence. It is now pertinent to follow the lead and find out more about the molecules involved and their *in situ* role.

REFERENCES

Bermúdez-Rattoni, F., & McGaugh, J. L. (1991). Insular cortex and amygdala lesions differentially affect acquisition of inhibitory avoidance and conditioned taste aversion. *Brain Research, 549,* 165–170.

Bliss, T. V. P., & Collingridge, G. L. (1993). A synaptic model of memory: Long-term potentiation in the hippocampus. *Nature, 361,* 31–39.

Braun, J. J. (1990). Gustatory cortex: Definition and function. In B. Kolb & R. C. Tees (Eds.), *The cerebral cortex of the rat* (pp. 407–430). Cambridge, MA: MIT Press.

Bures, J., Buresova, O., & Krivanek, J. (1988). *Brain and behavior: Paradigms for research in neural mechanisms.* New York: Wiley.

Catarsi, S., & Drapeau, P. (1993). Tyrosine kinase-dependent selection of transmitter responses induced by neuronal contact. *Nature, 363,* 353–355.

Davis, H. P., & Squire, L. R. (1984). Protein synthesis and memory: A review. *Psychological Bulletin, 96,* 518–559.

Dudai, Y. (1989). *The neurobiology of memory.* Oxford: Oxford University Press.

Dudai, Y. (1992). Why "learning" and "memory" should be redefined (or, an agenda for focused reductionism). *Concepts in Neuroscience, 3,* 99–121.

Dunn, L. T., & Everitt, B. J. (1988). Double dissociation of the effects of amygdala and insular cortex lesions on conditioned taste aversion, passive avoidance, and neophobia in the rat using the excitotoxin ibotenic acid. *Behavioral Neuroscience, 102,* 3–23.

Gallo, M., Roldan, G., & Bures, J. (1992). Differential involvement of gustatory insular cortex and amygdala in the acquisition and retrieval of conditioned taste aversion in rats. *Behavioral Brain Research, 52,* 91–97.

Garcia, J. (1989). Food for Tolman: Cognition and cathexis in concert. In T. Archer & L.-G. N. Isson (Eds.), *Aversion, avoidance and anxiety* (pp. 45–85). Hillsdale, NJ: Lawrence Erlbaum Associates.

Goelet, P., Castellucci, V. F., Schacher, S., & Kandel, E. R. (1986). The long and the short of long-term memory: A molecular framework. *Nature, 322,* 419–422.

Grant, S. G. N., O'Dell, T. J., Karl, K. A., Stein, P., Soriano, P., & Kandel, E. R. (1992). Impaired long-term potentiation, spatial learning, and hippocampal development in *fyn* mutant mice. *Science, 258,* 1903–1910.

Kandel, E. R., & Hawkins, R. D. (1992). The biological basis of learning and individuality. *Scientific American, 267,* 78–86.

Lubow, R. E. (1989). *Latent inhibition and conditioned attention theory.* London: Cambridge University Press.

Meiri, N., Rosenblum, K., Masos, T., Miskin, R., & Dudai, Y. (1994). Transgenic mice overexpressing urokinase-type plasminogen activator are defective in conditioned taste aversion learning. *Proceedings of the National Academy of Sciences* (USA), *91,* 3196–3200.

Mishkin, M., & Appenzeller, T. (1987). The anatomy of memory. *Scientific American, 256*(6), 62–71.

Miskin, R., Axelrod, J. H., Griep, A. E., Belin, D., Vassalli, J.-D., & Westphal, H. (1990). Human and murine urokinase cDNAs linked to the murine αA-crystallin promoter exhibit lens and non-lens expression in transgenic mice. *European Journal of Biochemestry, 190,* 31–38.

O'Dell, T. J., Kandel, E. R., & Grant, S. G. N. (1991). Long-term potentiation in the hippocampus is blocked by tyrosine kinase inhibitors. *Nature, 353,* 558–560.

Qian, Z., Gilbert, M. E., Colicos, M. A., Kandel, E. R., & Kuhl, D. (1993). Differential screening reveals that tissue-plasminogen activator is induced as an immediate early gene during seizure, kindling, and LTP. *Nature, 361,* 453–457.

Rosenblum, K., Meiri, N., Dudai, Y. (1993). Taste memory: The role of protein synthesis in gustatory cortex. *Behavioral Neural Biology, 59,* 49–56.

Rosenblum, K., Schul, R., Meiri, N., Hadari, Y., Zick, Y., & Dudai, Y. (1995). Modulation of protein tyrosine phosphorylation in rat insular cortex following conditioned taste aversion. *Proceedings of the National Academy of Sciences, 92,* 1157–1161.

Saksela, O., & Rifkin, D. B. (1988). Cell-associated plasminogen activation: Regulation and physiological functions. *Annual Review of Cell Biology, 4,* 93–126.

Schacher, S., Glanzman, D., Barzilai, A., Dash, P., Grant, S. G. N., Keller, F., Mayford, M., & Kandel, E. R. (1990). Long-term facilitation in *Aplysia*: Persistent phosphorylation and structural changes. *Cold Spring Harbor Symposium on Quantitative Biology, 55,* 187–202.

Schlessinger, J., & Ullrich, A. (1992). Growth factor signaling by receptor tyrosine kinases. *Neuron, 9,* 383–391.

Yamamoto, T., & Fujimoto, Y. (1991). Brain mechanisms of taste aversion learning in the rat. *Brain Research Bulletin, 27,* 403–406.

12 Time-Dependent Biochemical and Cellular Processes in Memory Formation

Steven P. R. Rose
Open University

There is an interesting way in which thinking about the physiological and cellular mechanics of learning and memory formation has become divorced from knowledge about the processes of remembering and of memory systems derived from neuropsychology. The conventional physiological wisdom, derived from the earlier molluscan studies of Alkon (1987) and Kandel (e.g., Hawkins, Kandel, & Siegelbaum, 1993) and from work on hippocampal long-term potentiation (LTP; McNaughton, 1993), is that memory formation is essentially a Hebbian process, although variants on the Hebb rules, such as homosynaptic and anti-Hebbian pairings, are permitted (Singer, 1990). Hebbian memory depends on the alteration of synaptic weights within, at best, small ensembles of neurons, so as to strengthen or weaken connections, and it is this type of memory that has been extensively modeled by connectionist theoreticians (Churchland & Sejnowski, 1992). The implication of such models for the cellular mechanics of memory formation is that a linear sequence of biochemical events, culminating in altered synaptic morphology, occurs within the neurons of the ensemble, and that these events form the cellular analogues of short- and long-term memory, although at least since the classic paper of McGaugh (1964), it has been recognized that the "phases" of memory may run in parallel, rather than sequentially.

In contrast to these physiological models, however, neuropsychological investigations of human amnesic patients and of "animal models" of amnesia—usually monkeys with specific brain lesions trained on versions of the delayed nonmatching to sample task—have revealed the existence of multiple memory systems (Squire, Knowlton, & Musen, 1993). At least in vertebrates, different forms of memory (e.g., procedural vs. declarative) involve different brain regions. Furthermore, a memory formed in one brain region soon becomes relo-

171

cated and distributed through many other regions in a content-specific and time-dependent manner. The classical example of this process is the role of the hippocampus in processing the transition between short- and long-term memory. Whatever the function of the hippocampus as a cognitive or spatial map (O'Keefe & Nadel, 1978), its role in learning water or radial mazes, or its capacity for LTP, it is abundantly clear that it does not serve as a long-term memory store, in either human or nonhuman subjects.

Most memory modeling at the neurophysiological level has focused on associative learning. (One of the critiques of the early *Aplysia* work was that the cellular mechanisms being studied were apparently those concerned with sensitization or habituation, which are forms of nonassociative learning, and the Kandel group for some years was under considerable pressure from psychologists to prove that the processes it was studying were relevant to associative learning as well.) Yet, despite the extent to which, since Pavlov and the behaviorists, associative learning has been seen as *the* definitive form of learning to which all others must aspire, it is clear that most human declarative memory, and much nonhuman animal learning, cannot be collapsed into simplistic associationism (Squire & Butters, 1992).

To be compatible with the phenomenology of memory, cellular and physiological models should make some effort to accommodate to the neuropsychological evidence. In the rush to present neurophysiological demonstrations of synaptic plasticity (notably LTP) as either models for or, more provocatively, mechanisms of memory, this effort has not often been made (e.g., Bliss & Collingridge, 1993). In what follows, I review recent work from my laboratory that helps decipher the molecular cascade leading to the synaptic reorganization that appears to form the neural representation of a simple form of memory, and tries to place our results in the more holistic context of time- and space-dependent brain systems subserving memory.

Since the late 1970s, my laboratory has been working with a one-trial learning task that makes use of the fact that young chicks peck spontaneously at small bright objects in their field of view. If the object is a colored bead dipped in a bitter-tasting liquid, the chick will subsequently avoid pecking at even a dry bead of that color and shape, although its general pecking activity remains unimpaired. It has thus learned to associate the sight of, and the pecking response to, the bead with the aversive taste of the bitter liquid. This behavior forms the basis of the one-trial passive avoidance learning task introduced by Cherkin (1969), and is an excellent model system in which to study the neural correlates of memory formation. Further, it is not necessary to pair the bead-peck directly with the aversive taste: Chicks will peck spontaneously at a dry colored bead, and if some time later, they are made sick by an intraperitoneal injection of LiCl, they will subsequently avoid beads of similar color (Barber, Gilbert, & Rose, 1989). This latter paradigm is a version of the well-known conditioned taste-(CTA) aversion paradigm; retention for these tasks persists for up to several days.

Learning to suppress pecking at the bitter bead initiates an intracellular cascade of cellular processes that—beginning with presynaptic and postsynaptic membrane transients, and proceeding by way of genomic activation to the lasting structural modification of these membranes—occurs in identified regions of the chick forebrain. I believe that these synaptic modifications form, in some way, the neural representations of the aversive bead-pecking experience and encode the instructions for the changed behaviour (avoidance of pecking a bead of these characteristics) that follows (Rose, 1992).

TRAINING PROCEDURES

In the basic experimental design as employed in our laboratory (Lössner & Rose, 1983), day-old chicks are placed in small pens under controlled illumination and, after a period of equilibration, may be injected intracerebrally with appropriate precursors or potentially amnestic agents, a procedure that is very simple, requiring no anesthesia because of the chick's soft, unossified skull. The birds are then presented with a small chrome bead dipped in either water (W) or the bitter aversant, methylanthranilate (M). After intervals ranging from 30 minutes to 24 hours posttraining, the chicks are tested and their brains are taken for analysis. More than 80% of W birds peck on test, and more than 75% of M birds avoid on test; the percent avoidance among the M birds, by comparison with W birds, is taken as a measure of recall. Variants of this procedure include comparing retention of avoidance in M-trained chicks injected with a putatively amnestic drug or metabolic blocker with M-trained birds injected with saline and the use of weaker aversants such as dilute solutions of methylanthranilate or quinine, for which the avoidance memory fades after a few hours. A further training task replaces the aversive with an appetitive learning procedure, in which the floor of the pen is covered with a perspex sheet, on which small pebbles have been stuck; interspersed with the pebbles are food grains. The chicks learn, after trials lasting 5 minutes or so, to distinguish edible food from inedible, and inaccessible, pebbles. Chicks are scored for "correct" and "incorrect" pecks (Andrew & Rogers, 1972). All training experiments are run "blind," in that two experimenters are involved, so the one testing the chick's behavior is unaware of its previous treatments. All replications involve balanced groups of chicks in any of the several conditions being studied. Statistical comparisons for behavioral groups are by χ^2, and for biochemical procedures by Student's t.

THE LOCI OF CHANGE

To localize the areas of the brain that might be involved in the response to pecking at the bitter bead, we gave chicks a 30-minute pulse of ^{14}C-2-deoxyglucose either just prior to or after training on the bead and compared autoradiograms of forebrains from M and W birds. Two regions, in particular, showed enhanced accumulation of radioactivity in the 30 minutes after training, the intermediate medial hyperstriatum ventrale (IMHV) and the lobus parolfactorius (LPO; Kossut & Rose, 1984). The IMHV, regarded as an avian homologue of striate cortex, is not a primary sensory area, but receives secondary projections from visual, gustatory, and other sensory areas, and on this basis, might be regarded as having an associative function. It is also the region in which cellular changes have been found in chicks trained on an imprinting task (Horn, 1985). The IMHV has also been shown to display, in vitro, properties analogous to mammalian hippocampal LTP (Bradley, Burns, & Webb, 1991). The LPO may be regarded as a basal ganglion homologue, but it also receives some olfactory inputs. There are no monosynaptic connections between the LPO and the IMHV, but a pathway via the archstriatum has been identified (Lowndes & Davies, 1994). Interestingly, and of considerable relevance to our subsequent studies, our 2-DG data gave evidence of lateralization in the IMHV, with the greatest training-associated increases in radioactivity within 30 minutes of the training procedure being seen in the left hemisphere (Rose & Csillag, 1985).

SYNAPTIC TRANSIENTS

Having identified IMHV and LPO as sites of enhanced neural activity in the minutes following training on the passive avoidance task, in subsequent experiments we have followed biochemical, physiological, and morphological changes in these regions. The working hypothesis is compatible with Hebbian models: that memory formation (if not subsequent memory expression) requires synaptic modulation, initially by way of changes in receptor activity, and subsequently by lasting changes in synapse structure or number. The IMHV is a region of the chick brain rich in receptors for N-methyl-D-aspartate (NMDA) glutamate receptors, and three lines of evidence point to these receptors being required for memory formation for the passive avoidance task. The first and most direct is that, within 30 minutes of training the chick, there is a significant up-regulation of NMDA receptors in the left IMHV (Stewart, Bourne, & Steele, 1992), with a reciprocal change in accumulation of inositol phosphates via non-NMDA-activated second messenger pathways (Bullock, Rose, Pearce, & Potter, 1993). The third piece of evidence is that administration of the noncompetitive NMDA antagonist, MK801, or 7-chloro-kynurenine, an antagonist of the glycine-binding site of the NMDA receptor, just before or just after training, results in amnesia for the avoidance task: That is, chicks trained on the bitter bead will subsequently peck at it, rather than avoid it. By contrast, blocking the non-NMDA glutamate receptors by posttraining injections of CNQX or NBQX, although producing transient but marked behavioral deficits, is quite without effect on subsequent retention (Burchuladze & Rose, 1992; Steele & Stewart, 1993).

Activation of the postsynaptic NMDA receptors is supposed to open post-synaptic calcium channels initiating a sequence of postsynaptic molecular processes and result in some retrograde message being transmitted to the presynaptic side, initiating a biochemcial cascade there, too. As is well known, nitric oxide (NO) has become a powerful candidate as such a retrograde messenger. In accordance with this idea, we have shown that blocking NO production with nitroarginine injected up to an hour prior to training results in amnesia for the avoidance, and that this amnesia can be alleviated by injection of excess arginine along with the nitroarginine (Holscher & Rose, 1992). Nitroarginine-induced amnesia sets in within 30 minutes of training and persists indefinitely thereafter. By contrast, although metabolic blockers of production of another putative retrograde messenger, arachidonic acid, such as nordihydroguaiaretic acid or quinacrine, do produce some amnesia if injected before training, this is not apparent until some 90 minutes posttraining, and even then, it is not as marked as is the effect of nitroarginine (Holscher & Rose, 1993).

It would seem likely that the signal provided by the arrival of NO affects calcium flux at the presynaptic membrane, as if prisms of IMHV are cut within 30 minutes of training the chicks and incubated *in vitro*, we can measure an increase in $^{45}Ca^{2+}$ uptake. The increase is transient, and is not observed in prisms cut either 5 minutes or 3 hours posttraining. The increased Ca^{2+} flux is probably mediated through presynaptic, conotoxin-sensitive, N-type calcium channels, because conotoxin, but not the postsynaptic L-channel blockers, nifedipine or nimodipine, produces amnesia for the passive avoidance task if injected at the time of training and also abolishes the increased Ca^{2+} flux (Clements & Rose, 1993). Within the same time frame (30 minutes following training), there is a change in the phosphorylation state of an exclusively presynaptic 52kD membrane protein, immunologically identical to the phosphoprotein, variously called B50, GAP 43, neuromodulin, or F1 (Ali, Bullock, & Rose, 1988). The enzyme responsible for the phosphorylation of B50, protein kinase C (PKC), exists in a number of isoforms and is partially membrane bound and partially cytosolic. One widely canvassed model for the regulation of the phosphorylation of its membrane substrates is by way of translocation of the enzyme from cytosol to membrane (Akers, Lovinger, Colley, Linden, & Routtenberg, 1986). We have used a specific antibody to the α/β (translocatable) forms of the enzyme to assay the enzyme in synaptic membranes, and have found a small but significant increase in the amount of membrane-bound PKC in the left IMHV 30 minutes after passive avoidance training (Burchuladze, Potter, & Rose, 1990). Further, if the phosphorylation step is essential for memory formation, intracerebral injection of PKC inhibitors, such as melittin or H7, which prevent the phosphorylation of B50, should result in amnesia for the passive avoidance. This, indeed, turns out to be the case: Localized unilateral injection of melittin or H7 into the left, but not the right, IMHV just before or just after training results in amnesia in birds tested 6–24 hours later (Burchuladze et al., 1990). Thus, in the forebrain, the early phosphorylation steps seem to be localized to the left IMHV. These processes are analogous to those occurring in LTP, where PKC inhibitors have been reported to affect the maintenance, although not the initiation, of the effect (Reymann, Schulzeck, Dase, & Matthies, 1988). As with LTP, retention of weak memories (which occurs, e.g., if the 100% methylanthranilate is replaced by a 10% solution of the aversant in alcohol) can be potentiated by the injection of activators of PKC, such as phorbol esters, at around the time of training (Gulinello & Rose, 1993).

FROM SYNAPSE TO NUCLEUS

Conversion of such transient modifications of membrane properties into more lasting presynaptic or postsynaptic modulations of connectivity must depend on the synthesis of new membrane constituents; thus, it has been shown in virtually every system in which it has been studied, including the chick (Freeman & Rose, 1993; Rosenzweig et al., 1991), that the formation of long-term memory is prevented by inhibitors of protein synthesis. The molecular biological mechanisms involved in triggering the synthesis of such membrane proteins are assumed to involve the initial activation of members of the family of immediate early genes, of which the protein oncogenes, c-fos and c-jun, are among the best known. C-fos and c-jun expression is believed to be initiated by signals emanating from the membrane, especially the opening of calcium channels and the activation of the PI cycle mediated by the phosphorylation steps described earlier (Chiarugi, Ruggiero, & Corradetti, 1989). Using northern blotting and *in situ* hybridization, we have shown that, 30 minutes after M training, c-fos and c-jun mRNAs are induced in the IMHV and the LPO (Anokhin, Mileusnic, Shamakina, & Rose, 1991). Because almost any disturbance to an animal can result in increased c-fos expression, it is important to emphasize that we have been able to devise experimental protocols, using the pebble floor task already described, to show that, at least in this protocol, the enhanced immediate early gene expression effect is learning- or novelty- and not merely experience-related (Anokhin & Rose, 1991).

FROM NUCLEUS TO SYNAPSE

Whatever the intervening intracellular signals and genomic mechanisms, within an hour after training there is enhanced synthesis of a variety of proteins (notably tubulin; Mileusnic, Rose, & Tillson, 1980; Scholey, Bullock, & Rose, 1992) intended for export from the cell body. Most of our attention has been directed toward the glycoproteins of the synaptic membrane, because of the major role that several glycoprotein families (i.e., the N-CAMs and integrins) play as cell recognition and adhesion molecules in stabilizing intercellular connections. There is enhanced incorporation of radioactively labeled fucose into presynaptic and postsynaptic membrane glycoproteins for many hours following training, which is regulated by increased activity of the rate-limiting enzyme, fucokinase (Lössner & Rose, 1983; Sukumar, Burgoyne, & Rose, 1980). Using double-labeling techniques, we have separated the glycoproteins on SDS gels and identified a number of fractions of interest. In particular, in the IMHV and the LPO, a presynaptic component of Mr around 50 kDa and postsynaptic components of Mr of 100–120 and 150–180 kDa seem particularly training sensitive (Bullock, Zamani, & Rose, 1992); these latter molecular weights are interestingly close to those of the N-CAMs.

Training-related glycoprotein synthesis has been reported in several species and tasks: For instance, increased fucosylation has been found following brightness discrimination training in rats by Matthies group in Magdeburg, which showed that the increased fucosylation occurred in two waves, separated by some 6 hours, the first hippocampal, the second cortical (Pohle, Rüthrich, Popov, & Matthies, 1979). We have become intrigued by the possible biochemical and behavioral significance of this second wave.

As with the phosphorylation and protein synthesis steps of the cascade, we would expect to find that, if the synthesis of glycoproteins was a necessary step in the formation of long-term memory, then inhibiting this synthesis should produce amnesia. Jork (in Magdeburg) has shown that 2-deoxygalactose (2-DGal) is a competitive inhibitor to galactose, which, once incorporated into the nascent glycoprotein chain, prevents terminal fucosylation, and we have found that intracerebral administration of 2-DGal during a time window of up to an hour or so following training produces amnesia for passive avoidance in the chick (Rose & Jork, 1987). Recently, we have gone further, and shown that there is a second time window, at some 5–8 hours after training, during which injections of 2-DGal result in amnesia in chicks tested 24 hours later. Furthermore, injections of a monoclonal anti-NCAM, which is without effect at the earlier time window, results in amnesia if injected 5.5 hours posttraining (Scholey, Rose, Zamani, Bock, & Schachner, 1993). A similar time period of sensitivity of memory to intervention by anti-NCAM has been shown by Doyle, Nolan, Bell, and Regan (1992) using a step-down avoidance task in the rat.

The significance of these two waves of glycoprotein synthesis in the context of memory consolidation becomes apparent from two further experiments. Methalanthranilate is a strong aversant. If it is replaced as the aversant by the less strong tasting quinine, chicks will avoid the dry test bead in the first few hours posttraining, but subsequently, memory declines and by 24 hours, the aversion is almost completely lost. Under these conditions, there are no lasting increases in glycoprotein synthesis above the level in the control birds (Bourne, Davies, Stewart, Csillag, & Cooper, 1991). A similar effect may be occurring in the CTA paradigm referred to earlier. Chicks pecking a dry green bead, and made sick 30 minutes later by ip injection of 1 M LiCl, avoid the bead on test 3 hours after the LiCl injection, although they no longer avoid the green bead if the presentation of the bead is delayed 24 hours. If, however, 2-DGal is injected intracerebrally at the time of the bead-peck (but not at the time of LiCl injection), the chicks are amnesic on test and peck the green bead. Thus even the "weak" learning of an unpaired experience, such as pecking at a taste-neutral but conspicuous object, seems to require the first wave of glycoprotein synthesis (Barber et al., 1989).

Our explanation for these observations is that the initial registration and memorizing of a new phenomenon or experience involving visual experience in the chick is associated with a cascade of macromolecular processes occurring primarily in the left IMHV, resulting in at least some synaptic restructuring, which demands glycoprotein synthesis. However, if the memory trace is to be "stamped in" more permanently, a more lasting synaptic reorganization is required, one that involves the mechanisms of presynaptic and postsynaptic recognition provided by the neural cell adhesion molecule and, presumably, other glycoproteins with similar functions, such as the integrins. A similar role has been postulated for the molluscan homologue of NCAM (ApCAM) by Mayford, Barzilai, Keller, Schacher, and Kandel (1992).

How might this intracellular biochemical cascade translate into altered presynaptic and postsynaptic morphology? Working on the hypothesis that changes in synaptic connectivity might be expressed in changes in the numbers or dimensions of axo-dendritic synapses, a series of studies by Stewart (1991) has quantitatively examined morphological parameters, at both light and electron microscope level, in the IMHV and LPO of chicks 24 hours after training on the passive avoidance task. At this time, there is a large (60%) increase in the density of dendritic spines on a class of large multipolar projection neurons of the left IMHV in the M-trained chicks, compared with the W chicks and somewhat smaller increases in a similar class of cells in the LPO. This lateralized change is superimposed on a left–right asymmetry that already exists in control chicks (Patel & Stewart, 1988).

Stereological analysis of the synapses of the IMHV and LPO has also shown training-related changes, the most striking of which include increases in synapse number in both the left and right LPO and a 60% increase in the numbers of synaptic vesicles per synapse in the left IMHV and the left LPO. Changes in synapse numbers in the right IMHV can be detected as soon as 1 hour after training, but they are transient, presumably involving only the first wave of glycoprotein synthesis (Doubell & Stewart, 1993). The changes in the LPO can be detected as soon as 12 hours after training. These changes are reminiscent of those found by Greenough and Bailey (1988) in rats exposed to enriched versus impoverished environments (Greenough and Bailey, 1988) and by Bailey and Kandel (1993) in the synapses involved in the gill withdrawal reflex in *Aplysia*; they have argued that changes in vesicle number are relatively transient, while those in synapse number are longer lasting.

PHYSIOLOGICAL CORRELATES

Such structural changes are among those that might be expected were the memory for the training experience to be represented by an alteration in the physiological connectivity of IMHV and LPO synapses. For instance, theoretical calculations show that spine synapses are more effective than shaft synapses in depolarizing the postsynaptic neuron, and the spine head diameter can limit the magnitude of the postsynaptic signal. The IMHV of the young chick shows interesting neurophysiological plasticity, notably its capacity to express LTP-like phenomena *in vitro* (Bradley et al., 1991). In accord with the prediction that the structural modification of synapses induced during memory formation is associated with changes in electrical properties, extracellular recordings from the IMHV (and LPO) of anesthetized chicks in the hours after training with the bitter bead show dramatic time-dependent increases in the incidence of bouts of high-frequency neuronal firing and bursting activity (Gigg, Patterson, & Rose, 1993, 1994; Mason & Rose, 1987).

It is, of course, essential to show that these substantial biochemical, morphological and physiological changes are in some way directly related to memory formation and are not simply the sequelae of the combination of sensory, motor, and aversive experiences associated with pecking a bitter bead. To check for this possibility, we have made use of the fact that a brief subconvulsive transcranial electroshock given in the minutes after training on the passive avoidance task results in subsequent amnesia, so that birds peck on test. If the electroshock is delayed, however, until about 10 minutes after training, birds show recall on test (Benowitz & Magnus, 1973). This phenomenon is presumably a consequence of the fact that the very earliest phases of memory formation are dependent on transient ionic fluxes at the synapse, which the electroshock disrupts. In any event, this effect makes it possible for us to dissociate the sequelae of the experience of pecking the bead from those of memory for the avoidance by simply comparing our presumed biochemical, morphological, or physiological markers in birds that have all pecked the bead and been shocked, but, because of the time of administering the shock, some of which show recall whilst others do not. Using this paradigm, we have shown that enhanced fucosylation, increased spine density, and neuronal bursting all occur only in birds showing recall; the mere tasting of the bead has no effect on these markers (Mason & Rose, 1987; Patel, Rose, & Stewart, 1988; Rose & Harding, 1984).

MEMORY STORAGE: LOCALISED OR DISTRIBUTED?

What do these data have to say about how memories for the passive avoidance response are stored in the brain? The biochemical and cellular cascade that I have described implies, as do most cellular models of memory formation, that a linear sequence of processes in a pair of neurons, or more realistically, in a small ensemble of such neurons, results in lasting modification of synaptic connectivity within the ensemble, a modulation that is the brain's representation of some association of events and experiences whose consequences are changed behaviors. Yet, I argued in the first part of this chapter that such physiological models of memory formation in cells are incompatible with the neuropsychological data on the phenomenology of memory, which reveals it to be dispersed in multiple brain systems. A series of lesion studies has also demonstrated that memory for the passive avoidance response is not simply localized to the left IMHV. Although pretraining left IMHV lesions are amnestic, posttraining ones are not, and although pretraining bilateral LPO lesions are not amnestic, bilateral posttraining lesions are (Gilbert, Patterson, & Rose, 1991; Patterson, Gilbert, & Rose, 1990). Based on our observations of the double wave of glycoprotein synthesis and the time-dependent shifts in neuronal bursting from left to right IMHV and LPO, I have interpreted these data by means of a rather simple dynamic model, in which the memory trace "flows" from the IMHV to the LPO (Rose, 1991). This did not, however, resolve the paradox of there being lasting changes in biochemistry and morphology in the left IMHV without that structure being apparently necessary for long-term memory. The resolution to the paradox lies in the fact that the chick makes complex representations of "the bead" that it pecks, based on color, size, shape, and location. By challenging the chick's memory appropriately, we have been able to show that the IMHV plays a role in remembering the bead as an object of a particular color, and that, in the absence of its left IMHV, the bird simply cannot make the necessary color discrimination (Patterson & Rose, 1992).

It is on the basis of such observations that I want to conclude that memory "traces" are not stably located within a single neuronal ensemble, but, following early synaptic changes within a locale, later become more widely distributed, dynamic, and fluid, even moving from site to site within the brain. Representations are multiple, and the very concept of a fixed locus may be misleading. (See, in this context, the alternative, global chaos model of memory proposed by Skarda and Freeman, 1990, and the critique of synaptic models of memory made by Tulving, 1991; see also Rose, 1992.)

During the processing and stabilizing of the memory trace for passive avoidance in the chick, there is a sequential activation of the right IMHV and LPO. The second wave of glycoprotein synthesis, probably occurring in the LPO, is responsible for producing the glycoproteins, including NCAM, that stabilize the changed synaptic connectivities by creating new synapses or dendritic structures or by altering the locations of preexisting ones. Understanding the molecular and cellular processes involved in this stabilization depends on interpreting the time dependencies, identifying the relevant glycoproteins and their cellular functions, and, perhaps more importantly, in rethinking the overly simple associationist models of memory that have, so far, guided experimental cellular approaches to memory mechanisms.

ACKNOWLEDGEMENTS

The experiments described here are based on collaborative work by many members of the Brain and Behaviour Research Group over the past decade; I thank all who are cited, and those others whose work forms part of the essential background to the results discussed here. Our research has been principally funded through the Open University, MRC, and SERC, and the ESF programme in the neural mechanisms of learning and memory.

REFERENCES

Akers, R. F., Lovinger, D. M., Colley, D., Linden, D., & Routtenberg, A. (1986). Translocation of protein kinase C activity after LTP may mediate hippocampal synaptic plasticity. *Science*, *231*, 587–589.

Ali, S., Bullock, S., & Rose, S. P. R. (1988). Phosphorylation of synaptic proteins in chick forebrain: Changes with development and passive avoidance training. *Journal of Neurochemistry*, *50*, 1579–1587.

Alkon, D. L. (1987). *Memory traces in the brain*. New York: Cambridge University Press.

Andrew, R. J., & Rogers, L. J. (1972). Testosterone, search behaviour and persistence. *Nature*, *237*, 343–346.

Anokhin, K., Mileusnic, R., Shamakina, I., & Rose, S. P. R. (1991). Effects of early experience on c-fos gene expression in the chick forebrain. *Brain Research*, *544*, 101–107.

Anokhin, K. V., & Rose, S. P. R. (1991). Learning-induced increase of immediate early gene messenger RNA in the chick forebrain. *European Journal of Neuroscience*, *3*, 162–167.

Bailey, C. H., & Kandel, E. R. (1993). Structural changes accompanying memory storage. *Annual Review of Physiology*, *55*, 397–426.

Barber, A. J., Gilbert, D. B., & Rose, S. P. R. (1989). Glycoprotein synthesis is necessary for memory of sickness-induced learning in chicks. *European Journal of Neurosciences*, *1*, 673–677.

Benowitz, L., & Magnus, J. G. (1973). Memory storage processes following one-trial aversive conditioning in the chick. *Behavioural Biology*, *8*, 367–380.

Bliss, T. V. P., & Collingridge, G. (1993). Long-term potentiation and memory. *Nature*, *361*, 31–39.

Bourne, R. C., Davies, D. C., Stewart, M. G., Csillag, A., & Cooper, M. (1991). Cerebral glycoprotein synthesis and long-term memory formation in the chick (*Gallus domesticus*) following passive avoidance training depends on the nature of the aversive stimulus. *European Journal of Neuroscience*, *3*, 243–248.

Bradley, P. M., Burns, B. D., & Webb, A. C. (1991). Potentiation of synaptic responses in slices from the chick forebrain. *Proceedings of the Royal Society of London* (Series B), *243*, 19–24.

Bullock, S., Rose, S. P. R., Pearce, B., & Potter, J. (1993). Training chicks on a passive avoidance task modulates glutamate stimulated inositol phosphate accumulation. *European Journal of Neuroscience*, *5*, 43–48.

Bullock, S., Zamani, M. R., & Rose, S. P. R. (1992). Characterization and regional localisation of pre- and postsynaptic glycoproteins of the chick forebrain showing changed fucose incorporation following passive avoidance training. *Journal of Neurochemistry*, *58*, 2145–2154.

Burchuladze, R., & Rose, S. P. R. (1992). Memory formation in day-old chicks requires NMDA but not non-NMDA glutamate receptors. *European Journal of Neuroscience*, *4*, 533–538.

Burchuladze, R., Potter, J., & Rose, S. P. R. (1990). Memory formation in the chick depends on membrane-bound protein kinase C. *Brain Research*, *535*, 131–138.

Cherkin, A. (1969). Kinetics of memory consolidation: Role of amnesic treatment parameters. *Proceedings of the National Academy of Sciences* (USA), *63*, 1094–1100.

Chiarugi, V. P., Ruggiero, M., & Corradetti, R. (1989). Oncogenes, protein kinase C, neuronal differentiation and memory. *Neurochemistry International, 14*, 1–9.

Churchland, P., & Sejnowski, T. (1992). *The computational brain*. Cambridge, MA: MIT Press.

Clements, M. P., & Rose, S. P. R. (1993). Increase in 45-Calcium uptake in slices prepared from the IMHV of one-day-old chicks following passive avoidance learning. *Brain Research Association Abstracts, 35*(4), 46.

Doubell, T., & Stewart, M. G. (1993). Short-term changes in numerical density of synapses in the intermediate medial hyperstriatum ventrale of the chick following passive avoidance training. *Journal of Neuroscience, 13*, 2230–2236.

Doyle, E., Nolan, P., Bell, R., & Regan, C. M. (1992). Neurodevelopmental events underlying information acquisition and storage. *Network, 3*, 89–94.

Freeman, F., & Rose, S. P. R. (1995). Time course of anisomycin induced amnesia for passive avoidance training in the day-old chick. *Brain Research Association Abstracts, 35*(5), 46.

Gigg, J., Patterson, T. A., & Rose, S. P. R. (1993). Increases in neuronal bursting recorded from the chick lobus parolfactorius after training are both time-dependent and memory specific. *European Journal of Neuroscience, 6*, 313–319.

Gigg, J., Patterson, T. A., & Rose, S. P. R. (1994). Training-induced increases in neuronal activity recorded from the forebrain of the day-old chick are time dependent. *Neuroscience, 56*, 771–776.

Gilbert, D. B., Patterson, T. A., & Rose, S. P. R. (1991). Dissociation of brain sites necessary for registration and storage on memory for a one-trial passive avoidance task in the chick. *Behavioral Neuroscience, 105*, 553–561.

Greenough, W. T., & Bailey, C. H. (1988). The anatomy of memory: Convergence of results across a diversity of tests. *Trends in Neuroscience, 11*, 142–147.

Hawkins, R. D., Kandel, E. R., & Siegelbaum, S. A. (1993). Learning to modulate transmitter release: Themes and variations in synaptic plasticity. *Annual Review of Neuroscience, 16*, 625–665.

Holscher, C., & Rose, S.P. R. (1992). An inhibitor of nitric oxide synthesis prevents memory formation in the chick. *Neuroscience Letters, 145*, 165–167.

Holscher, C., & Rose, S. P. R. (1993). Inhibiting synthesis of the putative retrograde messenger nitric oxide results in amnesia in a passive avoidance task in the chick. *Brain Research, 619*, 189–194.

Horn, G. (1985). *Memory, imprinting and the brain*. Oxford: Oxford University Press.

Kossut, M., & Rose, S. P. R. (1984). Differential 2-deoxyglucose uptake into chick brain structures during passive avoidance training. *Neuroscience, 12*, 971–977.

Lössner, B., & Rose, S. P. R. (1983). Passive avoidance training increases fucokinase activity in right forebrain tissue of day-old chicks. *Journal of Neurochemistry, 41*, 1357–1363.

Lowndes, M., & Davies, D. C. (1994). The effects of archstriatal lesions on one trial passive avoidance learning in the chick. *European Journal of Neuroscience, 6*, 525–530.

Mason, R. J., & Rose, S. P. R. (1987a). Lasting changes in spontaneous multi-unit activity in the chick brain following passive avoidance training. *Neuroscience, 21*, 931–941.

Mason, R. J., & Rose, S. P. R. (1987b). Passive avoidance learning produces focal elevation of bursting activity in the chick brain: Amnesia abolishes the increase. *Behavioral and Neural Biology, 49*, 280–292.

Mayford, M., Barzilai, A., Keller, F., Schacher, S., & Kandel, E. R. (1992). Modulation of an NCAM-related cell adhesion molecule with long-term synaptic plasticity. *Aplysia Science, 256*, 638–644.

McGaugh, J. L. (1964). Time-dependent processes in memory storage. *Science, 153*, 1351–1358.

McNaughton, B. (1993). The mechanisms of expression of long-term enhancement of hippocampal synapses: Current issues and theoretical implications *Annual Review of Physiology, 55*, 375–396.

Mileusnic, R., Rose, S. P. R., & Tillson, P. J. (1980). Passive avoidance learning results in changes in concentration of and incorporation into colchicine binding proteins in the chick forebrain. *Journal of Neurochemistry, 34*, 1007–1015.

O'Keefe. J., & Nadel, L. (1978). *The hippocampus as a cognitive map.* Oxford: Oxford University Press.

Patel, S. J., Rose, S. P. R., & Stewart, M. G. (1988). Training-induced dendritic spine density changes are specifically related to memory formation processes in the chick, *Gallus domesticus. Brain Research, 463*, 168–173.

Patel, S. N., & Stewart, M. G. (1988). Changes in the number and structure of dendritic spines, 25h after passive avoidance training in the chick, *Gallus domesticus. Brain Research, 449*, 34–46.

Patterson, T. A., Gilbert, D. B., & Rose, S. P. R. (1990). Pre- and post-training lesions of the IMHV and passive avoidance learning in the chick. *Experimental Brain Research, 80*, 189–195.

Patterson, T. A., & Rose, S. P. R. (1992). Memory in the chick: Multiple cues, distinct brain locations. *Behavioral Neuroscience, 106*, 465–470.

Pohle, W., Rüthrich, H. L., Popov, N., & Matthies, H. (1979). Fucose incorporation into rat hippocampus structures after acquisition of a brightness discrimination. *Acta Biologica Medica Germanica, 38*, 53–63.

Reymann, K. G., Schulzeck, K., Dase, H., & Matthies, H. J. (1988). Phorbol ester-induced hippocampal long-term potentiation is counteracted by inhibitors of PKC. *Experimental Brain Research, 71*, 227–230.

Rose, S. P. R. (1991). How chicks make memories: The cellular cascade from c-fos to dendritic remodelling. *Trends in Neuroscience, 14*, 390–397.

Rose, S. P. R. (1991). Memory: The brain's Rosetta stone? *Concepts in Neuroscience, 2*, 43–64.

Rose, S. P. R. (1992). *The making of memory.* London: Bantam Press.

Rose, S. P. R., & Csillag, A. (1985). Passive avoidance training results in lasting changes in deoxyglucose metabolism in left hemisphere regions of chick brain. *Behavioral and Neural Biology, 44*, 315–324.

Rose, S. P. R., & Harding, S. (1984). Training increases 3H-fucose incorporation in chick brain only if followed by memory storage. *Neuroscience, 12*, 663–667.

Rose, S. P. R., & Jork, R. (1987). Long-term memory formation in chick is blocked by 2-deoxygalactose, a fucose analogue. *Behavioral and Neural Biology, 48*, 246–258.

Rosenzweig, M. R., Bennett, E. I.., Martinez, J. L., Beniston, D., Colombo, P. J., Lee, D. W., Patterson, T. A., Schulteis, G., & Serrano, P. A. (1991). Stages in memory formation in the chick: Findings and problems. In R. J. Andrew (Ed.), *Neural and behavioural plasticity* (pp. 394–418). Oxford: Oxford University Press.

Scholey, A. B., Bullock, S., & Rose, S. P. R. (1992). Passive avoidance learning in the young chick results in time- and locus-specific elevations of a-tubulin immuno-reactivity. *Neurochemistry International, 21*, 343–350.

Scholey, A. B., Rose, S. P. R., Zamani, M. R.; Bock, E., & Schachner, M. (1993). A role for the neural cell adhesion molecule in a late consolidating phase of glycoprotein synthesis 6hr following passive avoidance training of the young chick. *Neuroscience, 55*, 499–509.

Singer, W. (1990). Ontogenetic self-organisation and learning. In J. L. McGaugh, N. M. Weinberger, & G. Lynch (Eds.), *Brain organisation and memory: Cells, systems and circuits* (pp. 211–224). Oxford: Oxford University Press.

Skarda, C. A, & Freeman, W. J. (1990). How brains use chaos to make order. *Concepts in Neuroscience, 1*, 275–286.

Squire, L. R., & Butters, N. (Eds). (1992). *Neuropsychology of memory* (2nd ed.). New York: Guilford.

Squire, L. R., Knowlton, B., & Musen, G. (1993). The structure and organization of memory. *Annual Review of Psychology, 44*, 453–495.

Steele, R., & Stewart, M. G. (1993). 7-chlorokynurenine, an inhibitor of the glycine binding site of

NMDA receptors, inhibits memory formation in day-old chicks (*Gallus domesticus*). *Behavioral and Neural Biology, 60,* 89–92.

Stewart, M. G. (1991). Changes in dendritic and synaptic structure in chick forebrain consequent on passive avoidance learning. In R. J. Andrew (Ed.), *Neural and behavioural plasticity* (pp. 305–328). Oxford: Oxford University Press.

Stewart, M. G., Bourne, R. C., & Steele, R. J. (1992). Quantitative autoradiographic demonstration of changes in binding to NMDA-sensitive [3H]glutamate and [3H]MK801, but not [3H]AMPA receptors in chick forebrain 30min after passive avoidance training. *European Journal of Neuroscience, 4,* 936–943.

Sukumar, R., Burgoyne, R. D., & Rose, S. P. R. (1980). Increased incorporation of 3H-fucose into chick brain glycoproteins following training on a passive avoidance task. *Journal of Neurochemistry, 34,* 1000–1007.

Tulving, E. (1991). [Interview]. *Journal of Cognitive Neuroscience, 3,* 89.

Author Index

Subject Index